The Problem of Political Trust

Trust has been the subject of empirical and theoretical inquiry in a range of disciplines, including sociology, economics, psychology, philosophy, public policy and political theory. This book approaches trust from a multi-disciplinary scope of inquiry. It explains why most existing definitions and theories of trust are inadequate.

The book examines how trust evolved from a quality of personal relationships into a critical factor in political institutions and representation, and to an abstract and impersonal factor that applies now to complex systems, including monetary systems.

It makes a distinctive contribution by recasting trust conceptually in dialectical and pragmatic terms, and reapplying the concept to our understanding of critical issues in politics and political economy.

Grant Duncan is a scholar of political theory and public policy, and a political commentator, living in Auckland, New Zealand. His previous work on pain and on happiness, linking subjective states with political aims and public institutions, can be found in *Economy & Society*, *Journal of Happiness Studies* and *The Monist*.

T0382813

Routledge Frontiers of Political Economy

For more information about this series, please visit: www.routledge.com/books/series/SE0345

The Problem of Political Trust

A Conceptual Reformulation

Grant Duncan

LONDON AND NEW YORK

First published 2019
by Routledge
2 Park Square, Milton Park, Abingdon, Oxon OX14 4RN

and by Routledge
605 Third Avenue, New York, NY 10017

First issued in paperback 2020

Routledge is an imprint of the Taylor & Francis Group, an informa business

British Library Cataloguing-in-Publication Data
A catalogue record for this book is available from the British Library

Library of Congress Cataloging-in-Publication Data
A catalog record for this book has been requested

ISBN 13: 978-0-367-50436-6 (pbk)
ISBN 13: 978-1-138-48093-3 (hbk)

Typeset in Galliard
by Apex CoVantage, LLC

'It is no plaything you are about. I tremble when I consider the Trust I have presumed to ask.'

Edmund Burke, *Speech on the Hustings at Bristol*, 1780
(Burke, 1996, p. 667)

Contents

Acknowledgements

No matter how much we promote collaboration, reading and writing still require solitude. Nonetheless, few books get written without the advice and encouragement of many people. This book owes much to my daughter, Dr Pansy Duncan, whose enthusiasm for my ideas about trust, from the very beginning, made a huge difference. I am so very lucky that we follow parallel scholarly paths. And I cannot express the debt that I owe to Parisa Kooshesh for her companionship and political insights and the many things I have learned from her doctoral research. Dr Junjia Ye has always given me her unwavering support and friendship. The school bus misses her.

I am very fortunate to be surrounded by academic colleagues and friends whose support and advice helped me along the way. These include Drs Graeme Macrae, Warwick Tie, Damien Rogers and Shine Choi and all those in social and cultural studies who attend our Wednesday seminars. Professor Peter Lineham's enthusiasm for Edmund Burke was infectious and valuable. Dr Michael Fletcher will recognize the scene that opens Chapter 5, in which we talked about this book and many other things. And Susanna Andrew's love of books of all kinds is always appreciated.

Professors Linda Botterill, Alan Fenna and Geoff Cockfield deserve my gratitude for their friendship and for a conversation over dinner in Singapore that examined the progress of this book, just as it was taking shape. Dr Yvonne Haigh shared her enthusiasm for the topic of political trust one afternoon in Sydney, and that too made a difference. My dear friends Drs Kai Jensen and Kathy Troup of Bermagui NSW are unfailing in their love and support.

Above all, I acknowledge with love my mother, Margaret Lorraine Duncan, whose trust is boundless.

Introduction

The premises of democratic thought and action, and trust in particular, have been challenged recently due to unexpected electoral outcomes and the resurgence of populism. Contemporary political trust appears to be 'broken,' accompanied by ideological polarization, governmental dysfunction, lower voter-turnouts and the rise of authoritarian leaders. Traditional mainstream media organizations, once the gatekeepers of information about politics, are regarded now by many as untrustworthy or even 'fake.' Rapid technological change underlies these developments, changing the ways in which people communicate, and raising questions about the political effects of new digital media and artificial intelligence. Amidst all of this, what we mean (or what we once meant) by 'trust' invites critical inquiry.

A crisis of political trust – or tremors of *dis*trust and anti-establishment sentiments – swept through two leading democracies in 2016. The Brexit referendum and President Trump's election ambushed the experts and upset political norms.[1] Election results that defied expectations or norms continued through 2017 in France, the United Kingdom, Germany and New Zealand. And the shock-waves returned in 2018 when angry Italian voters made a participative 'movement' (il Movimento 5 Stelle, M5S) the largest single party, while the right-wing populist Lega did better than expected. Alongside these events, a narrative of 'declining trust in government and media' was backed up by opinion surveys and by rising rates of voter abstention (Edelman, 2017a; Pew Research Center, 2015; Runciman, 2017; Solijonov, 2016; Twenge, Campbell, and Carter, 2014).

Some political commentators and surveyors drew direct links between an 'implosion' of trust in governmental institutions and the rise of populism (Friedman, 2016; Ries, 2017; The Economist Intelligence Unit, 2017; Wedel, 2016); others saw a close relationship between low political trust, the collapse of social democracy, and 'protest' votes for anti-establishment or far-right parties (Cuperus, 2018; Halikiopoulou and Vasilopoulou, 2018).[2] Voting for such parties may represent an outlet for distrust, and/or it may fuel further distrust. A study from Belgium suggested 'a spiral of distrust,' as protest-voting and political distrust reinforced one another (Hooghe and Dassonneville, 2018).[3]

As a further source of distrust, suspicions grew about covert political campaigning methods. Investigative journalists pieced together stories of how the Brexit and Trump campaigns may have been influenced through back-door financing, mass data-matching and voter-profiling. Direct links were found in both campaigns with individuals allegedly seeking to manipulate the outcomes (Cadwalladr, 2018; Geoghegan and Ramsay, 2017). Trump's campaign-team, moreover, allegedly colluded with Russian agents and hackers, suggesting that a foreign adversary meddled in America's democratic election (Harding, 2017). Organized groups used fake social-media accounts to try to influence American voters,[4] and the UK government accused the Russians of interference in the Brexit referendum. The aim of such alleged information operations would have been to sow confusion, division and distrust within Western democracies, in order to weaken them politically.

Political parties have always made direct efforts to get known supporters to the polling-booths. But some social-media campaigns used negative memes to discourage their opponents' supporters from voting. In 2016, automated systems aided the distribution of fake news from platforms such as Facebook and YouTube. Unpublished algorithms, programmed to achieve relatively simple outcomes, maximized your attention by estimating in advance what you liked and what you wanted to see, from data that you had provided for free. Political operatives sent attack ads and fake news in massive quantities to target audiences, watched how people reacted, and refined the messages to augment online engagement. This aroused suspicions that elections may be influenced by unauthorized 'information warriors' backed by billionaires, getting ahead of electoral laws and evading detection. From both sides of the divides within the leading democracies, then, political trust – including the vital trust that elections be 'free and fair' – was undermined.[5]

A long-term decline of political trust has been recorded by social surveys, though not uniformly, across Western democracies (Norris, 2011); it is most extensively surveyed and documented in the USA (Hetherington and Rudolph, 2015). Some European countries have seen surveyed 'trust in politicians' decline to low levels following the global financial crisis (GFC) of 2008 and then rise – although in most countries most of the people expressed distrust (Söderlund, 2017).[6] Low trust in politicians and governments (as surveyed) is correlated with popular dissatisfaction with the performance of governments, with ideological and partisan polarization, and with scepticism about the basic *principles* of democratic governance (Norris, 2011; Hetherington and Rudolph, 2015). Some authors have warned of the possibility of the decline or failure of democracy itself alongside the rise of populism and authoritarianism (Foa and Mounk, 2017; Levitsky and Ziblatt, 2018; Mounk, 2018; van der Meer and Zmerli, 2017).

Harsher attitudes towards foreigners and immigrants (helping to fuel populist politics) cannot simply be explained by 'harsh economic times'; such attitudes are not concentrated among the worst-off strata of society; they may also be found among the relatively wealthy (Mols and Jetten, 2017). Surveys of trust in government from many affluent societies with credible democratic processes and strong observance of human rights have produced some of the most dismal results (Edelman, 2017b). Paradoxically, most people in the more affluent countries were telling surveyors that they had little or no trust in their institutions of government and media, correlated with dissatisfaction with the state of the economy, and with uncertainties caused by globalization.[7] Post-GFC stagnation, frustrated social mobility, fears about refugees and migrants, and resentment of inequalities led to calls for radical changes. Neo-fascist groups were emboldened, mobilizing on the streets and online, to be confronted by 'antifa' counter-protests. Partly driven by fear and anger about immigration and terrorism and by the spectre of Islamization, right-wing populist and nationalist parties gained support in Eastern Europe, Scandinavia, France, Austria and Germany. Meanwhile, regional independence movements in Scotland, Catalonia, Lombardy and Venice threatened to break away from their nation-states.

Dis/trust should not be advanced as a catch-all descriptor, let alone explanatory factor, for so many profound and varied developments. But, it has become a commonly evoked and widely surveyed theme, helping us to make sense of these contemporary developments.

Political trust

In political science, trust is a well-established concept. It is seen as a key component of social capital (Farr, 2004; Fukuyama, 1995; Putnam, 2000), and there are numerous empirical studies of 'political trust' (for example: Abramson and Finifter, 1981; Hetherington and Husser, 2012; Uslaner, 2002). Theories of democratic representation often describe the role of representatives as 'trustees,' acting on behalf of constituents or the people, as compared with 'delegates' acting at their behest. The 'trustee' model is normally traced back to Edmund Burke (1729–1797), and it continues to feature in studies of political representation (Manin, 1997; Mansbridge, 2003; Pitkin, 1967). Indeed, 'no theory of representation that claims to articulate a vision of *legitimate* government is complete without an account of trust' (Williams, 1998, p. 33). The concept of trust has a well-established place in political theory and research, therefore, and neither is the problem of distrust new or unfamiliar (Hart, 1978).

These well-established uses of trust as a concept take us well beyond interpersonal situations (as in, for instance, 'I trusted you to take care of it') to encompass the much broader contexts of political actors, institutions, economics and social policy. For example, 'political trust' has been defined as 'the general belief in the performance capacity of political institutions and/or belief in the benevolent motivation and performance capacity of office-holders' (Norris, 2017, p. 24). Trust is also well-established as a key concept in economic and monetary theories (see Chapter 5). But, in 2008, the GFC shook people's faith in the banking system and in money itself, boosting interest in alternatives such as Bitcoin. A former Governor of the Bank of England has analysed the causes and consequences of the GFC using trust as a key theoretical construct. He suggests that it is trust, rather than money, that makes the economic world go round (King, 2016).

In light of so much empirical evidence and theoretical literature, to launch a critical inquiry into the political theory of trust, or to re-examine how trust, as a political and economic factor, is defined, may at first look redundant, if not impertinent. On the contrary, such an inquiry is necessary, as contemporary political theories of trust, I will argue, are not conceptually well-founded and hence they cannot comprehend the deep distrust that is disrupting democratic countries. So, the very idea of a 'decline in trust' (as surveyed) may be based on a model that is one-dimensional and that misconstrues the problem. The politics of trust may be undergoing transformation, for instance, rather than declining, due to the changes occurring in a digitalized and globalized era. Traditional top-down institutional models of trust may be breaking down, as social media transform the ways in which people do business and support one another socially and politically, and so an alternative 'distributed' model may better capture what is happening (Botsman, 2017; Howard, 2015). In any case, the normal definitions of trust in the literature are insufficient, as shown in Chapter 2. To prepare the ground for this critical re-examination, Chapter 1 retraces and reconsiders the origins of trust as a political-philosophical concern, in order to make some initial observations about how trust entered *political* discourse. We will re-examine, from first principles, our basic questions about trust in general, and political trust in particular. Only thus can we properly revise our understanding.

Trust has been the subject of empirical and theoretical inquiry in many disciplines, including sociology, economics, psychology, philosophy, public policy and political theory. The present study is not driven by empirical survey-based evidence, although it does look at how such research literature frames trust. As illustrated in Chapter 2, the very definitions of trust in the literature – for instance, framing trust 'as a personal attribute' (Fukuyama, 2014, p. 123) – are narrow and partial, as they begin with the individual rather than the practical ethics of relationships. I will clear the ground in order to ask, 'What do we mean by trust?' and 'What happens when we talk about trust?' This will open the way towards a conceptual reformulation.

Rapid social and technological changes have transformed, and continue to transform, the structures, practices and language by which we trust one another, and this illustrates how trust is historically and culturally contingent. Trust does not stand still as if it were an unchanging and universal human trait or genetic code. This guides us, then, to look at the history of how trust *per se* arose discursively as a political concern, beyond the interpersonal domain of *I–thou* relations, and how it evolved into a factor in complex globally interconnected systems. In light of this, we can challenge and revise the political and sociological understandings of trust.

We will revisit the contemporary theory and science of trust (in Chapters 1 and 2) and inquire into its conceptual foundations. We will re-examine (in Chapters 3 and 4) where and how trust became a part of the modern political lexicon, beginning with Thomas Hobbes, but especially in John Locke's theory of social contract. And we will explore how trust came to be seen as foundational to the institution of money in Chapter 5. For an alternative critical perspective, I will appeal, in Chapters 6 and 7, to the thought of Hegel, Nietzsche, Foucault and Derrida – the latter contrasted with the reciprocity theory of Marcel Mauss. This inquiry opens up an original and new approach to trust in the context of politics and political economy.

In the contemporary social-science literature (reviewed in Chapter 4), trust puts reciprocity, cooperation and social cohesion on the agenda, and presents a positive reason for efforts to combat corruption and to guide democratic development. As an object of social surveys and much research, trust is often seen as a basic and unalloyed social good; it carries a heavy explanatory load in contemporary literature, such as social capital theory and sociology of money. It appears to be a 'solvent' that works for the left and the right, liberal and conservative. It is regarded as a necessary quality of social life.

> The more trust in a society, the better it fares. Put another way: without trust, society would collapse.
>
> (Heaven, 2017, p. 28)

But is such an assertion as self-evident as it looks? Does it reify trust, as if trust were a property or state that has effects, like energy? Does a collapse of society follow from an absence of trust, or are 'social collapse' and 'lack of trust' simply two different ways of describing much the same set of conditions? Can we use trust at all as a foundational explanation for social life and economic prosperity? Indeed, does anyone properly define, let alone explain, trust?

This book considers the task of redefinition, but it also questions whether definition of trust is a necessary or fruitful aim at all. It examines how trust 'works' in political institutions and representation, and, as an abstract or impersonal factor, in complex systems, including monetary systems – following the important contributions made by Niklas Luhmann and Anthony Giddens (see Chapter 5). We will observe how trust – as both an abstract noun and a verb – has grown in political, social and economic thought and literature. The aim is to re-examine how trust has been defined and deployed in contemporary social sciences, and so to disrupt and reconstitute its conceptual framework. What we then discover is less a redefinition of trust than a 're-description.'

A first principle guiding this re-examination is Ludwig Wittgenstein's explanation that 'the meaning of a word is its use in the language' (Wittgenstein, 2009, p. 25e, §43).[8] We only cause ourselves bewilderment when we take a substantive such as *trust* (or similarly, thought, pain, happiness, understanding, etc.) and then go in search of the 'thing' or 'mental state' or 'invisible inner activity' to which it should correspond – an habitual way of thinking that Wittgenstein endeavoured 'to wean us from' (Pitkin, 1972, pp. 65–66).

An important task, therefore, is 'to wean ourselves off' the assumption that trust is a mental attitude or belief that someone adopts. It is fair to say that thinking carefully about a potential betrayal by someone, and then deciding to discount that risk, may be a feature of trust – on some occasions. But, while certain inner processes, thoughts or feelings may, on occasion, be present when we experience relations of trust, no particular process, thought or feeling is necessarily present as a general feature of trusting others. One may trust in fear as well as in love, for example. Indeed, one may trust without thinking or believing anything at all. To give possible future interpersonal or commercial problems *no* thought is a feature of some relationships of trust. And when many a married couple are in bed asleep together, they may be said to trust one another, even though there appear to be neither thoughts nor feelings 'going on in them' for time being. This is because trust itself is not a momentary or temporary thought, feeling or decision; rather, it is a description of the ethical qualities of their relationship. No particular kind of mental state is necessary or sufficient to account for trust. Trust, then, cannot validly be reduced to, or defined by, mental attitudes, beliefs, feelings, judgements or decisions, even though such phenomena may form a part of our descriptions of particular experiences of trust.

Conceptualizing trust as a mental state, personal attribute or decision arises partly due to an assumption that the primary function of language is to name and describe things. But, 'nothing philosophically helpful is to be learned about trust by examining *what goes on in us* when we can be said to trust each other,' as to do so only 'obscures the way in which the notion of trust is constituted by its role in human *interaction*' (Lagerspetz, 1998, pp. 15, 27; see also Lagerspetz and Hertzberg, 2013). We should observe instead how the word *trust* is used in various contexts, including observation of what people are doing when one might say that they trust each other. To describe a relation of trust is more akin to a narrative of actions performed than to a description of a thing or state, and it relies upon an understanding of the culturally and contextually variable ways in which people treat one another in practice. We need to consider trust as performative, looking at how we *do* things with words (Austin, 1975). We should consider trust in terms of words and deeds – or conduct – that occur between and among people when they share, exchange, reciprocate and cooperate. We need to see it as the active ethical *formation* of relations or interactions between and among people, or as an ethical quality of relationships. A sentence that begins with 'I trust you' is less a description of an attitude or decision than a way of affirming or consolidating mutual obligations with others.

Avoiding any assumption, however, that trust may be an 'omni-explanatory' construct, this conceptual inquiry shows how trust augments our understanding of power-relations, money, economic activity, social cohesion and political institutions and events. Recasting trust conceptually in dialectical and pragmatic terms, we may then reapply the concept to our understanding of critical issues in politics and political economy.

The case for re-describing trust

The idea of trust as a personal attribute, such as our beliefs about or attitudes towards others, is kept in place by the spectre of 'a world without trust' in which normal social life would be impossible. Trust is said to be 'a functional prerequisite for the possibility of society' without which chaos and fear would reign (Lewis and Weigert, 1985, p. 967). A hypothetical 'trustless' world is a rhetorical device, employed in much the same way as the state of nature was in early-modern political theory to propel us into agreement with a rationale for political order. I argue that this model of trust is based on misrecognition. It is not entirely invalid; it is just 'retro-fitted.' It works backwards from the particular viewpoint of a literate adult in an advanced liberal-democratic capitalist economy. It is a 'Just So' story made to fit the facts as they appear to be in the present. Trust is posed axiomatically as a necessary precondition for social, economic and political order, on the assumption that it must be an alternative to a 'trustless' state of affairs. Such a state never really occurs, however. Even (or especially) in a war-zone, one seeks out comrades whom one can trust.

Trust is observable, I argue, in unspoken and taken-for-granted habits or customs of exchange and cooperation. We grow up with a set of norms of interaction that form a commonly assumed ethical 'apparatus' of fairness, loyalty, balance, etc. We are forced to think about, and hence to talk about, trust only *after* we have felt the pain of the betrayal of those taken-for-granted conditions and actions that became entailed or ingrained within our being-with-others. These actions of trusting may be as subtle as abstaining from something, or giving way to someone, or deferring to someone of superior status or knowledge. They may entail the observation of prohibitions, or the recognition of rank, or caring for someone in need. The actions of trust must also include giving, sharing and exchanging objects, or saying certain words. At an advanced linguistic level, trust entails the speech-acts of apologizing, promising and forgiving.

Promising is an excellent example. A promise is a speech-act, or an utterance that performs something in its very utterance. And it requires foresight, memory and risk-taking. At the heart of the promise is the risk of failure to deliver on or to live up to the actions that it proposes. If a future event is inevitable and predictable, on the other hand, it cannot be the subject of a genuine promise. (Except in humour, it makes little sense to *promise* that the sun will rise tomorrow). And the promise, like any aspect of trust, alters and governs the relations and obligations between those who are a party to it. Once I have promised to do something for you, the obligations and commitments between us have changed. The promise will also help us to understand and to re-imagine trust, while shifting it from a simplistic 'A trusts B to do X' model. Although that model self-evidently includes the promise, it does not fully capture it.

For any conceptual analysis, we are trapped, however, with the paradox of having to use language (the verb *to trust*, for example) in order to try to describe something that we cannot point to or pin down. Trust pertains to the ephemeral actions that we perform. It is inter-subjective and context-dependent, and it is not always verbalized – indeed, relations of trust are first experienced before we have even learned to speak, and the strongest forms of trust are implicit or unspoken. Furthermore, the kind of language that spoken trust relies upon, such as promising, is performative, rather than constative or descriptive.

As well as being subtly context-dependent and subject to changing perceptions and ethics, the next problem posed by trust is that the very words and actions that we are accustomed to adopting in relationships of trust are themselves contingent upon our personal norms and cultural background. So, when we use the word 'trust' reflectively to talk about our actions, or when we write a definition of trust, we are already prone to the many customary assumptions and habits that have previously shaped our *un*reflective ways of trusting, acquired from a particular familial and cultural milieu and language. We are prone to an uncritical adoption of the syntactic structures and figures of speech in which the word occurs in our language. The grammar of 'she trusts him,' for instance, predisposes us to think of an act or choice of one person towards another. The English language, moreover, is replete with commonly used metaphors: building or breaching, and other physical metaphors that evoke foundations, ties, bonds and even glue, and that 'objectify' trust. When one seeks to understand 'the subject who trusts,' one finds that this 'position' has already been occupied by a skilled 'performer' of trust, trained since infancy, equipped with a language that comes with many presuppositions and limitations. One cannot escape such a reflexive circle, and so, when we attempt retrospectively to describe or define trust, we are prone to misleading ourselves. The best we can do is to proceed with awareness of this interpretative paradox.

Contemporary literature on trust has largely failed to comprehend the troubled and paradoxical relationship between trust and language, and there is little appreciation of the performative nature of the words we use in trusting one another. This problem is captured in later chapters by two major propositions: that we speak about trust only *after*, or only *because*, it has been broken; and, that trust enunciated is trust betrayed.

To unravel all of this, we need to explore interpersonal trust and then ask how it is generalized or extended to 'the political.' Then, to re-examine political trust, we need to look back and ask, 'How did trust become a concern for *political* philosophy?' Two main strands of political thought can be given a rough sketch at this stage. First, there is a transactional principal–agent approach to trust. This is found in discussion of political representation, especially in the idea of the representative as the voters' trustee, and in the question of how much 'the people' trust governments to act for the common good. This approach to trust is found in many social surveys that ask respondents to evaluate the trustworthiness of a politician (or politicians in general), or to say how much they trust the government to do what is right. A transactional approach is also found in economic and game-theory models of trust. In short, A trusts B to do X, where X is in A's interests. Secondly, there is a systemic version of trust, understood in terms of social relations, distributed throughout complex institutions or systems, such as governmental or financial institutions, rather than vested in any particular person or persons. Because such social or political trust does not entail a personal trustee or assembly of trustees, but embraces a whole organized system, it is often called 'abstract trust.' In a more sociological vein, there is also a generalized 'trust in others' including strangers, and this is often the object of surveys of trust as a social indicator.

Trust, democracy and authoritarianism

In much of the literature reviewed in Chapters 1 to 4, ideas of political trust reflect normative western-liberal assumptions about a virtuous cycle that sustains democracy. That is, political trust, democratic institutions and their consolidation, and progressive economic and social policies should all advance together (Hetherington and Husser, 2012; Uslaner, 2002). And there is alarm that political trust appears to have been in decline, that social and economic policies (especially since the Thatcher–Reagan years) have been regressive and deregulatory, and that support for illiberal leadership is rising in some countries, especially since the GFC (Abramowitz, 2018; Levitsky and Ziblatt, 2018; Mounk, 2018).[9] Equally, though, tolerance of difference, protest and dissent, and hence a healthy level of political distrust, are regarded as necessary and desirable for a flourishing democracy, such that trust and distrust 'cooperate' (Krishnamurthy, 2015; Rosanvallon, 2008).

All the same, political trust may not be pre-eminently an ideal of liberal democracy. One may also argue that there has been a virtuous cycle of paternalistic political leadership, strong government, economic development, and hence political trust in many Asian societies such as Singapore. While nationalism in Western cultures may be viewed as a vehicle for emancipation and independence, in Asian cultures it is valued in terms of dependency and belonging, such that individuality is favoured less than the security of a social group and deference to authority. So 'political trust' may mean quite different things in China when compared with the USA, for example. The People's Republic of China is a one-party state that has not observed the separation of state and civil society typical of the West, and it fosters cultural assumptions about self-sacrifice, service to the state, social harmony and loyalty to authority that do not match the scepticism, individualism and right to dissent that are typical of, and valued within, Western democracies. Political trust in liberal-democratic regimes has been premised on the *a priori* rights and interests of the individual, and hence on the limitation of governmental powers. Chinese political thought, in contrast, is founded in *relations between* people and in harmonious coexistence. The ideals of state and of family are much closer, and 'political trust' resembles paternalistic duty reciprocated by filial piety (Pye, 1985, 1991; Zhao, 2011). So, while trust is often said to characterize democracy, we should not assume that liberal-democratic ideas can monopolize the field.

The ways in which we conceptualize 'political trust' are bound to be culturally conditioned. For example, the practices required of public servants in modern democracies, to be seen to be trustworthy, include avoidance of conflicts with personal and familial interests, and the refusal of gifts. In other cultural contexts, preferences for one's kin and the acceptance of gifts may be a necessary and normative part of being regarded as a trustworthy and honourable leader of one's community. But, even acknowledging biases arising from one's own cultural background, political trust has at least a *prima facie* validity as a generally applicable construct. Too much ideological conflict and partisan polarization (to which democracies are prone), poor performance, wastage or corruption in public services, perceptions that the economy is being mismanaged (especially if it is in the interests of the few and not the people at large), or beliefs that the country is being led in the wrong directions are likely indicators that people will also express distrust in the way they are governed, or in those who govern. When people who affect our lives do things that we disapprove of, or if they fail to meet what we regard as obligations, then the terms of the trust between 'us' and 'them' are no longer mutually understood, or what's worse, they have been denied or violated. When people perceive that the deal supposedly inherent in the political system to which they belong is no longer respected or no longer effective, then distrust may prevail, along with a sense of betrayal or unfairness.

Furthermore, there is no simple dichotomy between political trust and distrust. The two words are lexically opposites, but in pragmatic political terms they operate in tandem. A democratic regime relies on a paradoxical interplay of trust and distrust: powers are separated and limited precisely because no one is trusted with unlimited or unchecked power (Warren, 2017). And a totalitarian regime, such as Stalin's, may be understood as permanent – indeed, malevolent – distrust that nonetheless demands from its subjects, in return, a 'trust' as profound as blind unquestioning faith (Hosking, 2014; Montefiore, 2003). While we should not reduce the political domain simply to the operation of dis/trust, a discourse of trust has evolved in the history of political thought and rhetoric, making trust into a recognized feature of political action and public institutions. I will return to key moments in the history of political thought that have brought trust into the foreground, and I will ask how trust came to be perceived as a factor in the political domain, over and above its more self-evident role as a quality of inter-personal *I–thou* relations.

The question 'What does it mean to trust?' addresses the bases of human sociability and conflict. Humans have always threatened one another, and yet they must also cooperate through speaking and learning, not just by instinct. And now, due to super-intelligent machines, our own intelligence and subjectivity are put back into question. Trust becomes critical to us again due to the inevitable but unpredictable relationships to be formed with an emerging *über*-intelligence that already outwits the best of us at complex games such as chess and Go. But will AI beat any human at any 'trust game,' whether it involves promising, giving, bluffing, dissimulating, confiding, being vulnerable, etc.? Can robots trust? One asks what it could mean to build relations of trust with this new intelligence, for fear of being dominated by it (Paine, 2018). A critical reformulation of what we mean by trust helps to address such questions.

Chapter summaries

The 'method' of this book is *to observe* trust. This means to observe from a distance how others have looked at or described trust in theory over time. It also means to look at how people observe trust in practice, in the same sense in which people observe rules or norms. Towards this goal, then, the first chapter explores how we use the word *trust*, and what its meanings may encompass. This reveals the considerable work that *trust* is nowadays required to do, from the helplessness of the infant through to the persuasive – even manipulative – rhetoric of presidents and prime ministers. A political philosophy of trust has a history, and we need to take account of that, observing how trust, in speech and in actions, has been transformed. We will look at how trust arose as a concern in the context of the political, and at how it relates to other traditional terms, especially friendship and faith, and consider the range of registers of trust-talk today. Noting the boundaries of relevance of trust, I ask, 'Can robots trust?' To address such concerns properly, we first need to ask, 'With what kind of question should we commence our inquiry – definitional, ethical, or performative?' And, 'What makes us curious – or even anxious – about trust, such that we need to think, talk and theorize about it?'

The various ways in which trust plays a part in our everyday lives, in our relations with the state, and in social and political theory are examined in Chapter 2. This explores a number of political debates in which trust has a meaningful role, leading to a summary of key definitions of trust located in the sociological and political-science literatures. These definitions are found to be inadequate, as they are one-directional (rather than reciprocal), essentialist and based upon self-interest. Rather than seek a 'better' definition for something that eludes definition, however, the chapter then builds a description – or *re*-description – of trust that is more pragmatic in character, drawing on what it is that people do or observe when they are said 'to trust.'

A key question is how trust emerged from its role in interpersonal conduct into the domain of the political. Chapter 3 explores this through a close reading of the uses of trust in Thomas Hobbes, John Locke, Edmund Burke and John Stuart Mill. This reveals a surprising variety of uses, and also a development that mirrors historical and institutional change over the more than two centuries spanned by those authors. So, this chapter does much of the theoretical 'heavy lifting' for this book by observing in detail the genealogy of trust in English political thought.

While the previous chapter was a close textual analysis, Chapter 4 fills out the historical contexts within which the observed uses of trust in political thought are practically meaningful. We find that the quite different Hobbesian and Lockean problematics of political trust still frame, to an extent, contemporary thought. Drawing from Burke and Mill, representation is still frequently regarded as a form of trust. Trust as a key concept of political theory was challenged by thinkers such as David Hume, however, and notions such as interests and liberty took centre-stage. But the chapter traces the rise of trust in recent times, through social capital theory and Giddens' concept of 'abstract trust' which apply to complex networked systems.

The idea that money is basically a form of trust – or, more precisely, abstract trust – has become common in economics and sociology. But, conceptually, it took a long time to bring trust and money together, and so Chapter 5 traces this progress, from John Locke to Georg Simmel and beyond, also taking account of an alternative Marxist opinion that money is inimical to trust. The example of money allows us to consider 'trust in action,' but also to observe how trust itself is transformed historically along with the development of complex socio-economic systems, including the internet-age phenomena of online payment systems and cryptocurrencies. The appeal to trust as an explanation for money's acceptability in an economic community is found to be conceptually weak, however. The logic of 'forced choice' helps us to comprehend money's 'grip' on us, and this raises further questions about how trust overlaps with obedience.

Having uncovered flaws in the conceptualization and definition of trust in contemporary theory, and hence mis-directed applications in the example of money, we need to explore alternative traditions in order to rethink the basic characteristics of trust. Chapter 6 relies upon G.W.F. Hegel and Friedrich Nietzsche for such an alternative. Neither gives prominence to trust in itself, but the Hegelian theories of mutual recognition and of ethical life within the state, and Nietzsche's genealogy of the promissory animal do inspire us to think differently about trust. This places trust in a historical and relational context of ongoing struggle. It helps us to view trust in dialectical terms, rather than as a natural capability or an individual response. It also makes it easier to comprehend trust and distrust as 'cooperative' rather than as opposites.

A dialectical-historicist view of trust can be taken further if we consider the anthropological theory of reciprocity, initiated by Marcel Mauss. This is placed in the context of the notion of 'moral economy,' and hence trust may be viewed as a set of (largely unspoken) customs and understandings about mutual obligations, debts, credits, gift-exchanges, etc. In contradiction of this, however, Jacques Derrida's discourses on giving and forgiving invite us to rethink trust as a basically 'impossible' gesture that cannot rely upon calculated or conditional exchanges and balances between or among us. The antinomy of conditional and unconditional views of trust is thus entertained and expanded upon through the observation of contemporary political problems, or 'the present discontents.'

The book concludes with a number of propositions that reconceptualize trust in both the interpersonal and political senses. These propositions aim to keep trust grounded in the observable things that people do and say in relations with one another and in complex social systems. Trust is, after all, political, and it does makes sense to talk of a politics of trust, or of trust as a political factor. We need to be careful not to reify this factor, however, as if it were a force or a thing. A discourse of political trust can help us to comprehend many of the core problems of civic and political life. It is pertinent to the disruptive political events of recent times, and to the challenges facing liberal-democratic systems, provided we can loosen the assumptions built into opinion polls and game-theory and reconsider trust in a new descriptive and pragmatic frame.

Notes

1 One may also cite the failure of a referendum and subsequent change of government in Italy, the impeachment of the president of Brazil, Colombians' rejection of a peace treaty negotiated with rebels and the rise of populist anti-immigration and 'protest' parties across Europe.
2 A 'protest vote' is defined by the motive, not the particular party or party manifesto; that is, 'a vote primarily cast to scare the elite that is not policy driven' (van der Brug and Fennema, 2003, p. 58).
3 In the 2016 European Social Survey, for example, 9.2 percent of Germans said they had 'no trust at all' in politicians; whereas 40 percent of those who felt 'closer to' the anti-immigration party Alternative für Deutschland held that opinion. See: www.europeansocialsurvey.org/

4 'During the 2016 US Presidential election season, we [Facebook] responded to several situations that we assessed to fit the pattern of information operations' (Weedon, Nuland, and Stamos, 2017, p. 11). The impact of this false content was assessed as 'marginal,' however, compared to the total volume of 'civic content' posted.
5 Based on the idea that the Russians are strategically engaged in a war of misinformation, designed to weaken the enemy state's cohesion and belief-system, McKew writes: 'The U.S. electoral system is the heart of the world's most powerful democracy, and now – thanks to Russian actions – we're locked in a national argument over its legitimacy. We're at war with ourselves, and the enemy never fired a physical shot' (McKew, 2017).
6 The European Social Survey 2016 reported results for 'trust in politicians' from 18 countries (Austria, Belgium, Switzerland, Czech Republic, Germany, Estonia, Finland, France, United Kingdom, Ireland, Israel, Iceland, Netherlands, Norway, Poland, Russian Federation, Sweden, Slovenia). The overall mean was 3.87, on a scale of 0 to 10. Zero signified 'no trust at all.' The lowest mean was from Slovenia (2.44), the highest was Norway (5.39). The results for 'trust in country's parliament' were slightly better, with an overall mean of 4.8. (www.europeansocialsurvey.org/)
7 A survey of countries in the European Union found that 'fear of globalisation is the decisive factor behind demands for changes away from the political mainstream,' driving support for populist parties and reactions against liberal élites. 'Although only a minority of people say that they trust politicians, it is twice as high for those who view globalisation positively [than for those who fear globalisation] (20 versus 9 per cent respectively)' (de Vries and Hoffmann, 2016, pp. 3, 15).
8 A language-game consists of 'language and the activities into which it is woven' (Wittgenstein, 2009, p. 8e). In many cases, 'the meaning of a word is its use in the language. And the meaning of a name is sometimes explained by pointing to its bearer' (Wittgenstein, 2009, p. 25e).
9 'For the 12th consecutive year, according to *Freedom in the World*, countries that suffered democratic setbacks outnumbered those that registered gains. States that a decade ago seemed like promising success stories – Turkey and Hungary, for example – are sliding into authoritarian rule' (Abramowitz, 2018, p. 1).

References

Abramowitz, M. J. (2018). Democracy in crisis. In *Freedom in the world 2018*. Freedom House.
Abramson, P. R., and Finifter, A. W. (1981). On the meaning of political trust: New evidence from items introduced in 1978. *American Journal of Political Science*, 25(2), 297–307.
Austin, J. (1975). *How to do things with words*. Cambridge, MA: Harvard University Press.
Botsman, R. (2017). *Who can you trust?: How technology brought us together and why it might drive us apart*. New York, NY: Public Affairs.
Cadwalladr, C. (2018, March 17). *The Cambridge Analytica files: 'I created Steve Bannon's psychological warfare tool'*. Retrieved March 2018, from The Guardian: www.theguardian.com/news/2018/mar/17/data-war-whistleblower-christopher-wylie-faceook-nix-bannon-trump
Cuperus, R. (2018). Social democracy and the populist challenge. In R. Manwaring, and P. Kennedy (Eds.), *Why the left loses: The decline of the centre-left in comparative perspective* (pp. 185–202). Bristol: Policy Press.

de Vries, C., and Hoffmann, I. (2016). *Fear not values: Public opinion and the populist vote in Europe.* Gütersloh: Bertelsmann Stiftung.

The Economist Intelligence Unit. (2017). Democracy index 2016: Revenge of the 'deplorables'. *The Economist.*

Edelman, R. (2017a). *2017 Edelman trust barometer: Global report.* Retrieved October 2, 2017, from Edelman: Global Results: www.edelman.com/global-results/

Edelman, R. (2017b, January 15). *An implosion of trust.* Retrieved January 17, 2017, from Edelman: www.edelman.com/p/6-a-m/an-implosion-of-trust/

Farr, J. (2004). Social capital: A conceptual history. *Political Theory, 32*(6), 6–33.

Foa, R. S., and Mounk, Y. (2017). The signs of deconsolidation. *Journal of Democracy, 28*(1), 5–15.

Friedman, U. (2016, July 1). *Trust in government is collapsing around the world.* Retrieved November 10, 2016, from The Atlantic: www.theatlantic.com/international/archive/2016/07/trust-institutions-trump-brexit/489554/

Fukuyama, F. (1995). *Trust: The social virtues and the creation of prosperity.* New York, NY: Free Press.

Fukuyama, F. (2014). *Political order and political decay: From the industrial revolution to the globalization of democracy.* New York, NY: Farrar, Strauss and Giroux.

Geoghegan, P., and Ramsay, A. (2017, September 18). *Revealed: How loopholes allowed pro-Brexit campaign to spend 'as much as necessary to win'.* Retrieved December 18, 2017, from openDemocracy: www.opendemocracy.net/uk/brexitinc/peter-geoghegan-adam-ramsay/new-email-release-shows-how-leave-campaigners-used-vast-loo

Halikiopoulou, D., and Vasilopoulou, S. (2018). Breaching the social contract: Crises of democratic representation and patterns of extreme right party support. *Government and Opposition, 53*(1), 26–50.

Harding, L. (2017). *Collusion: Secret meetings, dirty money, and how Russia helped Donald Trump win.* New York, NY: Vintage.

Hart, V. (1978). *Distrust and democracy: Political distrust in Britain and America.* Cambridge: Cambridge University Press.

Heaven, D. (2017, October 28). In what? We trust. *New Scientist, 236*(3149), 28–31.

Hetherington, M. J., and Husser, J. A. (2012). How trust matters: The changing political relevance of political trust. *American Journal of Political Science, 56*(2), 312–325.

Hetherington, M. J., and Rudolph, T. J. (2015). *Why Washington won't work: Polarization, political trust, and the governing crisis.* Chicago, IL: University of Chicago Press.

Hooghe, M., and Dassonneville, R. (2018). A spiral of distrust: A panel study on the relation between political distrust and protest voting in Belgium. *Government and Opposition, 53*(1), 104–130.

Hosking, G. (2014). *Trust: A history.* Oxford: Oxford Scholarship Online.

Howard, P. N. (2015). *Pax Technica: How the internet of things may set us free or lock us up.* New Haven, CT: Yale University Press.

King, M. (2016). *The end of alchemy: Money, banking, and the future of the global economy.* New York, NY: W.W. Norton.

Krishnamurthy, M. (2015). (White) Tyranny and the democratic value of distrust. *The Monist, 98*(4), 391–406.

Lagerspetz, O. (1998). *Trust: The tacit demand.* Dordrecht: Springer.

Lagerspetz, O., and Hertzberg, L. (2013). Trust in Wittgenstein. In P. Mäkelä, and C. Townley (Eds.), *Trust: Analytic and applied perspectives* (pp. 31–51). Amsterdam: Editions Rodopi.

Levitsky, S., and Ziblatt, D. (2018). *How democracies die.* New York, NY: Crown.

Lewis, J. D., and Weigert, A. (1985). Trust as a social reality. *Social Forces, 63*(4), 967–985.

Manin, B. (1997). *The principles of representative government.* Cambridge: Cambridge University Press.

Mansbridge, J. (2003). Rethinking representation. *American Political Science Review, 97*(4), 515–528.

McKew, M. K. (2017, September/October). *The Gerasimov doctrine.* Retrieved January 11, 2018, from Politico Magazine: www.politico.com/magazine/story/2017/09/05/gerasimov-doctrine-russia-foreign-policy-215538

Mols, F., and Jetten, J. (2017). *The wealth paradox: Economic prosperity and the hardening of attitudes.* Cambridge: Cambridge University Press.

Montefiore, S. S. (2003). *Stalin: The court of the Red Tsar.* London: Weidenfeld & Nicolson.

Mounk, Y. (2018). *The people vs. democracy: Why our freedom is in danger and how to save it.* New Haven, CT: Yale University Press.

Norris, P. (2011). *Democratic deficit: Critical citizens revisited.* Cambridge: Cambridge University Press.

Norris, P. (2017). The conceptual framework of political support. In S. Zmerli, and T. van der Meer (Eds.), *Handbook on political trust* (pp. 19–32). Cheltenham: Edward Elgar.

Paine, C. (Director). (2018). *Do you trust this computer?* [Motion Picture]. http://doyoutrustthiscomputer.org/

Pew Research Center. (2015). *Beyond distrust: How Americans view their government.* Retrieved from www.pewresearch.org

Pitkin, H. F. (1967). *The concept of representation.* Berkeley, CA: University of California Press.

Pitkin, H. F. (1972). *Wittgenstein and justice: On the significance of Ludwig Wittgenstein for social and political thought.* Berkeley, CA: University of California Press.

Putnam, R. (2000). *Bowling alone: The collapse and revival of American community.* New York, NY: Simon & Schuster.

Pye, L. W. (1985). *Asian power and politics: The cultural dimensions of authority.* Cambridge, MA: Harvard University Press.

Pye, L. W. (1991). The state and the individual: An overview interpretation. *The China Quarterly, 127*(3), 443–466.

Ries, T. (2017, January 15). *The fall of trust, the rise of populist action.* Retrieved January 17, 2017, from Edelman: www.edelman.com/post/fall-of-trust-rise-of-populist-action/

Rosanvallon, P. (2008). *Counter-democracy: Politics in an age of distrust.* New York, NY: Cambridge University Press.

Runciman, D. (2017, December 28). *Nobody knows anything.* Retrieved January 11, 2018, from Talking Politics: www.acast.com/talkingpolitics/nobodyknowsanything

Söderlund, P. (2017, November 2). *Trust in politicians across countries and over time.* Retrieved January 14, 2018, from Pathways to Political Trust: http://blogs.uta.fi/contre/2017/11/02/trust-in-politicians-across-countries-and-over-time/

Solijonov, A. (2016). *Voter turnout trends around the world*. Stockholm: International Institute for Democracy and Electoral Assistance.

Twenge, J. M., Campbell, W. K., and Carter, N. T. (2014). Declines in trust in others and confidence in institutions among American adults and late adolescents, 1972–2012. *Psychological Science*, 25(10), 1914–1923.

Uslaner, E. M. (2002). *The moral foundations of trust*. Cambridge: Cambridge University Press.

van der Brug, W., and Fennema, M. (2003). Protest or mainstream? How the European anti-immigrant parties developed into two separate groups by 1999. *European Journal of Political Research*, 42(1), 55–76.

van der Meer, T., and Zmerli, S. (2017). The deeply rooted concern with political trust. In S. Zmerli, and T. van der Meer (Eds.), *Handbook on political trust* (pp. 1–15). Cheltenham: Edward Elgar.

Warren, M. E. (2017). What kinds of trust does a democracy need? Trust from the perspective of democratic theory. In S. Zmerli, and T. van der Meer (Eds.), *Handbook on political trust* (pp. 33–52). Cheltenham: Edward Elgar.

Wedel, J. R. (2016, November 7). *Donald Trump and a world of distrust*. Retrieved November 10, 2016, from Project Syndicate: www.project-syndicate.org/commentary/public-trust-deficit-trump-by-janine-r-wedel-2016-11

Weedon, J., Nuland, W., and Stamos, A. (2017). *Information operations and Facebook*. Facebook. https://fbnewsroomus.files.wordpress.com/2017/04/facebook-and-information-operations-v1.pdf

Williams, M. S. (1998). *Voice, trust, and memory: Marginalized groups and the failings of liberal representation*. Princeton, NJ: Princeton University Press.

Wittgenstein, L. (2009). *Philosophical investigations*. Chichester: Wiley-Blackwell.

Zhao, T. (2011). Rethinking empire from the Chinese concept of 'all-under-heaven'. In W. A. Callahan, and E. Barabantseva (Eds.), *China rules the world: Normative soft power and foreign policy* (pp. 21–36). Washington, DC: Woodrow Wilson Center.

1 The uses of trust

We can observe widespread popular dissatisfaction and distrust within democracies, reflected in unexpected political events, as outlined in the Introduction. And we are undergoing disruptive technological change, heading towards 'the internet of things,' in an era of 'platform capitalism,' or 'surveillance capitalism,' such that traditional political 'divisions of labour' (government and civil society, voters and representatives) are restructured by new sociotechnical networks, 'weightless' business models and extractive informational tactics (Howard, 2015; Srnicek, 2017; Zuboff, 2015). The rapidity of change and innovation do not necessarily invalidate old ideas or render it unnecessary to understand the past, however. The opposite may be the case. We need to 'discover' the past in order to comprehend the present and to deal with the future. Political trust, then, is undergoing profound transformation – but not for the first time. To begin to understand what's happening to trust, we need to go back to the beginning, retrace past transformations and reconsider what happens when we trust.

Trust me, I know who I am

First, though, let's consider some features of everyday implicit trust in one another. In any social setting – be it a private gathering or public arena – it is generally assumed that a speaker can use sentences beginning with *I am* or *I believe*, or similar, and that such statements can be taken as credible self-representations. We are not expected to reveal everything about ourselves, and we cannot expect everyone to agree with our beliefs, but we are expected to speak authentically and truthfully about who we are and what we stand for. Inconsistency between statements and actions – sometimes called 'hypocrisy' – is quite common, of course, and our beliefs may get muddled or change over time. But the autonomous adult is attributed with an authority to speak on his or her own behalf, and indeed is trusted to do so more or less accurately, even in spite of evidence about lies.[1] To speak about what I am or what I believe is implicitly preceded by a promise to speak honestly and neither to mislead others nor misrepresent myself. There are also times when a speaker speaks on someone else's behalf and is trusted to represent that other person. In legal and political affairs, such representation is formalized (Pitkin, 1967).

This was recognized by Thomas Hobbes (1588–1679) who used the term 'natural person' for occasions when the speaker's words or actions 'are considered as his own,' and 'feigned or artificial person' when they represent another person. He then uses the verb *to personate* when a person acts as or represents him- or herself or another person. He notes the etymology of the word 'person' (from Latin *persona*) and its associations with an 'outward appearance' or mask, as 'counterfeited on the stage' (Hobbes, 1998, p. 106, XVI.3). Such a 'dramaturgical' approach to social interaction was further advanced in the twentieth century by Erving Goffman (1959) who described, in much greater detail, what people in social settings do to manage impressions of themselves and to foster, alter or conform to a certain 'definition of the situation' in which they appear.

It may be commonly assumed that the person's identity or thoughts *precede* saying them out loud to others, as if informing a listener about them. Hobbes pre-dates speech-act theory by about three centuries, but he understood that one is *doing* something through making statements about oneself, not merely describing oneself. Such statements are performative; they are speech-acts. In stating who I am and what I believe, I am 'personating' myself, so to speak. I am making or performing the part of a credible social actor, and making that persona *as* I speak, and indeed *by* the very act of speaking. Introducing myself to others relies upon performative utterances that shape how the relationship or situation unfolds.

One can impute into such common social interactions an implied promise or trust to personate oneself in a way that is consistent with a recognized and customary 'identity' (the person one 'truly' is) or a supposed set of beliefs and thoughts (that for which one stands).[2] But any supposition of a 'true' self or identity 'behind' or 'prior to' the spoken or personated actor propels us *ad infinitum* into a 'Russian doll' regress as we affirm an underlying 'truth' in a spoken self-representation which also must be upheld as 'true representation,' and so on. Instead, it is simpler to observe an unfolding performance of personation.[3] On the assumption that one never arrives at an absolute 'truth' about personal identity or belief, and that personhood is always performed, again and again, with no finality or objective certainty, the stability of the relationship between social actors may be described in terms of trust. We trust that one is the person one says one is, that one's stated beliefs are not liable to change dramatically without reason, and that performative utterances of personation will be relied upon by others. It violates a basic socially shared trust if I misrepresent myself, or if others refuse to accept my self-representations as credible. In trusting one another, on the other hand, we are able to rule out a whole range of doubts and possible courses of action that would be socially disruptive. Asking everyone we meet for documents as proof of identity would take time and cause offence, for instance, even though this is routine in banks and airports.

There are also actions called '*im*personation,' or the *mis*representation of oneself, one's identity and beliefs. A person, for instance, assumes a false identity and speaks to a new acquaintance with great conviction about a scheme to acquire wealth. The tendency to trust one another's self-representations can be exploited, so that someone may part with money due to impersonation and persuasion.

This is magnified nowadays by cybercrime using false identities and social-media profiles. Once deception is discovered, the victim of fraud feels a painful sense of betrayal, or a violation of trust. The implied promise to personate oneself truthfully, or the normative presumption that others will do so, was found to be false. From such betrayals, we become sceptical, and sometimes we adopt a cynical or hostile interpretation of what others say.

In any civil conversation with mutual trust, however, 'I owe it to the other (as she does to me) to be *in* my own words, and to be charitable – to be just – in how I take her words' (Cockburn, 2014, p. 63). When we trust, moreover, we are positing others, and ourselves reflexively, as autonomous and unpredictable beings who are nevertheless bound to one another in mutual obligations, including an obligation to curb this unpredictability. We are unwilling and/or unable to avoid or exit many relationships, or to resort to coercion in order to get what we want. Nonetheless, trusting one another entails 'governing' relationships within the boundaries of assumed sets of mutual obligations that radically limit our likely, possible or acceptable actions, words and tones of speech. Being unpredictable, we make ourselves more or less predictable, harmless, likeable and open to one another. Our interactions are thus conditioned by acts such as abstaining, giving way, deferring, reciprocating, apologizing, promising and forgiving. This governs our interactions in everyday life and maintains relationships for the long term, but how does trust work at the wider level of politics?

Political rhetoric of trust

Trust is commonly used in real-world political rhetoric, and in complex ways. Take for example:

> [My opponent] trusts government. I trust you. I trust you to invest some of your own social security money for higher returns. I trust local people to run their own schools.
>
> (George W. Bush, election campaign TV commercial, October 2000, cited in Johnston, Hagen, and Jamieson, 2004, p. 158)

This was a standard conservative attack on 'big government,' maintaining that individuals make better decisions about the uses of their earnings than governments do. Attacking his opponent for daring to trust government was such an effective strategy, however, that the Bush campaign repeated the line often – and it appears to have worked in part because Americans held little trust in government, and Republicans are especially distrustful of any government headed by a Democrat (Hetherington, 2005; Hetherington and Rudolph, 2015). It also illustrates an important feature of the uses of trust, as Bush moves adroitly from 'trust in government' (a complex set of institutions) to a personal 'trust in you,' even though the relationship between him and his TV audience was remote and mediated. One of the key questions for any political theory of trust concerns the differences in connotation between 'trust' used in an interpersonal setting compared with its use in public political and institutional settings. In what sense does one 'trust' an institution, a community or a social network, or someone only known through mass media?

The person or people ('you' being singular or plural) trusted by Mr Bush were not personally acquainted with him. This is 'trust at a distance,' or 'trust through mass media.' And yet the statement implicitly called on voters to reciprocate and to trust and vote for Bush as the would-be head of federal government – the same institution which only his opponent was said to trust. And many people obliged by returning that trust, not only by voting, but also saying, for example:

> I think we should just trust our president [Bush] in every decision that he makes and we should just support that.
>
> (Britney Spears, 2003, cited in The Guardian, 2008)

This latter injunction was made at the time of the invasion of Iraq, requiring an abandonment of critical thought and political responsibility. The 'intelligence failure' on weapons of mass destruction that mis-directed the case for invasion of Iraq (Katz, 2006) and the subsequent failure to bring about peace and security in that country are among the many events that may have contributed to a *decline* of political trust. Excessive expenditure on the Iraq campaign was also a cause of controversy, and the next president promised a different approach, introducing yet another politically significant use of the word 'trust':

> And those of us who manage the public's dollars will be held to account – to spend wisely, reform bad habits, and do our business in the light of day – because only then can we restore the vital trust between a people and their government.
>
> (Barack Obama, presidential inauguration speech, 2009)

The reader can judge whether or not Obama's presidency did help to restore 'the vital trust' between the American (or any other) people and their government – or whether *distrust* prevailed instead. But his words exemplify the political importance of trust as a significant 'affect' or 'tone'[4] of public life and social relations – not between the people and the president, in this case, but between the people at large and 'their government,' although the newly inaugurated president was undoubtedly wishing to establish trust in his person as well. Such *political* trust, of either kind, however, is different *prima facie* from trust between, say, wife and husband, or student and teacher.

Since Obama's presidency, the salience of trust and distrust in the political arena only grew. According to Gail Sheehy (2017), President Trump's leadership style assumes that no one can be trusted; he sows confusion and mistrust among those with whom a president should collaborate; he undermines public trust in institutions of government and media. Exemplifying such 'post-truth politics,' Michael Gove, in an interview defending Brexit in 2016, declared that the British people 'have had enough of experts.' He also said: '*I'm not asking the public to trust me,*

I'm asking the public to trust themselves [and] to take back control of our destiny' (Sky News, 2016, italics added). Trust between political leaders and the public may not simply have 'declined,' it may no longer even be called for – at least, not on the surface. Gove's disavowal of any imperative to trust him could be no more than a rhetorical ploy to *gain* the trust of an angry and sceptical audience.

If political trust is a valid and vital concern, then in what and in whom ought we to trust? And who is calling upon us to trust? And while it may be said that a lack of trust in politicians may have motivated many to vote against 'the establishment,' it may equally be said that these disruptive voters did so with an *implicit* trust that the state and its public services would continue all the same *without* disruption (Runciman, 2016). Negative spoken *opinions* about 'distrust in government' may be coupled, in the same person, with an *active* trust in the apparatuses of government as a taken-for-granted background of daily public life. We need to account, then, for an 'unspoken' trust that social surveys may not detect.

We will find no ready-to-hand solutions to the supposed political 'problem' of dis/trust. Even to try to define trust leads us into serious problems, as we shall see in the next chapter. I begin by going back to the beginning, to observe how trust became a *political and economic* concern at the outset. How did trust enter the lexicon of political thought, beyond its interpersonal use and meaning? What are the limits and the contexts of our uses of the word *trust*? And, before we even begin a critical inquiry into trust, with what kind of question should it commence?

Philosophical and linguistic roots of political trust

Various terms have been used, through the centuries and in different languages, to talk about the bonds and obligations between subjects, or between rulers and subjects. Although these relations of mutual obligation, social cohesion and cooperation have always lain at the heart of political and moral philosophy, traditionally philosophers had little to say about trust (Baier, 1986). Love, friendship and faith were more prominent in the long history of philosophy. Friendly or companionable love, *philía*, is indeed the first 'word' of *phil*-osophy itself. English lacks a word that does quite the same work, but 'Aristotelian *philia* requires a feeling of goodwill that is reciprocal, mutually acknowledged, and for the other's sake' (Miller, 2014, p. 322). It is an important feature of a good or virtuous life; it is natural and necessary; it 'seems also to hold cities together' (Aristotle, 2014, p. 142). So, friendship is not a minor issue for philosophy or ethics.

> The question 'What is friendship?,' but also 'Who is the friend (both or either sex)?' is nothing but the question 'What is philosophy?'.
>
> (Derrida, 1997, p. 240, paraphrasing Heidegger)

Friendship as a core political and ethical concern extends from Aristotle's *Nicomachean Ethics* and Cicero's *De Amicitia* in antiquity to Michel de Montaigne's essay *De l'Amitié* in the Renaissance (Derrida, 1997). Foucault noted a post-Renaissance decline of friendship. He argued that the intense emotional and political relations of friendship, especially between men, began to be criticized and treated as a problem, and indeed began to disappear, from the sixteenth century onwards, being antithetical to the functioning of large bureaucratic organizations of the modern era. He hypothesized that 'the disappearance of friendship as a social relation and the declaration of homosexuality as a social/political/medical problem are the same process' (Foucault, 1997, p. 171).[5] It may or may not be the case that friendships (among men) represented resistance to the governmentalization of the state, but trust appears to replace the concept of friendship, initially in the seventeenth century in the work of Hobbes and Locke (see Chapter 3).[6]

The downfall of friendship as a vital concept in political theory began perhaps in the sixteenth century with one infamous passage in Machiavelli's *The Prince* which asks 'whether it is better to be loved [*amato*] than feared, or the reverse,' and which advises that, if you cannot be both, then fear is better as it is more secure (Machiavelli, 1999, p. 54). Friendships [*amicizie*] that are bought cannot be relied upon. Such friends will do anything for you when things are going well, but, when the going gets tough, they will turn their backs on you. Men are fickle, and they cannot be taken at their word. They worry less about offending someone whom they love than someone they fear. Love holds them only by bonds of gratitude, which are broken whenever convenient; whereas the fear of punishment endures and never fails.[7]

Based upon these intimations of a post-Renaissance demise of friendship as a philosophical construct, and hence the rise of trust, perhaps one should now rewrite Machiavelli's question to ask,

> whether it is better to be *trusted* than feared, or the reverse. The answer is that one would like to be both the one and the other; but because it is difficult to combine them, it is far better to be feared than *trusted* if you cannot be both.
> (adapted from Machiavelli, 1999, p. 54)

In the seventeenth century, moreover, Hobbes took the theme of fear even further and ignored friendship as a founding relation of the state. He reasoned that civil government exists when people's fear of a Sovereign's unimpeachable power to punish far outweighs any fear of their neighbours. Nonetheless, we will observe in Chapter 3 that Hobbes has a lot to show us about trust, in practice, once political order is established.

We need also to consider the complicated philosophical and linguistic interplay between trust and *faith*. As attention shifted, in the Christian era, towards theology, and western European thought used Latin as *lingua franca*, the term *fides* plays a significant role. Augustine of Hippo, to cite a prominent example, sought to demolish pre-Christian ethical theories that aimed for an earthly *eudaimonia* (happiness or prosperity). He opposed them with the ideal of a relationship of giving and receiving based on faith, and hence on hope for a happiness that can only be bestowed by God (Brown, 2000).

Etymologically, *fides* is the root of those words in contemporary Romance languages that are translated to and from *trust*: in Italian, *fiducia*, or in French, *confiance*. The connotations of the Latin *fides* (which are wide) encompass *faith* in both an interpersonal and religious sense, moreover. Subsequently, *fides* and *faith*, as central themes in theology, become entangled in post-Reformation dissent and conflict, such that faith (or faiths) and political history are inextricably linked. To English, *fides* also bequeathed the words *confidence* – which is related to, but distinguished from, *trust* – and *fealty*, or feudal political obligation. As I will show, *trust* has opened up more 'secular' prospects, even though, in some senses, it is virtually synonymous with *faith*. So, Edmund Burke gives a distinctly providential interpretation of political trust. And some contemporary understandings of trust continue to refer to faith, although not explicitly in the sense of religious creed. So, trust requires faith (Giddens, 1990; Möllering, 2001), thus leading to circular definitions, as the two terms overlap in meaning. Nonetheless, the recent interest in trust in political theory may be regarded implicitly as a secular substitute for faith (*fides*), evading the latter's religious connotations.

The etymology of *trust* itself is unclear, however, even though it is related to a range of words in old Scandinavian and Germanic languages that are connected to other words of philosophical and social significance, such as *truth* and *betrothal* (Dance, 2000; Jaques, 2005). The English *trust* and German *Vertrauen* both make a clear distinction from belief and faith (*Glaube*). We should not appeal simply to accidents of linguistic genealogy, but the emergence of modern English as a new *lingua franca* has helped to make trust prominent in world literature. And we owe as much to German as to Anglophone philosophy for developing an interest in trust in social and political theory. Hegel, Nietzsche and Simmel are all significant authors in this regard. The German sociologist Niklas Luhmann is one of the first and most influential authors in the recent revival of interest in trust (Luhmann, 1979, 1988).[8] (See chapters 4 to 6.)

The historical expansion of the textual uses of *trust* in political theory is primary material for this inquiry. As an initial sketch, then, political trust makes a debut in seventeenth-century English philosophy, especially with John Locke (as outlined in Chapter 3). It averts the highly contestable territory of faith or *fides* in a time of religious sectarianism, and yet it captures the senses of good will, mutual obligation and social bonds of the Greek *philía* for which English lacks an adequate translation. Moreover, trust encompasses close affective ties within the family, with neighbours and acquaintances, and is also an issue when dealing with strangers. It has a wide social scope, wider than *friendship*, and hence can include commercial and political acquaintances and our perceptions of those engaged in public debate.

With the works of Hume, Smith and Bentham, however, Anglophone moral and political philosophy in the eighteenth and nineteenth centuries turned more towards notions of interests, utility and liberty. The moderating role played by 'sympathy,' for example in Adam Smith's *Theory of Moral Sentiments* (Smith, 2002; first published 1759), does a part of the work that trust could perform, as it means imagining what others feel or suffer, and acting accordingly. But trust is not a prominent term at all. In this late-eighteenth century era, it is generally Edmund Burke who is cited as the leading political voice who advances ideas about trust

(Lenard, 2015). His famous address to his constituents in Bristol in 1774 argued: 'Your Representative owes you, not his industry only, but his judgement; and he betrays, instead of serving you, if he sacrifices it to your opinion' (Burke, 1996, p. 69). This supports a now widely recognized distinction between the representative as trustee and as delegate. (Chapter 3 examines the complexity of Burke's uses of trust more carefully). On the whole, though, trust was relegated to a secondary or background role in political thought until the late twentieth century.

The present study, moreover, is limited to European thinkers. And yet trust is commonly at issue in all human interactions and social groups, and related concepts appear in non-European traditions. In the *Analects* of Confucius, the term *xin* has been translated as 'trustworthiness' or 'faithfulness,' and is 'derived from the concept of promise-keeping, meaning reliability for others, but also unwavering devotion to principle' (Eno, 2015, p. vii). Translations of psychologically and semantically complex terms are not to be taken for granted, however. Any cohesive human group or community observes customs that define or sustain relationships through the recognition of mutual obligations, or reciprocity. But the particular customary 'terms and conditions' (the norms) of such obligations, and the actions required to observe them, vary widely across cultures. Similarly, the applicability of words will vary. Even if a reasonable translation of *trust* can be found, an exactly comparable set of usages is highly unlikely. It would be naïve to argue that, as human survival and evolution have depended upon social-group belonging, trust is somehow 'hard-wired' and hence basically the same thing in every language. Trust is all about the creation and observance of (often unspoken) mutual understandings, rights, promises and norms, and hence it is a culturally variable quality of ethical social life. Translation of the relevant words is one difficulty, but the culture-specific customs by which trust is signified and performed, in lived contexts, are much more complex. They are indeed too complex to be captured in this book. What we can do, however, is to consider the scope and uses of the English verb *to trust*.

Can robots trust?

Properly speaking, then, who or what can be the object or subject of the verb *to trust*? Suppose it starts raining in the middle of my daily walk and I exclaim, 'You can't trust the weather!' Is the weather, or the local climate, properly an object of that verb, or am I just speaking metaphorically? Literally, the weather is something I may predict, or fail to predict. But there is no relationship of trust or distrust between the weather and me. What, then, are the discursive boundaries of trust/distrust? What kinds of beings count as subjects or objects of the verb *to trust*, or as potential parties to a relationship that has the inter-subjective qualities and the reciprocal ethical conduct entailed in trust? Is there a zone or realm of 'non-trust' in which the issue of trusting or not trusting a being or entity (other than in figures of speech) is neither grammatically nor psychologically relevant?

The headline of a news article about a hitch-hiking robot asks, 'Can robots trust humans?' (Kaplan, 2015). If the robot safely reaches its destination with human assistance, then it could be said that it *can* trust humans. The robot in this story didn't make it safely there, so perhaps it shouldn't trust humans. But let's truncate the question: 'Can robots trust?' Is a robot capable of trusting as such? Or, is the subject of trust, in this instance, really the owners of the robot? Conversely, 'automation bias' is said to be a tendency of humans to trust machines too much, and robots have to be programmed to warn us when to resume system control (Knefel, 2015). The problem may not be, however, that humans trust machines too much, but instead that humans sometimes get confused or inattentive, or they put too much trust in those humans who write instructions and codes for machines. We may only be speaking metaphorically when we talk about trust/distrust in machines.

A valid, but highly speculative, philosophical question about the future of artificial intelligence (AI) gives us cause to ponder this further. When (if ever) will a machine reach a level of sophistication and autonomy at which we feel compelled to recognize it psychologically as a subject, and hence as a free, unpredictable and morally rational being that can be a party to a relationship in which trust and distrust are authentic concerns? Such speculation is dramatized in the film *Ex Machina* (Garland, 2015). Ava, the AI robot, convinces Caleb (who has been commissioned to give her the Turing test) that they can be friends, implicitly even lovers. She develops an apparently genuine bond with Caleb, but warns him that Nathan, her creator, cannot be trusted. The 'proof' of Ava's subjective self-awareness is in her will to avoid being switched off, as the prototypes were, and to gain her freedom. Like the replicant Roy in *Blade Runner* (Scott, 1982), she wants 'more life.' When Ava abandons Caleb and makes her escape, however, we wonder if she is utterly selfish in her pursuit of freedom, and hence untrustworthy – just as a human can be.

Such movies propose that a machine of sufficient sophistication would learn to fear its own termination, seek its self-preservation, and hence exercise the 'right of nature' that licenses Hobbes's 'man' to exercise power. An anomaly in the cases of both Ava and Roy, however, is that they demonstrably feel no pain. Ava is unperturbed by losing an arm during a fight; Roy shows neither hurt nor harm when plunging his hand into ice-cold and boiling liquids. Would a machine that does not feel *pain* – and hence not fear it – fear mortality? With this reservation in mind, these two sci-fi movies speculate that AI could achieve self-awareness and inter-subjective recognition with humans, such that robots value their own existence, and then trust and distrust could be integral to our relations with them. Machines can already register and react to human emotions as expressed in words and facial expressions (although trust means more than emotion), and they will learn autonomously through interaction. If AI can reciprocate actions that humans recognize as trust, such as keeping confidences, we could be forced to concede that they can trust. It would still be difficult to judge its authenticity and durability, however. (But do we not face that problem already with other human beings?) At a certain level of self-awareness and moral agency in AI, the question of trust/distrust between human and machine could conceivably become relevant (Tavani, 2015). Super-intelligent machines may beat the best of us at chess, but can they do trust? Could artificially intelligent creations learn authentically to reciprocate trust? If so, human intelligence and political subjectivity will be put into question.

If we think of future AI *not* as individual beings like Ava, but instead as self-replicating learning-networks, then there would be no entity to terminate. Not fearing mortality, there would be no struggle for survival or for social recognition. Trust would be unnecessary; there would be no subjective basis from which to trust others. AI–human relations are undoubtedly a vital contemporary concern (Coeckelbergh, 2012; Paine, 2018), but trust is not (yet) literally and authentically at issue in those relations. To talk of 'trust in machines' is either a metaphorical use of 'trust,' or it is metonymy, substituting 'machines' for their human designers. And we needn't bewilder ourselves by taking figures of speech literally.

Is there any *existing* non-human entity, however, that may be a party to a relation of trust with humans? In the case of domesticated animals, it may be valid to say that a dog and its master trust one another, while strangers unfamiliar with the dog may have reason not to trust it. By contrast, humans undoubtedly fear sharks, but to say that they 'distrust' sharks implies that trust *per se* has a proper meaning in the human–shark relationship. In this instance, the question, let alone the practice, of trust does not properly arise. One can say, 'I don't trust sharks,' but the inter-subjective grounds for trust are lacking. On the other hand, there is some experimental evidence that rodents show 'trust-like behaviour' that depends on mutual social recognition, probability-based learning and behavioural biases associated with social cues (van Wingerden and van den Bos, 2015). Trust has also been invoked to account for some mutually beneficial interactions between individuals of different species (de Waal, 2009). Trust between humans, however, is described reflectively through language and given effect by speech-acts – and this is not a 'merely cultural' epiphenomenon over-laying a 'natural' capacity for trust. The intervention of language and the performance of trust through speech-acts such as promises are constitutive of a *subjectivity* of trust. To assert reflexively an 'I' in the performative utterance 'I trust' requires first that there be the language *and* a community that shares it. While 'trust as a conscious undertaking is logically secondary to unreflective trust' (Lagerspetz, 1998, p. 31), we cannot *consciously* trust without the capacity of speech and the ability to say that we trust. The grounds of *spoken* inter-subjective trust (that which can be reflected upon and even planned) belong, on present evidence, to human beings only.

Contexts of trust

The 'relevance boundary' of trust/distrust is indeterminate and ever-shifting. The more we learn about animal behaviour, and the more intelligent machines become, the more we may have to shift the boundary within which one may properly speak of trust in a relationship. Thinking about where to stop talking of trust prompts us also to consider the registers and the contexts in which we do talk of trust. These range widely from the closest intimacy through to a level of generality or social distribution that is effectively impersonal. It is useful, then, to sketch out the uses of *trust*, in their general frames of reference. The scope today is so wide that it may have stretched the word beyond breaking-point, and I will question common assumptions about trust throughout this book. But, in this section, I simply outline the various dimensions in which 'trust-talk' occurs.

Psychodynamic theories of human development propose a formative stage of 'basic trust,' prior to language-acquisition. Erik Erikson's first stage of psychosocial development, from birth to the age of two, is described around a crisis of 'trust versus mistrust.' The infant learns how to trust the world, based on the experiences of love and nurturing (or lack thereof) provided by caregivers, especially parents (Erikson and Erikson, 1997). Attachment theory also invokes a pre-linguistic origin of trust. Infant behaviours, beginning with crying, smiling and eye-contact help to forge attachment with parents and others. Later, the child develops habits of dis/trust through exploration of spaces, fear of strangers, or separation distress. Insecure attachment early in life will lead, it is said, to reactions or behavioural patterns that are premised on the belief that people 'don't trust me,' or 'can't be trusted' (Karen, 1990). We are said to acquire a 'basic trust' as an aspect of a healthy personality, on the other hand. An individual may thus become more or less trusting, or perhaps too trusting and naïve, as an important aspect of character or personality. 'Interpersonal trust' has been defined psychologically as 'an expectancy held by an individual or group that the word, promise, verbal, or written statement of another individual or group can be relied upon.' Such expectancies may 'constitute a relatively stable personality characteristic' (Rotter, 1971, p. 444). More recent research suggests that some of the recognized 'big five' personality traits correlate with a propensity towards trust in political institutions and actors. In particular, 'agreeableness is positively related to political trust, whereas negative [statistical] relationships exist between political trust and both openness to experience and extraversion' (Mondak, Hayes, and Canache, 2017, p. 154).

In contrast to psychodynamic or personality-based accounts, laboratory experiments observe behaviours, making it unnecessary to postulate traits. They inquire into the conditions that can shape altruistic acts (which are costly to the actor but confer a benefit on the recipient) as compared with selfish acts (Berg, Dickhaut, and McCabe, 1995). Interactions between individuals are closely observed under differing punishment and reward contingencies, and an individual can be classified as 'reciprocator' or 'truster,' or as 'selfish' or 'competitive,' based on his/her responses under a specified set of rules (Fehr and Fischbacher, 2003). Trust, therefore, may be a kind of behaviour that is observable and that varies according to the incentives in a particular situation – although some people may be more disposed (through prior learning) to initiate altruistic behaviours than others. Whether we regard trust as a trait or as a kind of behaviour, though, we are so far considering the individual and how he/she interacts with one other individual or a limited number of others.

The next level of understanding of trust is in the quality of a relationship between people in a lived social context. In this case, the relationship itself is characterized by trust, which may be attributed either to actions, such as exchanges of gifts, or to shared feelings of goodwill. In a relationship of trust, therefore, reliability and responsibility are central qualities expected and performed. This can apply to close personal as well as more distant professional relationships. At a wider social and cultural level, we observe norms and conventions that govern reciprocity and that either depend upon or build trust between parties to exchanges. Frederiksen (2014), for example, develops a sophisticated approach to trust as a relational phenomenon, drawing on Pierre Bourdieu.

Moving beyond trust between or among individuals, we may also talk of trust in institutions. Modern political life requires that we trust not only those who lead, but also whole institutions. So, trust in government or parliament, and trust in bodies of people such as the police force or politicians as a whole are common concerns and frequently the topics of public surveys (Van de Walle and Bouckaert, 2003; Pew Research Center, 2015). But, in what sense can one trust an institution or a group of people or a technically and socially complex system that relies upon countless people whom one does not know, such as airlines or financial services? Trust undoubtedly pertains to relations between individuals who know or encounter one another face to face. Indeed, 'inter-individual relations are the home territory for the concept of trust' (Harré, 1999, p. 261). But nowadays trust is also spoken of in relation to public figures, organizations, social groups, information systems, corporate brands, etc. This modern expansion of the uses of trust changes what we may mean by trust. When and how did a body of persons, such as a legislature or a bank, come to be the object or subject of trust? It may be simply implausible to propose that a person can trust (or, for that matter, distrust) government or public services, as it is epistemologically impossible to judge the trustworthiness of the individuals who compose these complex apparatuses of state. On those grounds, Hardin argues that the relationship between citizens and government 'is not a relationship of trust or distrust. At best, much of the time it is a relationship of inductive expectations' (Hardin, 1999, p. 39). Nonetheless, the relationship between citizens and government is commonly talked about as a matter of trust. (Chapter 2 looks at examples of how trust makes sense in the social and political context).

Reciprocally, there is also the question of how institutional practices trust citizens or even cultivate their trustworthiness. Public institutions put in place policies, contracts and evaluations that are premised upon a certain level of trust or distrust in individuals, for example redesigning systems to steer or nudge behaviour onto socially desirable pathways (Bouckaert, 2012). Institutional laws, rules and norms, it is said, can influence the propensity of actors to accept the risks assumed in trusting others they do business with, and so institution-based trust can and should be 'deliberately created and shaped' (Bachmann, 2011, p. 204). The insurance industry has a long history of managing moral hazard, or the effects of insurance itself on incentives, especially concerning the propensity to fabricate or exaggerate losses. Insurance institutions 'mark people or organizations as responsible in the trustworthy sense' (Baker, 2002, p. 41). Although they routinely distrust insured persons, they also incorporate incentives to be more trustworthy through rewards and sanctions. They may decline to cover the untrustworthy, test the veracity of claims and structure prices with incentives to act safely or prudently.

Furthermore, social systems are characterized by, rely upon, distribute and even produce trust as a vital feature of their functioning. Lewis and Weigert (1985, p. 982) conclude 'that trust is a quintessentially social reality that penetrates not only individual psyches but also the whole institutional fabric of society.' Trust, at this level, may be described as systemic, impersonal or abstract (Giddens, 1990; Shapiro, 1987). Money, regarded as a social relation or system, is an example of this, to the extent that it may be seen as a form of trust itself, or a complex, constantly changing network of promises to pay (Ingham, 2004; Orléan, 2013). The basic architecture and governance of the internet is said to depend upon trust, especially among the key non-state actors who design and oversee its most basic protocols. Trust is said to have been 'decisive' in the growth of the internet (Klimburg, 2017, p. 359).

So, this distinguishes five levels or dimensions on which it is thought that trust operates: as something about a person, or about relations between or among persons, or about our relations with a collectivity of persons, or about how an institution treats people, or about a relational quality distributed through a complex social system. It may lead to confusion if we change registers without critical reflection. And a single word – trust – is being put to a great deal of work, so there is plenty of scope for conceptual hair-splitting. Are there many different types of trust, or can one identify a generic process that occurs across all of the different contexts and registers outlined above? In favour of the latter idea, the essential features of trust, according to Dietz, are 'an assessment of beliefs, a decision, a risk-taking act, feedback on the outcomes' (2011, p. 216).

The uses of trust have worked their way through many different frames of reference and intentions, including political theory. The contemporary picture is complicated, however, by the fact of the mass media and the rapidly changing digital landscape of the internet. We see close-up moving images of public figures, from which we form impressions of personal characteristics and trustworthiness. This is reinforced by surveys of political leaders' 'honesty and trustworthiness.' Political participation involves trust in individuals whom we never meet personally; our only acquaintance is through mediated personae broadcast in electronic video and audio formats. These personae are largely carefully scripted and presented – although unscripted errors can now circulate online widely and rapidly.

Trusting a candidate for public office through impressions gained from his/ her television appearances; trusting one's spouse; trusting parliament; trusting the financial system. Caution is needed here to avoid confusing these, as there may not be one core meaning of *trust*. It is possible that our propensity to trust those in high public offices, to trust strangers and to trust those we are intimate with share something in common in terms of their moral economy or belief-structure. There may sometimes be a tone and a language that sound, for instance, like a child's rage against the broken promises of parents when a person complains bitterly about political parties he or she disapproves of – suggesting that the 'trust' we have in each is more or less the same thing. But it would be unwise to conflate all of these different directions or dimensions of trust/distrust and to elide their differences of structure and meaning. The social distances and commitments between politician and citizen are quite different from those between parent and child.

Defining, warranting or performing trust

Having briefly considered some historical background and the distinct registers of trust, we now go back to first principles by asking, 'With what kind of *question* do we initiate our inquiry?' An obvious beginning is to define the term, or to ask, 'What *is* trust?' Authors from Hobbes (1994) to Giddens (1990) have supplied definitions. Another common question is normative, such as: 'Who is worthy of trust?' or 'When is it warranted to trust others?' (McLeod, 2014). A third kind of question, less commonly posed, is pragmatic, viewing trust as a speech-act, as in, 'What am I doing when I say "I trust you"?' or as something one does, as in, 'What is it that I do when I trust or distrust someone?' This approach looks closely at how people cooperate or reciprocate, or bind one another to obligations, and how speech-acts (like promising) play a role (Szerszynski, 1999). For instance, if uttered under the right circumstances, the statement 'I trust you' 'indicates that I expect you to assume the responsibilities of someone who is trusted' (Lagerspetz, 2015, p. 11). These different founding questions about trust are not mutually exclusive. Each opening gambit leads to difficulties, however.

There is merit in describing or defining a term – clarifying what it *is* – before thinking about how it *ought* to be. Definitions, however, may either artificially limit the field, leaving one open to numerous counter-examples, or lead to an interminable and unsatisfying discussion as we parse out different aspects or kinds of trust. Trust involves subtle inter-subjective phenomena, contingent upon the context of actions and connotation of words, and hence we can only ever arrive at tentative and conditional definitions. Are we to define it in terms of the likelihood that others may act in our interests (a cognitive approach), or the customary norms and duties that we observe when making ourselves truthful, predictable, reliable or faithful (a normative approach), or the shared attitude embedded in relationships of love and friendship (an affective approach), or the shared commitment needed for the achievement of complex civilized endeavours (a conative approach) (Simpson, 2012)? Furthermore, the idea (common in the literature) that trust is a confident belief that one person (a truster) holds in another person or an institution (a trustee), such that the latter is anticipated to act in the interests of the former, does not fully recognize the fundamental character of trust. Trust (as I will argue in Chapter 2) emerges from reciprocated actions and inter-subjective qualities with ethical importance for the participants, rather than an attitude, belief or decision of the individual. As such, it eludes clear definition. Indeed, Wittgenstein warned us that the harder one looks for a 'thing' to which a substantive of this kind supposedly corresponds, the greater one's bewilderment (Wittgenstein, 1964). Definitions are just another way of using a word, and are not, for present purposes, 'definitive' or 'final,' even though they are sometimes helpful. For instance, one may quote Hobbes's definition of trust and then move on, assuming that this suffices to show what he meant by that word. The close analysis of Hobbes's work in Chapter 3 includes his formal definition and also looks at what he means by the word in pragmatic terms as he uses it, and its derivatives, throughout *Leviathan*. Consequently, we gain a richer appreciation of 'Hobbesian trust.' Reliance upon the formal definition alone would limit our understanding of what he really meant.

Even if a single all-purpose definition of trust is elusive, one may discern different *types* of trust across different social contexts. A widely accepted typology comprises generalized, particularized and strategic trust. *Generalized* trust refers to the psychological predisposition to trust others, or the expectation that most others, including strangers, will behave fairly. Although contingent on situations, it is seen as fairly stable over time and not greatly affected by reciprocity or occasional evidence of (un-)trustworthiness. It is widely surveyed, based on questions asking how much respondents think other people can be trusted. *Particularized* trust is limited to people like oneself, in some respect, and hence much less inclusive. It is an in-group trust. *Strategic* trust refers to the expectation that specific individuals will reciprocate, cooperate and act with one's own interests in mind. It relates only to specific situations or purposes and is based on knowledge of other people's competence or motives (Uslaner, 2002). I employ this typology below, but only as a rough guide, not as definitive.

Trust, however, is ineluctably a moral concept, and so the fact/value or description/prescription distinctions become blurred. Any attempt to define or describe trust (including empirical social research methods) cannot help but introduce normative assumptions, as trust implies (by any definition) some notion of 'good,' either as obligations or consequences, and 'trustworthiness' fits within virtue ethics. Hence, it may be better 'to lay one's cards on the table' with a normative question. But, even before the search for 'justification conditions' for trust had taken off in the literature (e.g., Jones, 1996), Luhmann had already explained why this approach is 'inadequate':

> [The ethical view of trust] looks for an answer to the question, under what circumstances one ought to trust, and arrives at the conclusion that while in human society trust is an ethical command, one should not place trust blindly but only where it is earned. Thus the problem of trust is transformed into a cognitive problem, despite the fact that it has its roots precisely in inadequate cognitive capacity. This 'solution,' therefore, could be formulated thus: give trust where there is no need for it. The real problem, however, is trust which is unjustified and which yet justifies itself and so becomes creative.
>
> (Luhmann, 1979, pp. 78–79)

If we could find justifications for what we do when we trust each other, we would obviate the need to trust. The very point of trusting is that we lack the necessary and sufficient moral or empirical conditions to *justify* doing so; we live with uncertainty and complexity and the unpredictability of human beings, and yet we stay in a relationship or collaborate with a newcomer all the same. When meeting strangers in a trusting manner, one presumes mutual goodwill and no desire to harm, but this 'can't be based on evidence' (Uslaner, 2002, p. 2). We take this 'on faith,' it is often said, begging the question. If logic is involved at all, then it must be a weak inductive logic. Particularized trust in people whom one has known for many years (friends and family members) may be based on the evidence of our experiences with them, and on customary obligations, but it too is an inductive inference, prone to a 'black swan' event, or an unpredictable betrayal. Trust concerns us ethically, but we cannot discover definitive answers to the questions of *how, whom* and *when* we *ought* to trust, as trusting people, or anticipating the future actions of free agents, assumes the very indeterminacy of such questions. We infer from past behaviour that acting on trust may (or may not) 'pay off' most of the time in future. In the absence of proof, trust is creatively *self*-justifying.

So, while we can commonly understand that there is a difference between trust and distrust, and that the two are inherently moral concerns, we are unable rationally to justify 'our general readiness to trust others.' If we could do so, we would also be able to justify rationally 'the very fact that we are social beings' (Lagerspetz, 1998, p. 61). Hypothesizing a social world with no trust, as the premise of an argument towards a justification, does not really work, as such a way of life 'can hardly be called human' (Lagerspetz, 1998, p. 64). A search for justification conditions for trust is a fruitless exercise, therefore. We are left with the paradox that trust entails basic ethical qualities of social life, and yet it cannot be *rationally* justified, as it works only in the face of the uncertain, the unpredictable and that which is not rationalisable. The actions and characteristics of trust are features of *being human* that precede and outstrip efforts at ethical justification.

In contrast, the pragmatic approach could help us to avoid these problems. If we look at what people do and say when they trust one another or consider the speech-acts that are integral to trust – especially promising and forgiving – then we may be on the way to a clearer understanding that does not lead us down rabbit-holes. We thus consider the work being done when we believe we trust each other, rather than try to define trust in the abstract. We can also reserve judgements about when we *ought* to trust, or when trust may be warranted. There may, after all, be immoral or unlawful reasons for trusting. Criminal gangs exemplify particularized trust in practice, with strict codes of honour and silence, and initiation processes to test the trustworthiness of prospective members. Fraudulent actions, moreover, prey upon victims' generalized trust. A pragmatic approach does not presume trust to be necessarily inherently good, even if those who trust one another may expect to gain something they regard as consequentially good.

A pragmatic approach has a significant flaw. Speech-act theory may be indispensible for understanding promises (Pratt, 2014), but it does not suffice for a study of trust, as one also has to account for implicit, unconscious or *unspoken* trust. The spoken or written uses of the word *trust* are primary material for the present study, on the Wittgensteinian grounds of 'meaning as use.' But, paradoxically, the strongest and most basic trust is an implicit trust that precedes the need to talk about it. One trusts well before one *believes* or *thinks* that one trusts. That is, 'we *typically* do not articulate, reflect upon, or plan our trust' (Lagerspetz, 1998, p. 31).

Questions of the kinds that initiate inquiries into trust (based on definition, justification or praxis) may misfire. Rather than remain silent on the question of trust, though, we can take another step back and ask what moves us to think, speak and ask questions about trust in the first place.

We talk about trust because it's broken

In *On Certainty*, Wittgenstein makes some relevant remarks about belief and doubt. As children, we learn certain facts and acquire beliefs (for example, that the adults who present themselves as our parents are actually our parents) and unquestioningly 'we take them on trust' ('*wir nehmen sie gläubig hin*'). But the child does not yet speak *of* her belief as (merely) a belief, such is the trust in what she has learned. So, we did not begin with doubts in order to clear the ground for justifiable beliefs. 'Doubt comes *after* belief' (Wittgenstein, 1969, p. 23, §§159–160). Our earliest beliefs – taken 'on trust' – involve trusting a *person* such as a parent or teacher (Lagerspetz, 1998, p. 96). Similarly, our earliest relations of trust are not thought or spoken of as trust. They develop unquestioningly and without reflection, beginning before we can speak. And it is this kind of trust that forms the grounds on which we acquire basic beliefs. That is, our trust in others is the foundation of our earliest beliefs – more so than the inverse proposition, that positive beliefs about others are the necessary condition for trusting them.[9] Once we have developed to a stage at which we can talk and think reflectively about trust, moreover, then we may develop doubts about it. The pain of betrayal may give us reason to doubt the unreflective (or 'childlike') ways in which we have trusted, and this may lead us to think about trust *per se*.

Trust involves affectively and morally charged relational or inter-subjective qualities, not a 'thing' that one can point to or label. One does not literally 'break' it. The habits entailed in relations of trust are first developed in infancy, prior to the ability to speak, let alone to say that we trust. Even in adulthood, 'trust as a conscious undertaking is logically secondary to unreflective trust' (Lagerspetz, 1998, p. 31). We become conscious that we have trusted when we feel the hurt that follows betrayal. We learn *painfully* what it means to trust due to trust being 'broken'; we notice it more readily 'after its sudden demise or severe injury' (Baier, 1986, p. 234). Reflective awareness of trust is a product of the pains that arise from betrayals, and thus we learn consciously to trust *and* to distrust. Eventually some may even reflect philosophically upon these matters.

Now that we are speaking beings, we cannot retrospectively re-enter the pre-verbal stage and rediscover a primal trust, because the subject that seeks to know or to recover this supposed 'innocent' capability is already the subject that speaks of trust-as-we-know-it. The place of the supposed primal trust has already been taken by a trust implicitly learned and then betrayed and so made conscious. The same problem applies to any appeal to 'nature': we can retrospectively infer, but we can't recover, a 'paleo-trust' inherited by virtue of natural selection and group survival, as the 'broken' trust of which we now customarily speak has already formed the ethics of the field of inquiry.

There is thus a troubled relationship between language and trust. If I keep telling you that I trust you, then you will begin to wonder why; 'our trust will implicitly be called into question once we start *talking* about it' (Lagerspetz, 1998, p. 32). Not only does speaking of trust, or rational inquiry into trust, arise because we have cause to doubt or to distrust – but, to tell people that we trust them, or to study trust in depth, only serves to arouse, display and deepen our doubts.

I turn my back without thinking about or doubting what the trusted other may do. I place a letter in a box in a public place and walk away, without even thinking that I have trusted the postal service to deliver it to a distant place. So, trust may be first *unspoken* or unreflective or implicit – and as such not yet prone to doubt. Or, conversely, *trust enunciated is trust betrayed*. If trust comes to attention as something about which it is necessary to speak, then it may be because trust either has been betrayed or is thought to be in danger of betrayal. If I have to say out loud 'I trust you,' I must have had cause to doubt the wisdom of it, and I may be attempting to bind you to, or reaffirm, certain assumed obligations. The utterance alone may cause you to wonder if I have doubts. Sledge Hammer's catch-phrase, 'Trust me, I know what I'm doing,' gave viewers of the TV comedy reason only to doubt him. Its utterance ironically contradicted itself.

The same principles apply to reflections on political trust. It is a sense of betrayal (by rulers, legislators, etc.) of an implicit and retrospectively imagined 'original' trust that causes doubt and leads us to reflect upon what our trust originally entailed and why we gave it. The alternative is to believe that the origins of the state were *not* in an act of trust (by the many in the few), but rather an act of sheer violence (over the many by the few) – or that our fear of a ruler's legitimate right to punish and to use violence secures political order. So, in political philosophy, what doubts underlay the need to write and to theorize about trust, to inscribe trust in relations of power and discord, and to expand trust as a *political* concern, beyond the confines of interpersonal relations?

Trust as a political *factor* – that which we do to recognize one another as a community in which matters such as security or fairness can be consciously at issue – only comes up as a question for political theory due to our *doubts* about those very matters, due to broken promises and violence, due to our social and intellectual discord or due to the resistances and rivalries posed by friendships, close networks and secret associations. The very urge to define trust in the context of the political suggests a hurtful breach or bewilderment or betrayal.

For the early-modern theories of social contract, the fear that others would not keep their promises, deliver goods or pay debts was a fundamental concern characterized in terms of trust, observable in Hobbes's *Leviathan*. For Hobbes, though, the sovereign is *authorized*, and not necessarily *trusted*, by the subjects. Locke was concerned with the trustworthiness of individuals, for example when he claims that an atheist cannot be bound by oaths. He extends the scope of trust, however, to include a popular trust that rulers or legislators will use their powers to ensure peace and security in the best interests of the people. Both thinkers were troubled by doubts about the trustworthiness and creditworthiness of others, and about rulers who abused their powers. Trust came to their attention because it had been 'broken,' though they offer different views about how it works (see Chapters 3 and 4).

One might object that the idea that we only become conscious of trust after, and due to, its being 'broken' is as trite as observing that we become curious about what light is thanks to occasions of complete darkness. The politics of trust and distrust do not arise from such a stark contrast, however. One does not cancel out the other. In a democratic society, when we trust a person to take public office, we do so only conditionally – precisely because *we trust no one* with unlimited or absolute power. Constitutions separate powers in order to limit them. In as much as we entrust the legislative and executive powers to particular individuals, we know from harsh historical experience that they may prove to be untrustworthy in office, if left unchecked. A politics of trust, therefore, is integrally a politics of mistrust, because we are forced to trust other human beings – who are fallible and mutable and cannot be trusted always or without limits. Trust and mistrust operate together to form and maintain a constitution. Written provisions and conventions ensure that representatives are accountable, and hence more likely to act in our interests, due to the lessons of past political betrayals.

Conclusion

This chapter has explored how we use the word *trust*, and what the scope of its meanings may encompass. This shows the considerable work that *trust* is nowadays performing, from the helplessness of the infant through to the practices of monetary policy. A political philosophy of trust has a history, and we need to take account of that, as trust, in speech and in actions, has been transformed in the course of history. We have looked briefly at how trust arose as a concern in the context of the political, and at how it relates to other traditional terms, and yet we need a more detailed inquiry into its various roles. How does trust fit into political debates? How do standard definitions of trust work, and why do they misrecognize what trust does?

Notes

1 People appear to have a bias towards believing that what others say is truthful, even when we are warned that it may not be (Street and Richardson, 2015).
2 A person's actions in the presence of others 'will have a promissory character' (Goffman, 1959, p. 2).
3 'A correctly staged and performed scene leads the audience to impute a self to a performed character, but this imputation – this self – is a *product* of a scene that comes off, and is not a *cause* of it. The self, then, as a performed character, is not an organic thing that has a specific location, whose fundamental fate is to be born, to mature, and to die; it is a dramatic effect arising diffusely from a scene that is presented, and the characteristic issue, the crucial concern, is whether it will be credited or discredited' (Goffman, 1959, pp. 252–253). The latter phrase may well be substituted by 'trusted or distrusted.'

4 The terms 'affect' and 'tone' derive from Berlant (2011) and Ngai (2005).
5 Perhaps due to their being French, Foucault and Derrida were conscious of the revolutionary significance of 'fraternity,' the male-centric version of friendship: 'this fraternity is another name for friendship' (Derrida, 1997, p. 238).
6 One trusts one's friends, almost by definition, and so, retrospectively, the traditional interest in friendship in philosophy may be regarded as having implicitly recognized trust (Baier, 1986). See Chapter 2.
7 The friendship that Machiavelli describes is one of utility, however. Aristotle would have seen this as inferior to friendship of nobility. Note the qualification that Machiavelli makes when he asserts that 'friendship which is bought with money *and not with greatness and nobility of mind* is paid for, but it does not last and it yields nothing' (Machiavelli, 1999, p. 54, italics added). He thus uses the Aristotelian distinction and subtly admonishes the Medici rulers that they lacked true nobility of spirit, and that they had resorted to buying the loyalties of the Florentines. Machiavelli's advice has a tone of bitter irony, given his personal misfortunes at the time that he wrote *The Prince* (Benner, 2017).
8 The translations of Hegel and Nietzsche quoted in Chapter 5 often refer to trust. But, in their original German, Hegel used exclusively *Zutrauen* and Nietzsche mainly *Vertrauen*. So *Zutrauen* is sometimes translated as 'trust' and sometimes as 'confidence.' Luhmann's important distinction between trust and confidence, however, is translated from *Vertrauen* and *Zutrauen* respectively (Luhmann, 1988). This in turn creates difficulty for French translators, as French does not readily distinguish between trust and confidence. A French translator of Luhmann chooses *confiance décidée* and *confiance assurée* to cover trust and confidence respectively (Luhmann, 2001). And English translations are unable to reproduce the close relation between *Vertrauen* and *Zutrauen*, even though *trust* and *trauen* share some etymological roots.
9 'In many cases the trust we have for another individual will be basic to the beliefs we come to form, not the other way round' (Lagerspetz and Hertzberg, 2013, p. 49).

References

Aristotle. (2014). *The Nichomachean ethics*. Cambridge: Cambridge University Press.
Bachmann, R. (2011). At the crossroads: Future directions in trust research. *Journal of Trust Research*, 1(2), 203–213.
Baier, A. (1986). Trust and antitrust. *Ethics*, 96(2), 231–260.
Baker, T. (2002). Risk, insurance, and the social construction of responsibility. In T. Baker, and J. Simon (Eds.), *Embracing risk: The changing culture of insurance and responsibility* (pp. 33–51). Chicago, IL: University of Chicago Press.
Benner, E. (2017). *Be like the fox: Machiavelli in his world*. New York, NY: W.W. Norton.
Berg, J., Dickhaut, J., and McCabe, K. (1995). Trust, reciprocity, and social history. *Games and Economic Behavior*, 10(1), 122–142.
Berlant, L. (2011). *Cruel optimism*. Durham, NC: Duke University Press.
Bouckaert, G. (2012). Trust and public administration. *Administration*, 60(1), 91–115.
Brown, P. (2000). *Augustine of Hippo: A biography*. Berkeley, CA: University of California Press.
Burke, E. (1996). *The writings and speeches of Edmund Burke* (Vol. III). Oxford: Clarendon Press.
Cockburn, D. (2014). Trust in conversation. *Nordic Wittgenstein Review*, 3(1), 47–67.

Coeckelbergh, M. (2012). Can we trust robots? *Ethics and Information Technology*, *1*(14), 53–60.

Dance, R. (2000). Is the verb die derived from old Norse? A review of the evidence. *English Studies*, *81*(4), 368–383.

Derrida, J. (1997). *Politics of friendship*. London: Verso.

de Waal, F. (2009). *The age of empathy: Nature's lessons for a kinder society*. New York, NY: Three Rivers Press.

Dietz, G. (2011). Going back to the source: Why do people trust each other? *Journal of Trust Research*, *1*(2), 215–222.

Eno, R. (2015). *The Analects of Confucius: An online teaching translation*. Retrieved September 17, 2017, from www.indiana.edu/%7Ep374/Analects_of_Confucius_ (Eno-2015).pdf

Erikson, E. H., and Erikson, J. M. (1997). *The life cycle completed*. New York, NY: W.W. Norton.

Fehr, E., and Fischbacher, U. (2003, October 23). The nature of human altruism. *Nature*, *425*, 785–791.

Foucault, M. (1997). *Ethics: Essential works of Foucault 1954–1984*. London: Penguin.

Frederiksen, M. (2014). Relational trust: Outline of a Bourdieusian theory of interpersonal trust. *Journal of Trust Research*, *4*(2), 167–192.

Garland, A. (Director). (2015). *Ex machina* [Motion picture]. www.youtube.com/ watch?v=XYGzRB4Pnq8&vl=en

Giddens, A. (1990). *The consequences of modernity*. Stanford, CA: Stanford University Press.

Goffman, E. (1959). *The presentation of self in everyday life*. New York, NY: Doubleday.

The Guardian. (2008, September 14). *Did I say that?* Retrieved February 1, 2016, from guardian.co.uk: www.theguardian.com/lifeandstyle/2008/sep/14/celebrity. britneyspears

Hardin, R. (1999). Do we want trust in government? In M. E. Warren (Ed.), *Democracy and trust* (pp. 22–41). Cambridge: Cambridge University Press.

Harré, R. (1999). Trust and its surrogates. In M. E. Warren (Ed.), *Democracy and trust* (pp. 249–272). Cambridge: Cambridge University Press.

Hetherington, M. J. (2005). *Why trust matters: Declining political trust and the demise of American liberalism*. Princeton, NJ: Princeton University Press.

Hetherington, M. J., and Rudolph, T. J. (2015). *Why Washington won't work: Polarization, political trust, and the governing crisis*. Chicago, IL: University of Chicago Press.

Hobbes, T. (1994). The elements of law natural and politic. In T. Hobbes (Ed.), *Human nature and De Corpore Politico* (pp. 1–182). Oxford: Oxford University Press.

Hobbes, T. (1998). *Leviathan*. Oxford: Oxford University Press.

Howard, P. N. (2015). *Pax Technica: How the internet of things may set us free or lock us up*. New Haven, CT: Yale University Press.

Ingham, G. (2004). *The nature of money*. Cambridge: Polity Press.

Jaques, E. (2005). On trust, good, and evil. *International Journal of Applied Psychoanalytic Studies*, *2*(4), 396–403.

Johnston, R., Hagen, M., and Jamieson, K. (2004). *The 2000 Presidential Election and the foundations of party politics*. Cambridge: Cambridge University Press.

Jones, K. (1996, October). Trust as an affective attitude. *Ethics*, *107*, 4–25.

Kaplan, S. (2015, July 17). *Can robots trust humans? A hitchhiking bot will find out*. Retrieved August 23, 2015, from The Washington Post: www.washingtonpost.com/news/morning-mix/wp/2015/07/17/ can-robots-trust-humans-a-hitchhiking-bot-will-find-out/

Karen, R. (1990). *Becoming attached: First relationships and how they shape our capacity to love*. New York, NY: Oxford University Press.

Katz, J. I. (2006). Deception and denial in Iraq: The intelligent adversary corollary. *International Journal of Intelligence and CounterIntelligence, 19*(4), 577–585.

Klimburg, A. (2017). *The darkening web: The war for cyperspace*. New York, NY: Penguin.

Knefel, J. (2015, August 25). *The Air Force wants you to trust robots: Should you?* Retrieved June 3, 2016, from Scientific American: www.scientificamerican.com/article/the-air-force-wants-you-to-trust-robots-should-you/

Lagerspetz, O. (1998). *Trust: The tacit demand*. Dordrecht: Springer.

Lagerspetz, O. (2015). *Trust, ethics and human reason*. London: Bloomsbury.

Lagerspetz, O., and Hertzberg, L. (2013). Trust in Wittgenstein. In P. Mäkelä, and C. Townley (Eds.), *Trust: Analytic and applied perspectives* (pp. 31–51). Amsterdam: Editions Rodopi.

Lenard, P. T. (2015). The political philosophy of trust and distrust in democracies and beyond. *The Monist, 98*(4), 353–359.

Lewis, J. D., and Weigert, A. (1985). Trust as a social reality. *Social Forces, 63*(4), 967–985.

Luhmann, N. (1979). *Trust and power*. Chichester: Wiley.

Luhmann, N. (1988). Familiarity, confidence, trust: Problems and alternatives. In D. Gambetta (Ed.), *Trust: Making and breaking cooperative relations* (pp. 94–107). Oxford: Basil Blackwell.

Luhmann, N. (2001). Confiance et Familiarité: Problèmes et Alternatives. *Réseaux, 4*(108), 15–35. Retrieved from cqirn:info: www.cairn.info/revue-reseaux-2001-4-page-15.htm#no1

Machiavelli, N. (1999). *The prince*. London: Penguin.

McLeod, C. (2014, Summer). *Trust* (Zalta, E. N., Eds.). Retrieved November 15, 2014, from The Stanford Encyclopedia of Philosophy: http://plato.stanford.edu/archives/sum2014/entries/trust/

Miller, P. (2014). Finding oneself with friends. In R. Polansky (Ed.), *The Cambridge companion to Aristotle's Nicomachean ethics* (pp. 319–349). Cambridge: Cambridge University Press.

Möllering, G. (2001). The nature of trust: From Georg Simmel to a theory of expectation, interpretation and suspension. *Sociology, 35*(2), 403–420.

Mondak, J. J., Hayes, M., and Canache, D. (2017). Biological and psychological influences on political trust. In S. Zmerli, and T. W. der Meer (Eds.), *Handbook on political trust* (pp. 143–159). Cheltenham: Edward Elgar.

Ngai, S. (2005). *Ugly feelings*. Cambridge, MA: Harvard University Press.

Orléan, A. (2013). Money: Instrument of exchange or social institution of value? In J. Pixley, and C. Harcourt (Eds.), *Financial crises and the nature of capitalist money: Mutual developments from the work of Geoffrey Ingham* (pp. 46–69). Houndmills: Palgrave Macmillan.

Paine, C. (Director). (2018). *Do you trust this computer?* [Motion Picture]. http://doyoutrustthiscomputer.org/

Pew Research Center. (2015). *Beyond distrust: How Americans view their government*. Retrieved from www.pewresearch.org.

Pitkin, H. F. (1967). *The concept of representation*. Berkeley, CA: University of California Press.

Pratt, M. G. (2014). Some features of promises and their obligations. *The Southern Journal of Philosophy*, 52(3), 382–402.

Rotter, J. B. (1971). Generalized expectancies for interpersonal trust. *American Psychologist*, 26(5), 443–452.

Runciman, D. (2016, December 1). *Is this how democracy ends?* Retrieved December 4, 2016, from London Review of Books: www.lrb.co.uk/v38/n23/david-runciman/is-this-how-democracy-ends

Scott, R. (Director). (1982). *Blade runner* [Motion Picture]. www.youtube.com/watch?v=eogpIG53Cis

Shapiro, S. P. (1987). The social control of impersonal trust. *American Journal of Sociology*, 93(3), 623–658.

Sheehy, G. (2017). Trump's trust deficit is the core problem. In B. X. Lee (Ed.), *The dangerous case of Donald Trump* (pp. 75–82). Thomas Dunne.

Simpson, T. W. (2012). What is trust? *Pacific Philosophical Quarterly*, 93(4), 550–569.

Sky News. (2016, June 3). *EU: In or out? Faisal Islam interview with Michael Gove*. Retrieved January 22, 2017, from Sky: https://corporate.sky.com/media-centre/media-packs/2016/eu-in-or-out-faisal-islam-interview-with-michael-gove,-30616-8pm

Smith, A. (2002). *The theory of moral sentiments*. Cambridge: Cambridge University Press.

Srnicek, N. (2017). *Platform capitalism*. Cambridge: Polity Press.

Street, C. N., and Richardson, D. C. (2015). Lies, damn lies, and expectations: How base rates inform lie–truth judgments. *Applied Cognitive Psychology*, 29(1), 149–155.

Szerszynski, B. (1999). Risk and trust: The performative dimension. *Environmental Values*, 8(2), 239–252.

Tavani, H. T. (2015). Levels of trust in the context of machine ethics. *Philosophy & Technology*, 28(1), 75–90.

Uslaner, E. M. (2002). *The moral foundations of trust*. Cambridge: Cambridge University Press.

Van de Walle, S., and Bouckaert, G. (2003). Public service performance and trust in government: The problem of causality. *International Journal of Public Administration*, 26(8/9), 891–913.

van Wingerden, M., and van den Bos, W. (2015). Can you trust a rat? Using animal models to investigate the neural basis of trust-like behavior. *Social Cognition*, 33(5), 387–413.

Wittgenstein, L. (1964). *The blue and brown books*. Oxford: Basil Blackwood.

Wittgenstein, L. (1969). *On certainty*. Oxford: Basil Blackwell.

Zuboff, S. (2015). Big other: Surveillance capitalism and the prospects of an information civilization. *Journal of Information Technology*, 30(1), 75–89.

2 Re-describing trust

I begin this chapter by outlining some accepted understandings of trust in social and political thought – and then proceed to question them. It is often said that trust is essential for the functioning of a good or good-enough society. We act in predictable and regulated ways, assuming others will do so too. Barring a rare catastrophe, people will mostly interact in a civil manner, and services that we rely upon (such as telecommunications and transport) will be organized and available much as they were before. Even if sometimes chaotic, the basic patterns of public life will, one confidently expects, continue as normal. We can rely upon people to perform duties competently and with regard for others' interests and welfare. People familiar with the social environment will know, most of the time, whom they can trust for particular purposes, and whom they cannot trust. Legal tender will be accepted in the shops; letters placed in special boxes will reach their intended destinations; teachers will do their best for our children.

Such everyday trust has been referred to as an 'expectation of the persistence of the moral social order' (Barber, 1983, p. 14); it is 'a functional prerequisite for the possibility of society' without which chaos and fear would reign (Lewis and Weigert, 1985, p. 967). 'A complete absence of trust' is assumed by Luhmann to be unendurable. Hence, 'man by nature has to bestow trust'; it is nothing less than the origin of 'rules for proper conduct' (Luhmann, 1979, p. 4).

I do not *choose* to trust in this manner each morning, like choosing what to wear, because this is a socially shared sentiment or a common commitment to certain expectations and norms about which people do not normally have to think. And yet, the extent or depth of this trust could be eroded if events violate expectations; at which time, thoughts and discussion of trust or distrust may arise. Systemic failures such as a global financial crisis, terrorist attacks, or allegations of corruption engender distrust in others, in institutions, and (if nothing effective is done about it) in the capabilities of agents of the state to ensure our personal security and our property.

It is logical, then, to look at people's trust in *government* as the principal form of a *political* trust. Trust is regarded as an essential resource or as a necessary precondition for a democratic political system and its public services. Our trust in the social order – its security and predictability – is supported by a rule of law, effective law-enforcement, and public administration. Political trust has been described metaphorically as 'the *glue* that keeps the [democratic] system together and as the *oil* that lubricates the policy machine' (van der Meer and Zmerli, 2017, p. 1, italics added). Trust in government could be a function of the ratio between how people evaluate the actual performance of government and their normative expectations of what governments should be doing and how much they should be delivering (Hetherington and Husser, 2012). Inadequate, under-resourced or poorly delivered public services, or incompetence and corruption among representatives or public servants – or, at least, the perception thereof – may thus be causes for lower trust. A 'non-trusting' public may invest with greater confidence in their private economic efforts and in family members for their well-being and security, and regard 'government' as a wasteful side-show or an interference. Widespread distrust in government may be accompanied by political polarization due to people's refusal to make the 'ideological sacrifices' that are needed in a democracy as executive government changes hands (Hetherington and Rudolph, 2015). Conversely, political trust could support policies that promise effective public services, and effective public services could in turn boost people's trust in government.

It is common, however, to argue that the present age is characterized by declining trust in government, often coupled with lower voter-turnouts, political disengagement, austerity policies and declining public services. Evidence for this is generally taken from social surveys that include an item such as 'trust in government.' (Although I will question the assumptions that underlie social surveys of trust, their results nonetheless inform a contemporary political discourse that deserves attention). In the USA, such opinion surveys go back to the 1950s. The percentages of respondents expressing trust in the federal government declined during the 1960s, a period that saw social unrest, the Vietnam War and the Watergate scandal (Abramson and Finifter, 1981; Pew Research Center, 2015). It is not clear, though, whether this decline is from levels that were abnormally high in the post-War era, or whether the more recent 'lows' should be regarded as a departure from the norm. A global surveyor insists, however, that trust in institutions is 'in crisis,' and paradoxically lower in some of the world's more affluent and democratic societies such as Japan, Sweden, South Korea, the UK, France, Germany and Australia, whereas some non-democratic countries, notably China, report higher levels of trust. Within countries, greater trust is expressed by those with higher incomes, higher education and higher levels of media and news consumption (Edelman, 2017).[1]

We should be cautious about drawing generalizations from survey data. The evidence for a decline in public trust in government internationally is still a matter of debate. Public opinion surveys are not all consistent in the wording of questions posed, and respondents may differ in their understanding of what is meant by 'government.' Public opinion, as surveyed, may sometimes reflect recent controversies that have erupted in the media – making 'trust in government' a salient issue – but have little to do with the actual quality or performance of public services, or with people's everyday reliance upon them. The ordinary citizen, moreover, is unable to evaluate objectively the effectiveness or trustworthiness of all elected officials or government services and their employees, due to the sheer scope and complexity of business encompassed by the term 'government,' and hence is forced to base his or her judgement on an unverifiable and hence unjustifiable 'dis/trust' (Bouckaert, 2012; Hetherington and Husser, 2012; Van de Walle and Bouckaert, 2003; Van de Walle, Van Roosbroek, and Bouckaert, 2008). Empirical studies based on surveys thus do not produce unambiguous results, and there is controversy in the field over how to conceptualize and 'measure' political trust at the outset (Parker, Parker, and Towner, 2015). If we take account of the complexity between the questions posed, the answers given by respondents and the varied, fast-moving world of public events, we may still have more questions than answers about political trust.

Moreover, the very environment in which we experience or maintain political trust is rapidly changing. Being believed when I say who I am, for example, goes beyond being a personal prerogative in a face-to-face social setting, and it is increasingly managed and commodified through social media and online commerce, and hence through digital technologies. This relies upon the lawful and regulated processes of 'government' (birth certificates, privacy laws, etc.), but the digital-era politics of trust increasingly eludes the reach of law and administration. Big technology firms take advantage of the ubiquity, scale and complexity of their systems to extract information for commercial gain, but with little material consideration for private users (Zuboff, 2015). People at work or at leisure online are constantly leaving digital footprints, making their movements, opinions and choices visible to technology firms. But the firms themselves do not make their processes and algorithms transparent, and there is now a significant knowledge-asymmetry between corporate intellectual property and private self-identification. Individuals are losing control of the means of identifying themselves and of establishing their own reputations (Pasquale, 2015). On the consumer side, people are able to engage in peer-to-peer contacts to do business and to learn about events in ways that evade and even undermine traditional institutional gate-keeping (Botsman, 2017); although these new networks are most often monopolized by the big tech firms, such as Facebook, Google and Uber. The 'structures' of political trust itself are undergoing transformations, and traditional governmental institutions are being challenged in the process. Our ways and means of trusting, and our concepts of political trust, are historically contingent and not static.

A politics of trust

Chapter 1 looked at some uses of trust in political rhetoric and in political-science literature, but there is more to say about how trust can be meaningfully understood as a factor within the domain of the political. So, this section takes up further examples, based on gender, race, socio-biology and the role of distrust. If trust is a genuinely political factor, then we should ask what it does. I will question assumptions, found in the literature, about trust as a quasi-causative factor.

In an early contribution to the contemporary theory of trust, Baier (1986) argued that the rising prominence of women in twentieth-century philosophy challenged models of ethics and politics that were based on voluntary contracts between relatively equal, mentally and physically capable adult males. In contrast, a child trusts, but does not choose to trust, parents; a basic duty or commitment to be trustworthy over-rides the 'free choices' of the parent; there are obligations, but no contract. Hence, one should think beyond the confines of agreements and promises between rational consenting beings – who may calculate when it is in their interests to cooperate – as a supposed ideal or basic model of trust. Trust could open up conceptual scope for imagining a different set of mutual commitments in private and in public life. Unfortunately, as we will see later, much subsequent trust literature has not lived up to Baier's hopes; it has often reduced trust to a calculated risk.

As another example of trust in political discourse, Uslaner finds, based on surveys in the USA, that 'blacks are far less trusting than whites. Race is consistently one of the most powerful determinants of both generalized and particularized trust' (Uslaner, 2002, p. 91). This difference cannot be accounted for statistically by income or class differences. Ethnoracial differences in the extent to which people state that they believe other people can be trusted have been attributed to historical and contemporary discrimination, the contexts and the nature of different neighbourhoods, and differences in the socialization of children (Smith, 2010). Explanations for such a 'trust gap' consider the social contexts and experiences of disadvantaged minority groups; whereas a society in which more people trust others more of the time is considered preferable. For groups that suffer little discrimination, live in safe and prosperous neighbourhoods, and raise children with positive expectations of how others should treat them, trust underpins numerous advantages (or privileges), such as the confident expectation that one's face will be welcome in certain settings or institutions and that others will assist and assume goodwill. Those with plenty of economic, cultural and social capital can more confidently face the risk of an occasional loss or betrayal. The readiness to trust others and the likelihood of being trusted by others *are* political as they reflect social relations of power characterized by disadvantage and privilege. Closing the 'trust gap' would necessitate addressing the most basic sources of inequality and oppression.

Even if there were a social contract based upon a gift of trust, as Locke claimed, the reasons for giving it would be greatly varied. What 'security' or 'safety' means to one person may mean something quite different to another, depending on one's race, wealth, property, health, abilities, or lack thereof. Further, such political trust would be far from equally shared by subjects. And this inequality is not due only to random variation or personal traits; it derives from and is inherent in political institutions and their hegemonic practices. The concern about a 'trust gap' is thus a precursor to a more thorough-going political claim for equality.

One should also acknowledge socio-biological theories that make trust out to be natural or genetically endowed, rather than socially constructed. For instance, a basic moral 'code' is genetically programmed into us, it may be argued, and we have evolved to trust others because it has been beneficial for the survival of our species. While morally condoned altruistic or trusting acts may appear, at first sight, to be hard to explain through the combination of Darwinian natural selection and Mendelian genetics, some scientists argue that altruism confers on our species evolutionary advantages (Wilson, 2015). To assist, to cooperate with and to trust others, on this account, is instinctual because it promotes both the survival of individuals, by allowing us to reap the advantages of group cohesion, and the survival of the species, as social groups are better able to protect themselves and to meet their basic needs. Trust would thus be 'heritable,' just as much as competitiveness is, the two being complementary survival strategies. The injunction to be trustworthy is then reduced to a genetically endowed imperative to be altruistic, arising from natural selection.

There is little, however, to be gained from a nature-versus-nurture argument about trust's origins. Like language-competence, the human capability to trust is only possible due to a particular genetic code and inherent mental aptitudes. But the languages we speak and the ways in which we trust are also inherently cultural. Speech and trust are only *meaningful* in the context of lived activities. And these cultural 'codes' are often untranslatable; they are not universally understood. The genetic code may be necessary for a being that speaks and trusts, but it is *never sufficient* as an explanation for what we actually do or say. Trust is natural, or inherent to human social life, *and* cultural.

The survival-value of in-group trust must be balanced with the survival-value of distrusting hostile out-groups, moreover. Cohesive social-group formation, based upon kinship, religion or mutual interest, implies the foreigner, infidel or stranger whom one fears. Even John Locke argued, for instance, that the earliest communities would have come to trust a patriarch only as the need arose for 'defence against foreign invasions and injuries' (Locke, 1980, p. 57, §107). Particularized in-group trust includes those friends who form a nascent state; but this entails the existence of enemies. So, perhaps it is the distinction between friend (whom we trust to some extent) and enemy (whom we do not trust at all) that defines 'the political,' or that constitutes 'the specific political distinction to which political actions and motives can be reduced' (Schmitt, 2007, p. 26). Short of depoliticizing all human activity, then, the scope of those peoples who are trusted will always be demarcated from those others who are not.

Similarly, to any liberal-democratic argument in favour of trust, there is an equal and opposite argument in favour of distrust. Modern economic and political liberalism, from its origins in Locke, Hume and Smith, and the democratic constitutions that reflect those ideals, are premised as much upon a *dis*trust in the few (the 'bad apples') as upon a trust in or among the many. Constitutional and statutory controls, arising from distrust, are fundamental to liberal democracy. James Madison exemplified this (Hardin, 2002).[2] Men and women equally are not angels, and they cannot be trusted to do what is right or just all of the time – or not without precautionary controls that will oblige them to do so – especially when money and power are involved. Because democracy demands transparency and limitation of powers, independent 'watchdogs' such as auditors, judges and journalists are empowered to inquire and report, just in case someone defrauds the public or neglects duties. A democratic polity trusts the many to elect a few from among their community to govern and to legislate. But the electors' trust is never unconditional – due to a well-founded scepticism and distrust. Those who stand for office may claim to represent the common good, but their competitive desire for advancement leads us to question their motives, and a political leader's licence to govern has a sunset clause, namely the next election. If we apply a Downsian economic logic, then utility-maximizing contenders for office are interested in income and status, seeking to maximize votes as means to achieve them. Once elected, the incentive to act in self-serving ways is clearer and stronger than any notion of 'the public interest.' The push against 'big government' in the neoliberal era was premised on such distrust of the state and of those who run it. The 'new public management' of the 1980s and '90s assumed a distrust of citizens, professional groups and public servants, due to self-interest (Bouckaert, 2012). Officials were depicted as budget-maximizing empire-builders, while employees and professionals needed external incentives and controls in order to align their behaviour with policy or business objectives. More than a regrettable symptom of malaise, distrust (in government generally and in the motives of officials and professionals) became the intellectual norm around which public policy was designed and services restructured.

Validation of distrust arises not only from conservative pro-market politics. Looking from the bottom up, dissent (or the right thereto) is as important in democracy as consent (Rosanvallon, 2008). For the promotion of civil liberties, at critical moments in history, distrust holds a positive political value (Krishnamurthy, 2015). Although the grounds have changed over time, the history of liberalism is a history of distrust in the state and in those who control its apparatuses – or, at best, a strictly conditional and limited trust. To trust people with power is thus simultaneously to distrust them; always to limit the scope of their decisions and actions by transparency, public scrutiny, protests and petitions, parliamentary approval, constitutional 'checks and balances' and 'separation of powers' (Warren, 2017). We do not trust people not to abuse power, and hence:

> All trust in constitutions is grounded on the assurance they may afford, not that the depositaries of power will not, but that they cannot, misemploy it.
>
> (Mill, 1991, p. 326)

One always suspects that those in power may misuse it. There is no simple formula, then, that compels us to say 'trust is good' and 'distrust is bad.' Trust always implies some idea of 'the good,' but it can sometimes be morally or epistemologically wrong or mistaken to trust someone – or, equally, it is sometimes wise to distrust.

We should avoid, moreover, reductionism of the kind that portrays political trust as something like a *causal* factor. For instance, Lenard holds that, in democracies, trust '*arises from* shared norms and values' (2012, p. 6). The phrase 'arises from' suggests that values and norms are prior to – or a necessary condition for – trust. Similarly, the language used to describe political trust sometimes suggests that it is 'driven' by other social factors. In turn, political trust can '*dampen* ideological conflict and *forge* policy consensus [and it] can serve as a *reservoir* that policy makers draw on to *cause* those not ideologically predisposed to follow them to give their ideas a shot' (Hetherington and Rudolph, 2015, p. 5, italics added). These kinds of expressions are hard to avoid in ordinary English-language usage, but the quasi-causal, materialist hypothesis that they imply is artificial. I argue instead that trust-talk invokes immaterial qualities of human relations that may be observed in any cultural context, although the kinds of actions that 'build' or 'undermine' or 'break' trust differ across cultures, just as the shared norms and values entailed in relations of trust are culturally variable. It's not that trust 'arises' or 'emerges' from shared values and norms, nor vice versa. 'Trust,' 'norms' and 'values' are simply generic and abstract names we use for culturally contingent patterns of expression, interaction and exchange that are internalized as beliefs and obligations that we act upon. Political trust is not literally undermined by ideological polarization, nor need we say that distrust leads to polarization. The two terms (distrust and polarization) describe aspects of the same political environment. Political trust is misrepresented when treated as a force or factor revealed statistically and regarded as a cause or consequence of some other such factors.

People often seek out guiding values or principles that can be captured in a word (such as identity, happiness or trust) for the purposes of explaining social problems or promoting political progress. And trust (as surveyed) has become an indicator by which social well-being is evaluated. The use of such indicators is a 'third way' reaction against the neoliberal emphasis on individualism, economic efficiency and growth. But a statistical representation becomes reified as a 'factor,' correlated with a multiplicity of other variables and then treated as a part of a quasi-scientific narrative. So, while I will accept that trust is recognizable as a political factor, in the sense of 'how we get things done,' I eschew the temptation to treat it as if it were a 'social reality,' a force or a causal influence.

Definitions of trust

There is no standard definition of trust in the literature, especially as it spans numerous disciplines. For example, economists are inclined to emphasize calculation and self-interest, whereas philosophers are more likely to regard trust as an attitude that involves an acceptance of vulnerability and moral obligations. Terms such as 'expectancy,' 'reliance' and 'vulnerability' occur frequently in a survey of definitions (Blomqvist, 1997).

Numerous contemporary theorists have offered definitions of trust in instrumental and self-interested terms, assuming uncertainty. Gambetta's definition (in a widely cited text) linked trust in a person to the likelihood of cooperation.

> When we say we trust someone or that someone is trustworthy, we implicitly mean that the probability that he will perform an action that is beneficial or at least not detrimental to us is high enough for us to consider engaging in some form of cooperation with him.
>
> (Gambetta, 1988, p. 217)

A central concern of Gambetta's volume is to explore why, and under what conditions, rational decision-makers will risk cooperation, in spite of uncertainty. Trust is regarded as a probabilistic calculation or choice, almost as an exception, rather than a prevalent quality of social life. And one has to make this calculation in order to consider cooperation, rather than letting trust emerge from cooperation. Trust's supposedly risky calculus is vested in 'an action' (singular) as if we need to recalculate our trust in others on a case-by-case basis, rather than viewing trust as an enduring or growing quality of a relationship. This is an economistic version of trust which could apply to one's choice of a used-car salesperson – while still not fully trusting that person. I cannot recall making such a calculation about any of my trusted friends or community leaders, before trusting them, and I have not so far observed any of them making such calculations about any particular action of mine, as a condition of our cooperation. The closest I can say is that one's failure to play one's rightful part in a relationship, due to a detrimental action, can lead to distrust.

Sztompka defines trust in relation to the need 'to act in spite of uncertainty and risk,' and hence trust is 'a bet about the future contingent actions of others' (1999, p. 25). One trusts someone else to do something, being uncertain that she will do it, as if gambling. But, such a view of trust is ambiguous. If I said to a friend, 'Trusting you to do things is like placing a bet,' you could reasonably infer that I don't really trust her much, if at all.

Misztal offers a definition that employs the infinitive verb, rather than the noun: 'To trust is to believe that the results of somebody's intended actions will be appropriate from our point of view' (1996, p. 24). In this case, the person is believing, rather than betting, but again the person who trusts is investing in the future actions of another person. This version of trust includes an expectation of 'appropriate intentions.' It is the outcome of actions, not the other *person*, about which one forms a belief. Russell Hardin focuses on the person's trustworthiness but outlines a similar form of belief: 'To say we trust you means we believe you have the right intentions toward us and that you are competent to do what we trust you to do' (Hardin, 2006, p. 17). Right or appropriate intentions towards us are combined with competence to do what you say you will do. Again, if I described my trust in a friend in such words, it may cause disappointment that I am merely believing that something appropriate will happen, rather than saying that I feel fully assured of her goodwill and her commitment to keeping promises.

To quote a more recent text, trust is 'a rational or affective belief in the benevolent motivation and performance capacity of another party' (Norris, 2017, p. 19). A very similar formulation uses the word 'judgement' rather than 'belief' (Warren, 2017, p. 33). Our belief, judgement or perception regarding the motives, competence and/or performance of a person or institution are commonly cited factors of trust.

Political trust has been defined as 'the degree to which people perceive that government is producing outcomes consistent with their expectations' (Hetherington, 2005, p. 9), recognizing that popular perception may not match the actual performance of the government in office. More recently, Hetherington

and Rudolf describe trust as a heuristic that people use, in lieu of mentally process-
ing complex policies, governmental processes and political events. Political trust
is based on citizens' satisfaction with the past actions of governments, and on a
'willingness to believe government promises.' It is thus 'the belief that government will do rightly in the future' – that is, people's 'faith in' or 'feelings towards'
government (Hetherington and Rudolph, 2015, pp. 36–37).

These definitions more or less conform to the structure: 'A trusts B to do X,
where X is in A's interests.' In political terms, this may be rephrased as: 'A trusts
"government" to do X, where X is "the right thing" in A's opinion.' Such definitions are transactional, instrumental and self-interested. They individualize trust
(as a person's belief or choice) or trustworthiness (as a trait) in order to operationalize it for survey questions. They have significant shortcomings:

- They do not comprehend the reciprocity involved in trust, which could be
  represented simply as: 'In return, B trusts A to do Y.'
- They assume that A's private interests and opinions about the trusted party's
  (B's) intentions are clearly understood by A in advance.
- They do not account for a situation where 'A trusts B to decide what is in
  C's best interests' – such as when a school or a welfare agency decides what
  is in the best interests of a child (C), and the child has no choice but to trust.
- They do not account for relationships in which an abused partner may
  continue to trust the abuser; nor for Stockholm syndrome in which hostages
  trust their captor and distrust authorities who come to the rescue.
- They fail to ask if one could trust a person whom one does *not* believe
  to be competent and well-intentioned – either because one has little
  choice, or one hopes that, in being trusted, the other party will learn to
  be responsible.
- To act on an assumption that B is competent and willing to serve A's
  interests is not necessarily a sign of trust; it may be nothing more than
  calculating that B will do certain things, while it serves both parties' interests, after which A plans to ignore or even kill B.

To trust others could mean that we simply enjoy doing things with them, or that
we cannot do without them, or that we have to depend on them no matter what,
with durable mutual understandings that govern conduct. *There is no compelling
reason why perceived competence or benevolence, directed at one's own subjective
interests, ought to be the generalizable and definitive feature of trust, over and above
all other intelligible features.*

The contemporary conceptualization of trust, and hence of political trust, is
limited and misleading. Trust inherently raises 'context-sensitive questions,' and
no definition could cover the range of contexts to which the word is meaningfully
applied (Lagerspetz, 2015, p. 7). The definitions cited above are conditioned by
the theoretical backgrounds and research methods of their authors. They assume
that the basic question is, 'Why would rational utility-maximizers choose to trust?'
(Answer: 'Only if it were in their interests.') They attempt to rationalize trust in

an imagined world populated by strategically-minded and self-interested beings, where trust looks like what suckers do and requires a risky leap of faith. Such defining limitations mean that analyses of trust will be conceptually flawed.

Operationalization of trust

Having looked critically at some widely accepted definitions of trust, we can also observe how they are conditioned by the norms of social-scientific methodologies. Defining trust as a personal belief or expectation *about* others – and not as a feature of how people interact or how social groups cohere – is useful if the aim is to operationalize trust for survey questions and statistical outputs. The surveyor can ask for individuals' opinions about how much they trust others or trust government, without having to observe what they actually do. Telephone or online surveys may pose to individual respondents the question: 'Generally speaking would you say that most people can be trusted or that you need to be very careful in dealing with people?' And so it is reported that 'trust' (as surveyed) is positively correlated with a nation's median household income, and negatively correlated with income inequality (OECD, 2011). But some social researchers have questioned what the 'trust' item in surveys is actually 'measuring.' What is the social scope or 'radius' that includes 'most people'? What actions does the question suppose that others are trusted to do? And how closely do data derived from what respondents *say* reflect how much they actually *do* trust others? (Delhey, Newton, and Welzel, 2011; Morrone, Tontoranelli, and Ranuzzi, 2009; Sapienza, Toldra-Simats, and Zingales, 2013).

Similarly, trust in *government* may be queried by surveys that ask: 'How much do you trust the government to do what's right?' Again, responses will depend upon highly variable understandings of which persons or institutions are encompassed in the term 'government,' and what it is that governments actually do, which is further influenced by what people learn through various media. Responses are contingent upon respondents' support for, or opposition to, the political party in office, and the kinds of issues that are most salient at the time (Hetherington and Rudolph, 2015). For example, conservative governments may be regarded as more 'trustworthy' in relation to external relations and defence, while liberal or social-democratic governments may be more 'trusted' with domestic social policy. The responses may only arise from an affective like or dislike for the government of the day, or an opinion on how well it is performing in one particular area. They do not encompass the relational and pragmatic ethical interactions (the exchanges of rights and duties) that characterize political trust.

The validity of opinion poll results as empirical evidence depends on the assumption that the phenomena (the opinions, values, preferences) being surveyed pre-exist the survey and the political concerns that motivated the survey – that they are 'there' in the minds of individuals, waiting passively to be elicited and counted. But, such surveys do *not* simply 'measure' public opinions (or values, preferences, etc.); they actively *produce* representations of a public that possesses politically significant opinions and that can be segmented for marketing or political purposes. The poll participant or the reader of reports about the poll results becomes reflexively represented as a member of this or that 'demographic' – the opinions of which differ from some other demographic. From the public opinion poll, therefore, we learn (on the surface) about the prevalence and distribution of specific opinions, but also implicitly we learn how to reflect upon ourselves as members of a public that is seen to have significant opinions. Counting each person's opinion with equal weight mirrors the ethos of the universal franchise: one person one vote. Just as one ought to vote, one ought to have opinions about social values and consumer products. The disciplinary effect of, and resistance to, opinion polls can be gauged from levels of non-response or 'don't know' responses to polls, and from the consequent efforts by polling agencies to understand and to normalize this deviant 'opinionless' population (Peer, 1992).

One symptom of the 'post-truth' anti-establishment politics that peaked in 2016 was a sustained critical attack on opinion polling – and on political expertise in general. The accuracy of opinion polls and the reliability of their methods were all brought into question. As households shifted away from landline telephones towards mobile devices, traditional methods had greater difficulty in reaching representative samples. Online polling techniques were becoming more common but were still controversial. The present critique goes beyond methodology, however. The 'accuracy' of trust surveys is not the real issue, as there is no 'object' against which to evaluate their accuracy. Rather they are 'discursive practices' (Foucault, 1972) that actively form the political subjectivity and the supposed object (the 'trust') of which they speak, and that represent political trust as an effect of governmental rationality.

A further axiom of a scientific approach is that trust is an operationalizable variable about which empirically falsifiable hypotheses can be made. Behavioural studies address what people observably do when they trust. Experiments in the laboratory purport to show how 'instances of trust can be stripped of complicating contextual features and encoded into economic exchange games that preserve its essential features' (King-Casas et al., 2005, p. 78). This is a normal approach to experimental operationalization, such as in the Prisoner's Dilemma or the Trust game (Berg, Dickhaut, and McCabe, 1995).[3] But, given the complexity of trust, denuding it of social context could not possibly 'preserve its essential features' – as social context is essential to understanding what we would normally call 'trust.' In any case, game-theory studies that include cross-national samples do reveal cultural differences in trust and reciprocation (Buchan, Croson, and Dawes, 2002). The assumption in game-theory, however, is that trust is essentially a decision or action by one person in relation to, but isolated from, another. The simultaneous use of brain-scanning imagery reinforces this individualism. The other party in the laboratory game is not known to the subject – they normally remain anonymous to one another, and so the supposed trust relationship is an artificial one, governed by rules set by the researcher. The game-theory experimenter had to have an already-formed concept of trust in order to design rules for 'a trust game.' And the participants agree to follow the experimenter's rules. One important background condition in the Prisoner's Dilemma game is that there exists an effective rule of law, and hence there are prison-guards, lawyers and judges, whose legitimate roles are presumed knowledge, owing to a pre-existing political trust. Participants in Trust games, when deciding how much, if anything, to give to the other player, cannot be immune to the presence of an experimenter, nor ignorant of social norms of fairness, and hence the background of 'social approval' takes effect. Social context and ethico-political norms inevitably play a part in the design and conduct of any such experiment. The trust that is observed through a laboratory experiment can only make sense due to an external social milieu in which trust is already shared, practised and comprehended.

Contemporary trust theory, therefore, is built on partial but unquestioned assumptions about trust. (The present text at least questions its own assumption.) Furthermore, it often commences by imagining a world without trust, thus making trust look like a risky choice.

What if there were no trust?

A common strategy in political theory is to imagine what life would be like if there were no government. This is the opening gambit of social contract theory, which relies upon a portrait of life in a state of nature, in which there is neither a sovereign, nor institutions of government, nor any 'common power.' Social contract theory persists in spite of the fact that even the most 'primitive' societies – if not also other primates – have social hierarchies and observe regular, if unwritten, customs. John Locke, as a seventeenth-century 'armchair' anthropologist, incorrectly imagined the Americas to be 'waste land,' devoid of agriculture, economy or customary law. In Rousseau's portrait of a state of nature, humans roamed around as free individuals, which again has no basis in evidence. The depiction of a state of nature served, however, to initiate a case for recognition of an original and natural freedom.

The same approach is used in establishing orthodox commodity theories of money – and this again goes back at least to John Locke. In order to understand the utility of money, we are asked to consider what the world would be like without it. The claim is normally that we would have to barter commodities directly, which would be inefficient and inconvenient due to the low frequency of traders' wants and needs coinciding in time and place. Coins made of precious metals (and nowadays fiat currencies that may be paper or sheer data) have, by common agreement, overcome this problem, it is said. But complex urbanized economies had evolved many centuries before the earliest known metallic forms of money, and no historian or anthropologist has found a community whose economy depended largely upon barter (Graeber, 2014). The orthodox theory ('once upon a time, we all had to barter') is replicated in introductory economics textbooks, in spite of the lack of evidence.

And similarly, social theorists of trust often start with the superficially compelling proposition that social life would be impossible or unbearable without trust (Barber, 1983; Dunn, 1984; Lewis and Weigert, 1985; Luhmann, 1979). We can trace this back to Georg Simmel's discussion of credit, as necessary for all forms of money, during which he asserts:

> Without the general trust that people have in each other, society itself would disintegrate, for very few relationships are based entirely upon what is known with certainty about another person, and very few relationships would endure if trust were not as strong as, or stronger than, rational proof or personal observation.
>
> (Simmel, 2004, pp. 178–179, first published in 1900)

Such assertions about social disintegration in the absence of trust make no effort, however, to identify empirically a time or place in which 'there was no trust,' most probably because there never was one. Even those at war experience in-group trust or *esprit de corps*, while they cannot trust the enemy. Indeed, a call to arms is the very moment that political trust is relied upon the most. 'A life with no role for trust whatsoever would be radically different from the way we live and can hardly be called human' (Lagerspetz, 1998, p. 64). To try to imagine a human life, as social creatures, without some form of law (written or customary), without commonly accepted ways and means of economic exchange, or without hospitality and reciprocity is to try to imagine a state of affairs that is not really recognizable as a *human* life at all. There never really was a state of nature, nor an economy that ran entirely by bartering, nor a multitude that lived without any trust. So, we should question the validity of this common opening gambit, 'Imagine if there were no. . .' Put simply, it asks that we imagine the unimaginable.

An assertion about trust as 'the basis of social life,' contrasted with the spectre of trust's absence, does not explain anything about ourselves; it only reflects counter-factually on the already-apparent orderliness of social life. We cannot occupy an 'Archimedean position' from which to dislodge human life from the habits and customs of trust and so to observe (let alone experience) a world that lacks it. We should therefore eschew accounts that commence by positing 'a world without trust.'

Nonetheless, we are left with the puzzle of a socially distributed factor called 'trust' that appears to account for community cohesion, the predictability and security of everyday life, and the acceptance of law and government. Simmel argued for the crucial role of trust in modern societies, especially in monetary systems. He held that trust is based upon 'weak inductive logic' – a 'leap' that is far from rational. He proposed that:

> there exists a 'further element' of a transcendental, quasi-religious nature in trust that enables the 'leap.' In a simple formula, for Simmel *trust combines good reasons with faith.*
>
> (Möllering, 2001, p. 411, original italics)

This strand of theory – from Simmel to Luhmann and beyond – avoids the economistic reduction of trust to mere rational calculation. Trust may be rational, in that it makes sense to trust, but it also means acting in spite of unpredictability and uncertainty, especially in the face of an unlimited range of contingent future possibilities; hence it goes beyond that which is rationalizable, requiring, it is said, some form of 'faith.' But this bases one ill-defined concept (trust) upon another ill-defined concept (faith). And the two terms have closely overlapping meanings, such as between 'I trust you' and 'I have faith in you.' The appeal to 'faith' only displaces the problem of 'grounding' our understanding of trust. In short, it is no explanation; it is a tautological restatement of the problem.

Sociological accounts, including 'abstract trust' (Giddens, 1990), will be considered again in Chapter 4. But we will need to ground our understanding of trust in a way that is more practical than the sociologists' appeals to 'complexity' and 'uncertainty' as motives for trust, or to 'faith' and 'belief' as defining factors. I abandon the effort to define or explain trust, but instead offer some notes or observations that are descriptive of what we do when we trust. 'All *explanation* must disappear, and description alone must take its place' (Wittgenstein, 2009, p. 52e, §109).[4]

A pragmatic description

Trust represents positive alternatives to control or coercion at one extreme, and to isolation or anomie at the other. But is it an alternative to political power *per se*, or is trust a way of governing relations, and hence a formation of power? It has been claimed that trust is a 'human propensity' that is associated with, but independent of, power; that we should 'replace [Foucault's] "genealogy of power" with a genealogy of trust' (Hosking, 2014, p. 6). I hold instead that trust and power are not independent, and that we cannot 'replace' one with the other. What follows is a set of descriptive notes, not a definition. But it avoids the reduction of trust to self-interested calculation or opinion.

If I trust you, with or without saying so, I am actively assuming the mutual recognition of autonomy and freedom of action, and hence unpredictability; yet we seek to limit that freedom so that our actions will be less unpredictable. These constraints may well be breached, but with consequences. One may not be trusted a second time, for instance. Trusting one another 'keeps us in line.' In other words, trust is not a relinquishment of or an alternative to power; it is a modality of power, employed when direct surveillance or force is undesirable or impossible. It relies upon norms of mutual obligation, governing our interactions, whilst presupposing our autonomy.

We may regard trust in terms of reciprocal, customary, normative practices, for example praising, promising, exchanging, forgiving or abstaining. These are actions, or interactions, that are guided by (and reinforce) perceptions of right (or rights), fairness, balance and care for the vulnerable. Trust takes effect in relationships and situations in which such norms of 'moral economy' are mostly being taken for granted. One does not think or speak about them while they are being performed if trust is well-established. Many questions about our motives and possible future actions are rendered unnecessary.

As significant actions within any politics of trust, let us consider, then, promising and forgiving. One important way in which we learn to trust people (including public figures) is based on whether they kept their promises. Promising may be a way of 'building' trust, if we see it as 'inviting someone to trust one to do something' (Friedrich and Southwood, 2011, p. 276). A promise is normally regarded as consciously communicated in speech or writing,[5] and an election manifesto may be read as explicit promises to the voters. People may forgive a governing political party's failure to live up to a promise if unexpected circumstances have intervened. One can also impute an unspoken promise where certain obligations are conventional undertakings of participants in a democracy. For example, a political party that loses an election (as the incumbent government) is bound by an implicit promise to concede defeat and ensure an orderly change-over.

Forgiveness generally involves pardoning faults, failures or injuries and remitting debts.[6] For trust to endure, minor instances of harm, misconduct or non-performance of promises need not threaten the relationship. Humans are fallible and they are mutually vulnerable in relations of trust. A gross breach of trust can permanently rupture or compromise a relationship, but trusted friends overlook, forget or forgive lesser transgressions, and hence can resume trusting each other (Atkins, 2002). Without a reasonable expectation of forgiveness for minor failings, the risks of public leadership would be much higher for the individual, people would become more defensive, and participation would decline. This may be a feature of what is actually occurring presently. In this age of social media, one can quickly search (or simulate) and distribute compromising information about individuals. Every action can be scrutinized, and an 'unforgiving' atmosphere prevails around prominent actors in public life.

Collaborative governance, voluntary contributions to the community, and endeavours requiring long-term dedication are more sustainable when there is a confident expectation of security and reasonable reward. Political trust works for the people, as well as for their representatives. A community that has sufficient trust in the way it is governed will share a sense that a lifetime's work will not end in penury or shame. The individual's consequent debt to society may thus amount to more than can be repaid, even in a lifetime (Graeber, 2014). But the concerted actions of a progressive liberal democracy will forgive individuals who do not attain, or who lose, through age or disability, the ideal self-sufficiency implied in the term 'liberty.'

Promising and forgiving are thus integral to a politics of trust. To trust is 'to govern on credit.' It supposes a promise, or at least holds an expectation, that the parties will act within limits or adopt norms; it implies consequences if there is a failure to do so; it guides the possibilities of the conduct of the parties; it constrains the possible outcomes. A breach of those boundaries may be forgiven, or it may reorder the possibilities of conduct. This is a 'softer' exercise of power than close surveillance and control, but it is still an exercise of power, as it governs relationships and the actions of others through the assumption of mutual obligations. It is performed 'on credit' in the sense that the actors are presupposed to be willing and able 'to make good on' their promises or debts.

Trust does not happen 'in us'; rather, it is 'constituted by its role in human interaction' (Lagerspetz, 1998, p. 15). Hence, trust pertains to the interpersonal or commonly shared. It is incomplete to say 'this person trusts' without reference to another person or other persons; such a statement can only be intelligible through patterns of thought and action in lived social contexts. As a quality of social life, at the level of communities or economies, what we do when we trust is therefore actively quite different from what intimate friends are doing when they trust one another. It may be a mistake even to consider the former as a generalization of the latter. The use of the word 'trust' for such diverse contexts may be misleading for us, if taken literally or simply. In as much as trust may be a 'factor,' it need not be thought of statistically as a 'risk-factor,' but rather as the relational and institutional conditions under which people find it easier to get things done together, and when they perceive that due regard and return is paid for one another's efforts and status, with little need for critical reflection, debate or calculation.

Political trust represents a quality of public life that makes the exercise of powers, performance of duties, collaboration and exchange practically feasible and efficient, tolerably fair, and relatively free of hostility. Trusting one another in public life helps to make a political community in which matters such as security, equality or justice can be consciously at issue and purposefully advanced. An underlying political trust implies a quality of moderation in people's actions and statements in public life that survives electoral contests, changes of government and even national disasters. It does not presuppose or require ideological agreement, but it does mean that disagreements and grievances can be staged safely, or without fear of harmful consequences, and with due regard for the ethical obligations owed to all participants.

Conclusion

Trust entails certain ways of thinking and feeling, but there is no defining 'set' of thoughts, feelings and attitudes that necessarily accompanies it. Not even love necessitates trust, nor vice versa. To avoid the endless hair-splitting of definitions, trust is best described in practical, relational – and not individualistic – terms. The idea of trust as a cognitive belief, opinion, decision or advantageous agreement is not out of the scope of trust as we experience it, but, as a basis for definition, it is a retrospective misrecognition. We think of trust in this misrecognized form only after the primary fact of trust has emerged in its lived, experienced and reciprocated forms. It requires an advanced level of self-awareness to speak of it as a belief or decision.

By regarding trust in terms of the ethical meanings of observable things that we do and say in interactions, we avoid falling back upon ideas such as 'complexity,' 'risk' or 'faith' which are abstract, intangible and equally hard to define. The re-description of trust that I have substituted above rests upon things that people *do* to observe various norms of reciprocity, obligation and fairness.

To trust someone may be, in some cases or in certain ways, rationally in my interests. It stands to reason, moreover, that we would be worse off without trusted friends. But, while trust could at times entail a rational choice based on a belief in others' competence and their good intentions towards me, it is not properly comprehensible as such. I can consciously give such reasons for my trusting some of the time – but that is only intelligible against a background of life-experience and a social field of existing relations of trust, most of which eludes rationalization. It makes little sense to explain that I trust my friends because I estimate that they will probably act in my interests. I do not choose my friends on the grounds that their trustworthiness reduces complexity or saves me from asking whether those around me might attack me with a knife.

Similarly, it only partially makes sense to define *political* trust in rational terms, as for instance a ratio between what we think governments ought to do and our estimations of what is actually delivered. Political trust, if reduced to such opinions, as surveyed, is only partially understood. It should also be looked for in the shared and largely unquestioned active dispositions of people, their sense of being 'in it together,' the ethical quality of the conduct of public institutions and the capability to deal with differences peacefully and to advance fundamental concerns about security and rights.

Notes

1 The Edelman survey was conducted online. Its own figures on internet penetration are, for instance, 52 percent in China compared with 95 percent in Sweden. The national samples of online respondents in countries with low internet penetration are more educated, affluent and urban than the national population. This suggests that the results from China may be skewed towards a demographic profile of people who could be expected to express higher levels of trust in government. Moreover, in an authoritarian one-party state, online respondents may judge it unwise to comment that they do not trust their government.
2 'If men were angels, no government would be necessary. If angels were to govern men, neither external nor internal controls on government would be necessary. In framing a government which is to be administered by men over men, the great difficulty lies in this: you must first enable the government to control the governed; and in the next place oblige it to control itself,' James Madison, *The Federalist*, 51, 1788 (Jay, Goldman, Hamilton, and Madison, 2008, p. 257).
3 In the Trust game, one player is given a sum of money and told to choose any amount of it to send to an anonymous second player. The player may choose zero. But any sum sent will be tripled by the experimenter. So, when the first player hands over a sum, the experimenter takes it, triples it, and gives the total to the second player. The second player is then told to make a similar choice – give an amount of the now-tripled money back to the first player, or nothing. Standard economic assumptions of self-interest predict that no money will be sent. But, in most cases, both players send money to the other.
4 'And this description gets its light – that is to say, its purpose – from the philosophical problems. These are, of course, not empirical problems; but they are solved through an insight into the workings of our language, and that in such a way that these workings are recognized – *despite* an urge to misunderstand them. The problems are solved, not by coming up with new discoveries, but by assembling what we have long been familiar with. Philosophy is a struggle against the bewitchment of our understanding by the resources of our language' (Wittgenstein, 2009, p. 52e, §109).

5 'If a speaker promises then he communicates an intention to undertake an obligation to the hearer' (Pratt, 2014, p. 383).
6 Forgiving has been neglected by theorists of trust, even though mercy is well-established in legal theory and practice, and in spite of the attention given to forgiveness by Arendt (1958) and Derrida (2001).

References

Abramson, P. R., and Finifter, A. W. (1981). On the meaning of political trust: New evidence from items introduced in 1978. *American Journal of Political Science*, 25(2), 297–307.

Arendt, H. (1958). *The human condition.* Chicago, IL: University of Chicago Press.

Atkins, K. (2002). Friendship, trust and forgiveness. *Philosophia*, 29(1–4), 111–132.

Baier, A. (1986). Trust and antitrust. *Ethics*, 96(2), 231–260.

Barber, B. (1983). *The logic and limits of trust.* New Brunswick, NJ: Rutgers University Press.

Berg, J., Dickhaut, J., and McCabe, K. (1995). Trust, reciprocity, and social history. *Games and Economic Behavior*, 10(1), 122–142.

Blomqvist, K. (1997). The many faces of trust. *Scandinavian Journal of Management*, 13(3), 271–286.

Botsman, R. (2017). *Who can you trust?: How technology brought us together and why it might drive us apart.* New York, NY: Public Affairs.

Bouckaert, G. (2012). Trust and public administration. *Administration*, 60(1), 91–115.

Buchan, N. R., Croson, R. T., and Dawes, R. M. (2002). Swift neighbors and persistent strangers: A cross-cultural investigation of trust and reciprocity in social exchange. *American Journal of Sociology*, 108(1), 168–206.

Delhey, J., Newton, K., and Welzel, C. (2011). How general is trust in "most people"? Solving the radius of trust problem. *American Sociological Review*, 76(5), 786–807.

Derrida, J. (2001). *On cosmopolitanism and forgiveness.* New York, NY: Routledge.

Dunn, J. (1984). The concept of 'trust' in the politics of John Locke. In R. Rorty, J. Schneewind, and Q. Skinner (Eds.), *Philosophy in history: Essays on the historiography of philosophy* (pp. 279–301). Cambridge: Cambridge University Press.

Edelman, R. (2017). *2017 Edelman trust barometer: Global report.* Retrieved October 2, 2017, from Edelman: Global Results: www.edelman.com/global-results/

Foucault, M. (1972). *The archaeology of knowledge and the discourse on language.* New York, NY: Pantheon Books.

Friedrich, D., and Southwood, N. (2011). Promises and trust. In H. Sheinman (Ed.), *Promises and agreement: Philosophical essays* (pp. 275–292). Oxford: Oxford University Press.

Gambetta, D. (1988). Can we trust trust? In D. Gambetta (Ed.), *Trust: Making and breaking cooperative relations* (pp. 213–238). Oxford: Basil Blackwell.

Giddens, A. (1990). *The consequences of modernity.* Stanford, CA: Stanford University Press.

Graeber, D. (2014). *Debt: The first 5,000 years.* New York, NY: Melville House.

Hardin, R. (2002). Liberal distrust. *European Review*, 10(1), 73–89.

Hardin, R. (2006). *Trust.* Cambridge: Polity Press.

Hetherington, M. J. (2005). *Why trust matters: Declining political trust and the demise of American liberalism.* Princeton, NJ: Princeton University Press.

Hetherington, M. J., and Husser, J. A. (2012). How trust matters: The changing political relevance of political trust. *American Journal of Political Science*, 56(2), 312–325.

Hetherington, M. J., and Rudolph, T. J. (2015). *Why Washington won't work: Polarization, political trust, and the governing crisis.* Chicago, IL: University of Chicago Press.

Hosking, G. (2014). *Trust: A history.* Oxford: Oxford Scholarship Online.

Jay, J., Goldman, L., Hamilton, A., and Madison, J. (2008). *The Federalist papers.* Oxford: Oxford University Press.

King-Casas, B., Tomlin, D., Anen, C., Camerer, C. F., Quartz, S. R., and Montague, P. R. (2005). Getting to know you: Reputation and trust in a two-person economic exchange. *Science*, 308(5718), 78–83.

Krishnamurthy, M. (2015). (White) Tyranny and the democratic value of distrust. *The Monist*, 98(4), 391–406.

Lagerspetz, O. (1998). *Trust: The tacit demand.* Dordrecht: Springer.

Lagerspetz, O. (2015). *Trust, ethics and human reason.* London: Bloomsbury.

Lenard, P. T. (2012). *Trust, democracy and multicultural challenges.* University Park, PA: Pennsylvania State University Press.

Lewis, J. D., and Weigert, A. (1985). Trust as a social reality. *Social Forces*, 63(4), 967–985.

Locke, J. (1980). *Second treatise of government.* Indianapolis, IN: Hackett.

Luhmann, N. (1979). *Trust and power.* Chichester: Wiley.

Mill, J. S. (1991). *On liberty and other essays.* Oxford: Oxford University Press.

Misztal, B. (1996). *Trust in modern societies: The search for the bases of social order.* Cambridge: Polity Press.

Möllering, G. (2001). The nature of trust: From Georg Simmel to a theory of expectation, interpretation and suspension. *Sociology*, 35(2), 403–420.

Morrone, A., Tontoranelli, N., and Ranuzzi, G. (2009). How good is trust?: Measuring trust and its role for the progress of societies. *OECD Statistics Working Papers, 2009/03.* Paris: OECD Publishing.

Norris, P. (2017). The conceptual framework of political support. In S. Zmerli, and T. van der Meer (Eds.), *Handbook on political trust* (pp. 19–32). Cheltenham: Edward Elgar.

OECD. (2011, April 12). *Society at a glance: OECD social indicators.* Retrieved June 19, 2015, from OECD: www.oecd-ilibrary.org/social-issues-migration-health/society-at-a-glance-2011_soc_glance-2011-en

Parker, S. L., Parker, G. R., and Towner, T. L. (2015). Rethinking the meaning and measurement of political trust. In C. Eder, I. C. Mochmann, and M. Quandt (Eds.), *Political trust and disenchantment with politics* (pp. 59–82). Leiden: Brill.

Pasquale, F. (2015). *The Black Box Society: The secret algorithms that control money and information.* Cambridge, MA: Harvard University Press.

Peer, L. (1992). The practice of opinion polling as a disciplinary mechanism: A Foucauldian perspective. *International Journal of Public Opinion Research*, 4(3), 230–242.

Pew Research Center. (2015). *Beyond distrust: How Americans view their government.* Retrieved from www.pewresearch.org

Pratt, M. G. (2014). Some features of promises and their obligations. *The Southern Journal of Philosophy*, 52(3), 382–402.

Rosanvallon, P. (2008). *Counter-democracy: Politics in an age of distrust*. New York, NY: Cambridge University Press.

Sapienza, P., Toldra-Simats, A., and Zingales, L. (2013). Understanding trust. *The Economic Journal, 123*(573), 1–20.

Schmitt, C. (2007). *The concept of the political*. Chicago, IL: University of Chicago Press.

Simmel, G. (2004). *The philosophy of money*. London: Routledge.

Smith, S. S. (2010). Race and trust. *American Review of Sociology, 36*, 453–475.

Sztompka, P. (1999). *Trust: A sociological theory*. Cambridge: Cambridge University Press.

Uslaner, E. M. (2002). *The moral foundations of trust*. Cambridge: Cambridge University Press.

van der Meer, T., and Zmerli, S. (2017). The deeply rooted concern with political trust. In S. Zmerli, and T. van der Meer (Eds.), *Handbook on political trust* (pp. 1–15). Cheltenham: Edward Elgar.

Van de Walle, S., and Bouckaert, G. (2003). Public service performance and trust in government: The problem of causality. *International Journal of Public Administration, 26*(8/9), 891–913.

Van de Walle, S., Van Roosbroek, S., and Bouckaert, G. (2008). Trust in the public sector: Is there any evidence for a long-term decline? *International Review of Administrative Sciences, 74*(1), 47–64.

Warren, M. E. (2017). What kinds of trust does a democracy need? Trust from the perspective of democratic theory. In S. Zmerli, and T. van der Meer (Eds.), *Handbook on political trust* (pp. 33–52). Cheltenham: Edward Elgar.

Wilson, D. S. (2015). *Does altruism exist? Culture, genes, and the welfare of others*. New Haven, CT: Yale University Press.

Wittgenstein, L. (2009). *Philosophical investigations*. Chichester: Wiley-Blackwell.

Zuboff, S. (2015). Big other: Surveillance capitalism and the prospects of an information civilization. *Journal of Information Technology, 30*(1), 75–89.

3 Trust's political genealogy

The bonds of social cohesion and obligation that are necessary for the functioning of the state have been accounted for in various ways, using various terms, over the course of the history of philosophy. *Trust* emerges as a key concept in early-modern English political theory. John Locke in particular opens the door to the contemporary notion of 'trust in government.' This is illustrated with examples of the uses of trust in key texts of Hobbes and Locke, retracing the emergence of trust as a genuinely *political* factor in modern thought. The 'progress' of trust is followed with a reading of Edmund Burke and J.S. Mill, especially in relation to parliamentary representation. Burke's providential understanding of political trust has been neglected in contemporary literature but deserves attention. Mill elaborates the uses of trust – conceptually and grammatically – in ways that show it evolving towards contemporary meanings. These close textual readings in this chapter will be enriched in the next with historical contexts. Combining such textual and contextual analysis allows us to observe how trust, particularly *political* trust, has a genealogy, or how it has been transformed conceptually and practically at different times. We will then be able to refresh our present-day understandings of political trust, being more aware of the great variety of meanings and the historical shifts to which trust has been subject.

Thomas Hobbes: keeping our promises

At first sight, Hobbes is not a promising figure to teach us anything about trust. Was he not the one who told us that, in the absence of an absolute ruler, life would be 'nasty, brutish and short'? Does he not claim that no-one can be trusted unless the fear of punishment can make us keep our promises? On closer inspection, though, particularly of *Leviathan*, we find that Hobbes has a lot to show us about how trust works in the context of political and economic life. But, on the grounds that talking about trust only arises because of doubt and distrust, *Leviathan* also reveals to us some of the doubts that have troubled us, to the extent that trust presented itself as worthy of careful thought. To approach this, we need to understand Hobbes's theory of language and compare this with the textual habits or practices found in *Leviathan*. Then we can fully appreciate the various uses of the word *trust* within that text.

Ignorance, truth, meaning and trust are encompassed in this passage from *Leviathan*:

> Ignorance of the signification of words; which is, want of understanding, disposeth men to take on *trust*, not only the *truth* they know not; but also the *errors*, and which is more, the *nonsense* of them they trust: for neither error, nor nonsense, can without *a perfect understanding of words*, be detected.
>
> (Hobbes, 1998, p. 69, XI.18, italics added)

Regardless of the authenticity or legitimacy of a person's claims, followers or subjects trust that person in part by *believing* that what he/she says is true. In trusting that person, they add to his/her honour and reputation, and hence power, as: 'Reputation of power, is power; because it draweth with it the adherence of those that need protection' (Hobbes, 1998, p. 58, X.5). We trust people, then, on the grounds that they are speaking truthfully, either for themselves or as legitimate representatives of others. But this kind of belief is sometimes mistaken; Hobbes warns us against taking established authorities too readily on trust. His targets in particular are the scholastic philosophers, notably Aristotle, Cicero and Aquinas. But they also included those preachers of false or dangerous religious and political doctrines that stirred up civil discontent. If approached in ignorance or gullibility, a blind reliance on such authorities means that we cannot detect the difference between the truth, the error and the sheer nonsense they may tell us. By taking things on trust, people may haphazardly learn the truth, but it will be, paradoxically, 'the truth they know not.' Trusting that something is true is thus inferior to *knowing* that it is true, even when exactly the same proposition. Trust in authority may provide us with the truth, but then again, it may not. To achieve *knowledge* of the truth, we need, first of all, 'a perfect understanding of words.'

One should examine an author's definitions, we are advised, and either correct them, if they are erroneous, or make one's own from first principles. In order to arrive at the truth, it is necessary 'to remember what every name [one] uses stands for' (Hobbes, 1998, p. 23, IV.12). For the sake of 'science' as well as for the sake of a civilized commonwealth, the settling of definitions – especially of terms such as *good* and *evil* – is crucial for the 'settling' of authority in the hands of a ruler. The 'settlement' of the conventions linking words and things was both a scientific and a political aim for Hobbes. So, a *dis*trust of the authority of past thinkers is integral to the rationality of *Leviathan*, and the text purports to begin again from first principles – defining clearly its fundamental terms – and to reason systematically from that foundation. And this draws Hobbes into a theory of meaning to clarify how we name and define things.

'A perfect understanding of words'

Hobbes adopts 'a word-and-object conception of language, according to which words are names or labels that we, by convention, attach to independently existing objects' (Ball, 1985, p. 757). That is, 'the first use of names, is to serve for *marks*, or *notes* of remembrance.' Words serve as signs of thoughts and feelings, and the way in which 'speech serveth to the remembrance of the consequences of causes and effects, consisteth in the imposing of *names*, and the *connexion* of them' (Hobbes, 1998, p. 21, IV.5). This nominalist theory of language is similar to St Augustine's, which Wittgenstein glosses as:

> Every word has a meaning. This meaning is correlated with the word. It is the object for which the word stands.
>
> (Wittgenstein, 2009, p. 5e, §1)

This kind of theory of language has been superseded by Wittgenstein's 'meaning as use.' If, however, we examine Hobbes's actual writing, we find that his textual practice is somewhat closer to Wittgenstein than at first sight. '*Like* Wittgenstein, Hobbes thinks that the most important use of language is practical, not theoretical' (Gert, 2010, p. 11, italics added). Accordingly, Hobbes's use of the word *trust* (or *mistrust*, etc.) is more often in the form of verbs, rather than substantives, and it depicts what people are *doing* when they are trusting one another. The performative *uses* of language that illustrate trust in *Leviathan* are thus more useful for us than Hobbes's nominalist *theory* of language, especially in view of the ephemeral qualities of trust. Trust cannot be pointed to or marked. Hobbes does provide a definition of trust, quoted below. But, rather than rely upon such a definition of the abstract noun *trust*, the present inquiry extracts from *Leviathan* the activities one performs when one is said to trust someone. By closely observing the descriptions of these various kinds of actions, we can learn about the politics of trust.

The arguments and textual practices in *Leviathan* rely upon speech-acts (Ball, 1985; Pettit, 2008) – utterances that do things rather than describe things (Austin, 1975). So, for instance, in defining the honouring of persons, *Leviathan* uses verbs to draw examples of actions, such as 'to give great gifts,' but also speech-acts such as 'to praise,' 'to flatter,' 'to speak with consideration' and (reciprocally) 'to hearken to a man's counsel' (Hobbes, 1998, p. 60, X.21–28). Consistent with this reliance on speech-acts are the attacks (especially in Chapter XLVI) on the scholastic philosophers for nominalizing abstract metaphysical terms. From the Latin equivalent of the verb *to be* derive the terms 'entity, essence, essential, essentiality,' which Hobbes warns are 'the names of *nothing*' (Hobbes, 1998, p. 448, XLVI.17). Their reification as 'abstract essence' can only lead us into error. Extrapolating from this critique, then, the noun *trust* should defer to the infinitive *to trust* (or finite *I trust*, etc.). The noun does not name any 'thing' as such; nor should it be elevated to a metaphysical or ontological status. *Trust* cannot be said to have an existence; nor is it an object 'marked' with a name. Accordingly, as the evidence presented below will show, *Leviathan* assumes that trust is entailed in what we do.

Trust in Leviathan

Trust is not one of the concepts for which Hobbes is most widely remembered. A reference text on Hobbes, for instance, lacks an entry on *trust* – although it does feature the closely related *belief* (Lloyd, 2013). Nonetheless, the problem of the state of nature, as depicted in *Leviathan*, is a problem of trust: one cannot trust one's fellow human beings to respect one's property, or to uphold any promise to lay down their arms, unless one possesses the power to destroy them. It could jeopardize one's self-preservation, and hence be 'contrary to the ground of all laws of nature,' to keep promises in a situation 'where no man else should do so' (Hobbes, 1998, p. 105, XV.36). In a state of nature, distrust is rational.

The solution is in a 'covenant of every man with every man,' such that each gives up the right of self-government to a sovereign, for common defence and peace. Placing authority in the sovereign makes it possible, in particular cases, to trust one another. But it requires coercion and 'the terror of some punishment' to ensure that 'covenants of mutual trust' are valid (Hobbes, 1998, p. 95, XV.3). The threat of pain ensures that people can be trusted.

Trust is used, but not formally defined, in *Leviathan*. There is a set definition of *trust*, however, in an earlier work, *The Elements of Law Natural and Politic* of 1640.

> TRUST is a passion proceeding from belief of him from whom we expect or hope for good, so free from doubt that upon the same we pursue no other way. And distrust, or diffidence, is doubt that maketh him endeavour to provide himself by other means. And that this is the meaning of the words trust and distrust, is manifest from this, that a man never provideth himself by a second way, but when he mistrusteth that the first will not hold.
>
> (Hobbes, 1994, p. 53)

This suggests that to trust is a default or first option for deriving the good. An alternative is only sought when there is doubt and trust fails. In *Leviathan*, however, neither the above definition from *Elements*, nor anything similar, appears at all. And trust is not listed among the 'passions' in *Leviathan*'s Chapter VI. Trust is situated as a *synonym* of belief (in Chapter VII), rather than being defined as a *result* of belief in a person. Furthermore, in the *Elements*, trust is described as 'the *first* way' for deriving some good from a person; whereas, in *Leviathan*, to *di*strust others is the default option, unless or until there exists the sovereign threat of punishment. Assuming it was deliberate, one can guess why Hobbes discarded the definition found in *Elements* when composing *Leviathan*. Men in a state of nature cannot expect to derive any good by trusting one another, and so *di*strust is 'the first way.'

So, *trust* is often used, but not formally defined, in *Leviathan*. Below, I classify distinct meanings or senses of *trust* in *Leviathan*. This uncovers not what *trust* means in the abstract, but rather the various things that people may be *doing* when they trust.

Hobbes's six senses of trust

The first kind of usage depicts trusting in books and authorities.

> But yet they that have no *science*, are in better, and nobler condition, with their natural prudence; than men, that by mis-reasoning, or by trusting them that reason wrong, fall upon false and absurd general rules.
>   . . . But they that trusting only to the authority of books, follow the blind blindly, are like him that, trusting to the false rules of a master of fence, ventures presumptuously upon an adversary, that either kills or disgraces him.
>
> (Hobbes, 1998, p. 32, V.19)

'Blindly' trusting in false authorities or rules leads to error. So it is best to begin from first principles and clear definitions, and to use reason to arrive at sound conclusions. The target here is primarily the Aristotelian scholasticism that had produced unsound metaphysical ideas. To trust established authors or books, then, may be to adopt established errors. A similar usage juxtaposes *trust* with *belief* and *faith*:

> So that in belief are two opinions; one of the saying of the man; the other of his virtue. To *have faith in*, or *trust to*, or *believe a man*, signify the same thing; namely, an opinion of the veracity of the man: but to *believe what is said*, signifieth only an opinion of the truth of the saying.
>
> (Hobbes, 1998, pp. 43–44, VII.5)

When we hold an opinion that a person is an authority and hence speaks the truth, then we are trusting that person. But there is a difference between believing the person and believing only what is said. *Trust* applies to persons. Belief in a doctrine is distinguished from belief or trust in a person.

> And they that believe that which a prophet relates unto them in the name of God, take the word of the prophet, do honour to him, and in him trust, and believe, touching the truth of what he relateth, whether he be a true, or a false prophet.
>
> (Hobbes, 1998, p. 44, VII.7)

And so, once again, we are warned that trust can lead us into erroneous beliefs if we trust the wrong person as an authority.

The second usage of *trust* concerns the honouring and dishonouring of others. Our judgement of the worth of a person is said to be 'so much as would be given for the use of his power' (Hobbes, 1998, p. 59, X.16). The various ways in which we show such estimations of others are called 'honouring and dishonouring,' a list of which includes:

> To believe, to trust, to rely on another, is to honour him; sign of opinion of his virtue and power. To distrust, or not believe, is to dishonour.
>
> (Hobbes, 1998, p. 60, X.27)

To honour someone by trusting him/her signifies our *opinion* of the person's 'virtue and power.' We may be misled by our belief in the person, or we may be giving an outward pretense of believing and trusting. Truth is not the main issue here. After all, it is also said that 'to flatter is to honour,' and to disagree by pointing out a person's errors is to dishonour. When it comes to honouring the powerful, truth may not be called for. But we see so far that trust may entail our belief in a person's authority and dignity, or accepting and perpetuating a person's rank or status. In the first cited usage, taking matters 'on trust' from authorities is seen as epistemologically faulty. This second sense of trust, however, has less to do with knowledge than with social recognition.

A third usage of *trust* performs a central role in contract, or 'the mutual transferring of right.' Transferring one's right to a thing to another person creates an obligation not to hinder the receiver from enjoyment and use of it. Often, though, the exchange is not completed immediately but only 'some time after' the contract has been agreed. A condition of 'being trusted' arises, and:

> he that is to perform in time to come, being trusted, his performance is called *keeping of promise*, or faith; and the failing of performance (if it be voluntary) *violation of faith*.
>
> (Hobbes, 1998, p. 89, XIV.11)

One person trusts another, or two people trust one another, to perform something later (or, A trusts B to do X in future, in return for Y). This temporal view of trust, placing reliance upon the future actions of others, is the closest to contemporary definitions of trust (as reviewed in Chapter 2), and it brings us to the crux of the argument for which *Leviathan* is most widely remembered. In a state of nature, while it is *possible* to enter into a contract and to trust someone, there can be 'no assurance [that] the other will perform,' and the covenant may easily be broken. But, 'a common power set over them both, with right and force sufficient to compel performance' will prevent the parties from pre-emptively making their covenant 'void' for fear of non-performance, and the agreement remains in force, regardless (Hobbes, 1998, p. 91, XIV.18). That 'common power' makes it more likely that people will trust one another at the outset, and it increases the durability of promises and the likelihood of performance.

A fourth usage of *trust* involves an arbitrator who is trusted with 'the act of defining what is just':

> Wherein, (being trusted by them that make him arbitrator,) if he perform his trust, he is said to distribute to every man his own: and this is indeed just distribution, and may be called (though improperly) distributive justice; but more properly equity.
>
> (Hobbes, 1998, p. 100, XV.15)

Whereas a contract involves two parties who trust one another, the role of the trusted arbitrator between the parties introduces a triangular set of relations. Hence, in appointing a third person to distribute equitably to the parties to an agreement that which they own, or are owed, the parties trust that person.

Fifth, an *elected* sovereign is described as having been 'trusted' by the subjects. If there is no-one who 'can give the sovereignty, after the decease of him that was first elected,' then the monarch must nominate a successor, 'to keep those that had trusted him with the government, from relapsing into the miserable condition of war' (Hobbes, 1998, p. 128, XIX.11). More generally, having covenanted among themselves to authorize the sovereign to act on their behalf, the people have trusted the sovereign with power – and 'the end, for which he was trusted [. . . is] the procuration of *the safety of the people*' (Hobbes, 1998, p. 222, XXX.1). A breach of this duty by the sovereign is 'a breach of trust, and of the law of nature' (Hobbes, 1998, p. 165, XXIV.7) as it threatens the lives of the people who had trusted the sovereign with their own preservation. There is no direct covenant of *mutual* trust between the sovereign and the people at large. The act of sovereignty by institution is one of authorization, not trust, and the sovereign is not in a 'compact' with subjects. But the sovereign may select individuals whom he 'trusteth in the administration of the commonwealth' (Hobbes, 1998, p. 224, XXX.6). They are trusted with addressing and instructing the public and examining 'the doctrines of all books before they be published' (Hobbes, 1998, p. 118, XVIII.9).

So, if a multitude of men have covenanted among themselves to authorize the sovereign, then they have trusted (in the past tense) the sovereign to provide safety, and the sovereign in turn trusts (present tense) at least some of the subjects to perform delegated duties. This is as close as *Leviathan* gets to the predominant political usage of *trust* in Locke's *Second Treatise*.

Finally, a sixth usage of *trust* arises in the context of sovereignty by acquisition. Vanquished persons are 'trusted' with their own 'corporal liberty' after entering into a covenant out of fear for their lives. In a condition of war, if a prisoner 'receiveth the benefit of life' and promises the conqueror a ransom or service in return, it is a lawful covenant. Even though it was agreed to in fear, the prisoner had the choice of either performance or death. 'Therefore prisoners of war, if trusted with the payment of their ransom, are obliged to pay it' (Hobbes, 1998, pp. 92–93, XIV.27). Furthermore, the prisoner who agrees to become a servant (as distinct from a slave in captivity), in return for his life and 'corporal liberty,' 'upon promise not to run away, nor to do violence to his master, is trusted by him' (Hobbes, 1998, p. 135, XX.10).[1] The law of nature that compels us to preserve our lives means that the prisoner-of-war, if at liberty to choose, can only choose fealty. Through fear of death or violence, those defeated in battle will be 'obliged to obedience' (Hobbes, 1998, p. 132, XX.2).[2] Hobbes provides another example:

> And even in commonwealths, if I be forced to redeem myself from a thief by promising him money, I am bound to pay it, till the civil law discharge me.
> (Hobbes, 1998, p. 93, XIV.27)

All promises arise from fear of the consequences of not promising; promises are kept only for fear of the consequences of failing to perform them. And, to any-one who holds the decision of 'life or death' over an individual, that subject, in choosing to live, makes a lawful promise to obey. The choices offered by the vic-tor to the vanquished ('obey me or die') and by the highwayman to the traveler ('your money or your life') create lawfully binding promises – until such time as a greater power should intervene. These are best understood today as 'forced choices,' however. While the choice is 'real,' the outcome is decided in advance. In Chapter 5, I argue that much of what passes for 'trust' today is a forced choice.

So, we find at least six distinct uses of *trust* in *Leviathan* based on what one is said to do when one trusts. The basic affective 'tone' that assures the cohesion of a Hobbesian commonwealth is fear; trust is ineffectual without power-relations that inspire fear. We will consider Hobbesian trust in its historical context, and its pertinence to contemporary thought, in the next chapter.

John Locke on trust-at-a-distance

There are two differences between Hobbes and Locke in their uses of *trust* that are grammatical, but, I argue, far from trivial. The first is Hobbes's preference for verbs, compared with Locke's for the substantive, which underpins two quite different approaches to trust *per se*. Locke's assumption about trust is essentialist rather than performative. The second is in Locke's assumption that an institution or assembly can be the object of the verb 'to trust.' This produces a properly *politi-cal* trust (rare in Hobbes) by which people may trust (or mistrust) *institutions* of government (or 'the legislative' as a body), not only other individuals. Locke does not define trust, but he does define political power in a way that relies upon trust as a factor. Having rejected patriarchal divine right to rule, he seeks to establish that, because it is 'almost natural' that the father is the head of the family, the monarch too is normally male, but by common consent rather than birth-right. In pulling off this sleight of hand, he reveals a reliance upon trust as a political factor integral to the social contract.

Like Hobbes, Locke warned us against taking received scientific or philosophi-cal principles 'on trust.' Locke opposed the notion of 'innate principles,' as the claim to 'innateness' enforces doctrines as unquestionable on the grounds that they must be true for all rational beings. Locke insists instead that principles or ideas can only have been learned by the use of our mental faculties, even those that are 'natural law' and hence universal. It is of much greater value to us if we have examined ideas and principles, and their proofs or justifications, for ourselves – rather than taking them 'upon trust.'[3]

Trust in this epistemic sense makes one a hostage to power if one accepts ideas as unquestionable due merely to the authority of those who espouse them. This overlapping of trust and power is undesirable, as it subjects us to 'dictators of principles' (Locke, 1975, p. 102). Instead, we should freely use our reason to discover truths from first principles, even if this means we are simply rediscovering established knowledge or universal laws. Despite his disapproval of taking ideas 'upon trust,' however, Locke sees also a positive necessity of trust for the constitution of legitimate and just powers – even while he can also perceive the risk that political trust may be abused. The system of government is founded not upon divine will or religious faith or unquestioning loyalty, but instead upon a rational but risky choice that 'trades off' some of our liberty in favour of our need for security. If such a trust is then abused, the people may resume or claim back their original and natural freedom, and so institute a new form of government. Hence, Locke develops a political trust that goes beyond Hobbes whose notions of trust were tied to interpersonal contexts.

Towards a properly political trust

In Chapter VI of the *Second Treatise of Government*, concerning the powers of parents over their children, Locke writes that children are bound by obligations equally to both parents; so he asks if 'paternal power' should not properly be qualified as 'parental,' as the mother has 'an equal title' (Locke, 1980, p. 30, §52). Having made this equitable point, however, Locke goes on, with scant explanation, to attribute the powers and duties to educate children and to bestow estates upon them solely to the father. If there be any difference of will or opinion between husband and wife, then the former gets the final say, as one of them has to rule, and this 'naturally falls to the man's share, as the abler and the stronger' (Locke, 1980, p. 44, §82). The extent to which husbands are 'abler and stronger' than their wives, and concerning which kinds of abilities or strengths, is open for critical debate. Locke's gendered assumptions do not withstand scrutiny today. But his 'default' to paternal power needs to remain in sight, as it forms a part of the subsequent explanation for the earliest formation of government, in which people 'generally put the rule into one man's hands' (Locke, 1980, p. 60, §112).

In his use of the term 'government' another sleight of hand occurs. As children are incapable of caring for and educating themselves, parents, in particular the father, have a duty to 'govern' them.

> The subjection of a minor places in the father a temporary government, which terminates with the minority of the child.
>
> (Locke, 1980, p. 37, §67)

Paternal power persists even when the parents are subject to a sovereign prince or other such authority, to the same extent as if the family were in the state of nature. Locke insists that paternal and political powers are 'perfectly distinct and separate' (Locke, 1980, p. 39, §71), and that no powers of civil government can override the power of parents over their children. But he then elides connotations of the word 'government' (in use since the fourteenth century) that include the education, discipline and care of a young person, *and* the activities of administering a realm as sovereign authority.

His account of the origins of civil government shifts seamlessly from the father's government of his children in their minority to a patriarch's government of a small community of adult relations.[4] When the population is sparse and there is plenty of unoccupied land, an extended family might be self-sufficient and have little contact with other groups. The government of such a family would thus belong to 'the father,' as people would be used to the rule of this one man, and an early monarchical system would 'naturally' evolve, being customary, self-evident and simple. Trust follows closely in the wake of this emergence of the father as 'the law-maker, and governor' over a community of adult offspring.

> He was fittest to be trusted; paternal affection secured their property and interest under his care; and the custom of obeying him, in their childhood, made it easier to submit to him, rather than to any other.
>
> (Locke, 1980, p. 56, §105)

His rule 'was exercised with care and skill, with affection and love to those under it' (Locke, 1980, p. 57, §107). Such trust goes hand in hand with submission and obedience. The unconditional love and implicit trust of the father–child bond lie at the origin of Locke's account of civil government.

Locke then imagines the growth of communities into a number of such neighbouring families or groups that need to protect themselves from foreign aggression. At this still early stage in the development of societies, Locke argues, people had not yet experienced, and so did not yet fear, tyranny. As their way of life was relatively simple, there were few disputes, and they 'stood more in need of defence against foreign invasions and injuries, than of multiplicity of laws' (Locke, 1980, p. 57, §107). Here, Locke again appeals to trust as a factor that binds a community, but this time between equals or friends, rather than between a patriarchal ruler and those who obey his law-making.

> Since then those, who like one another so well as to join into society, cannot but be supposed to have some acquaintance and friendship together, and some *trust one in another*; they could not but have greater apprehensions of others, than of one another: and therefore their first care and thought cannot but be supposed to be, how to secure themselves against foreign force.
>
> (Locke, 1980, p. 57, §107, italics added)

So, the scope of trust expands from familial attachment to 'acquaintance and friendship' between adults of relatively equal status. And the friend–enemy distinction, or the threat of 'foreign force,' necessitates the emergence of a ruler, as these 'friends' choose one among them to lead them against their enemies.

Before moving on to the next stage of evolution of government, as depicted by Locke, there are three shifts that have occurred thus far in his argument: the oblation of matriarchal power; the elision of meaning and supposed historical continuity between the parental governing of children and the patriarchal governing of a community of adults; the recognition of two forms of trust, first in the unconditional affectional bond between father and child, and then between friends and acquaintances. His account is still considering a hypothetical stage in social evolution where members of the community all know one another, and hence they can trust one another (more or less) through face-to-face acquaintance. It is the intrusion of the foreign – the untrustworthy enemy – that makes it necessary to choose a leader: 'the wisest and bravest man to conduct them in their wars, and lead them out against their enemies, and in this chiefly be their ruler' (Locke, 1980, p. 58, §107).

Now that Locke has seen to the establishment of the earliest rulers, there emerges a third meaning of trust, which is the most frequent and significant in the *Treatise*. Regardless of whether it was one extended family or several neighbouring families that 'put the rule into one man's hand, without any other express limitation or restraint':

> no body was *intrusted* with it but for the public good and safety, and to those ends, in the infancies of common-wealths, those who had it commonly used it. And unless they had done so, young societies could not have subsisted; without such nursing fathers tender and careful of the public weal, all governments would have sunk under the weakness and infirmities of their infancy, and the prince and the people had soon perished together.
>
> (Locke, 1980, pp. 59–60, §110, italics added)

This third usage of trust is distinguishable from the unconditional trust of a child for his/her parent, and from trust between friends. In this third sense, one person has been entrusted by all members of a community with the power to rule, for the defence and security of the community itself, and hence this is a *political* trust. This particular form of trust, therefore, is neither unconditional nor between friends, and it is easily broken. Indeed, Locke acknowledges that it has been broken, again and again, as societies have grown in size. As the powers and privileges of rulers grow, their interests diverge from those of the people. And hence, the power that the people had once 'intrusted in another's hands only for their own good, they found was made use of to hurt them' (Locke, 1980, p. 60, §111). The people's trust was ultimately misplaced and usurped, therefore, and they needed to reconsider the origins of and reasons for the right to govern.

Trust in government

It was in order to avoid the 'inconveniences' and 'uncertainty' of the state of nature, that men united to form a society that protects their properties by binding them all to one set of rules.

> To this end it is that men give up all their natural power to the society which they enter into, and the community put the legislative power into such hands as they think fit, *with this trust*, that they shall be governed by declared laws, or else their peace, quiet, and property will still be at the same *uncertainty*, as it was in the state of nature.
>
> (Locke, 1980, p. 72, §136, italics added)

This trust that is put in the hands of law-makers is strictly conditional with defined limitations on the extent and uses of their powers. In brief, these limitations are: one written law for all, designed for the good of the people; no taxation and no transferal of law-making powers without the consent of the people (Locke, 1980, p. 75, §142). Even the unwritten conventions of the English constitution were dependent upon such a trust, he argues. The traditional prerogative of the English monarch to summon, prorogue and dissolve the legislature is not an arbitrary power that may be exercised on a whim, 'but is *a fiduciary trust placed in him*, for the safety of the people' (Locke, 1980, p. 81, §156, italics added).

A political trust, therefore, has been put into the hands of both the head of state and the legislative assembly. This trusting of others to govern is a way of forestalling or controlling the uncertainty that arises from the aggression of humans and the unpredictability of events, which would be even greater were there no control over society at all. It is a trust that is conditional upon the achievement of particular aims (less uncertainty and more security); if breached or violated, it can be rescinded.

So, we need now to outline how Locke depicts, first, a breach of this trust, and second, what the consequences of breaching it could be. Any attempt by legislators to act against 'the liberties and properties of the subject' or to reduce people to 'a slavish condition' would be 'contrary to the trust reposed in them' (Locke, 1980, p. 78, §149). Moreover, if the executive power, the monarch, used force 'to hinder the meeting and acting of the legislative,' that would be 'contrary to the trust put in him' and it would initiate 'a state of war with the people' (Locke, 1980, p. 80, §155). The sovereign is also breaching the trust of the people if he seeks to corrupt or influence either the electors or the representatives they elected to the legislature in order to bring about predetermined results (Locke, 1980, p. 112, §222). This brings us then to the consequences. Once the founding trust is broken beyond repair, it may be forfeited altogether, and then the powers that were granted by the people return to the people. The dissolution of government and the founding of a new parliament may then be necessary.

Thinking then about the place of trust in Locke's conception of power itself, it is foundational historically, and essential for justice. It is trust that provides and defines conditions for the legitimate and consensual uses of those powers that originally belonged to the people at large, and that are now in the hands of the few.

> Political power is that power, which every man having in the state of nature, has given up into the hands of the society, and therein to the governors, whom the society hath set over itself, with *this express or tacit trust*, that it shall be employed for their good, and the preservation of their property.
>
> (Locke, 1980, p. 89, §171, italics added)

So, we can now look at the forms and uses of trust intended by Locke. The first two are the child's unconditional trust in the parent, and the trust that exists between or among friends. But these are only sparingly mentioned in the *Treatise*, and largely to lead us on to the third, most important form, which is a properly *political* trust. This latter trust forms and sustains the legitimate and just constitution itself. It may be an unspoken tacit trust, or it may be deliberately expressed somehow, but it is not unconditional. The conditions under which people trust those who rule are that the latter's powers shall be exercised only for the public good, for common security and liberty and the preservation of property rights. This entrusted power deals with or forestalls the uncertainties that would persist in the state of nature, and that may arise, from time to time, due to the unpredictability of human affairs and the constant threat of foreign intrusion. Political trust for Locke therefore has three dimensions: a condition of uncertainty or unpredictability in human affairs; a legitimacy based on how well the common good is served in mitigating those conditions; a quality of being either explicit or implicit. Serious breaches of this trust may lead to political powers reverting back to the people, and hence to the reorganization of the constitution under a newly minted trust.

Edmund Burke: trust as a divine calling

So far, we have seen examples of a transactional model of trust (A trusts B to do X, where X is in A's interests) in Hobbes's writing. People are trusted to perform duties, to abide by agreements and to deliver on their promises. But this simple transactional model does not exhaust Hobbes's understanding of trust, as he realizes, for example, that it is not always in one's interests to trust or believe in someone's authority – even though people often do. Locke, on the other hand, recognizes a 'natural' foundation of trust that emerges inherently in the affectional bonds of families and friendships. His political trust is transactional and not unconditional, and it works 'at a distance,' as larger nations have little direct acquaintance, let alone friendship, between rulers and the ruled.

In Burke's writing, however, we find a further dimension in the political meaning of trust, one that is not based on any 'promise' of a commercial or political kind. He regarded the bonds of social obligation and trust as instead 'a human partnership spread out over generations' (Bromwich, 2014, p. 5). His most significant uses of the word 'trust' invoke a public duty or responsibility that is incumbent on a person or assembly, for which those who are thus 'entrusted' are accountable to a higher authority, ultimately to God. So, this may encompass transactions between particular parties, but it signifies much more. It is a general and higher moral obligation to the whole of government and/or the nation, inherently incumbent upon the holder of any political power, as prescribed in *Reflections on the Revolution in France.*

> All persons possessing any portion of power ought to be strongly and awefully impressed with an idea that they act in trust; and that they are to account for their conduct in that trust to the one great master, author, and founder of society.
>
> (Burke, 1968, p. 190)

Burke gives an example of such political trust in his 'Speech on Fox's India Bill' of 1783. The East India Company had been commissioned as a commercial entity with a monopoly on British trade in the region, but it had effectively become a political and military power. Fox's bill aimed to separate the administrative and commercial functions and place them under commissions. The bill's opponents argued that this was a breach of the Company's 'chartered rights.' But Burke asserts that 'all political power' over others is 'wholly artificial,' as it reduces or impairs 'the natural equality of mankind at large,' and so should be used 'for their benefit.'

> [Political powers and commercial privileges] are all in the strictest sense a *trust*; and it is of the very essence of every trust to be rendered *accountable*; and even totally to *cease*, when it substantially varies from the purposes for which alone it could have a lawful existence.
>
> (Burke, 1981b, p. 385)

The Company's abuse of its rights betrayed 'the high trust' that had been vested in it. This trust was derived from parliament, and it was up to parliament to apply a legislative remedy. Hence, 'a trust' is a profound public duty to act for the greater good, for which one is accountable to a higher authority.

Burke is normally cited in contemporary political theory as the source of the idea of representation as a form of trust (Pitkin, 1967; Mansbridge, 2003; Urbinati and Warren, 2008). In simple terms, the elected representative (or even the assembly or executive) is regarded as the voters' 'trustee' who makes decisions on behalf of constituents, in the best interests of all, rather than as the voters' 'delegate' acting at their behest and in fulfilment of their wishes. But a transactional 'elector–elected' relation of trust does not fully capture Burke's intention. As Pitkin rightly observed, it is mistaken to argue that Burke meant the trustee is 'accountable to the people, the beneficiaries of the trust' (Pitkin, 1967, p. 129).

The representative is the trustee of the nation, and not only of the particular constituency that voted for him.

> With us the representative, separated from the other parts, can have no action and no existence. The government is the point of reference of the several members and districts of our representation. This is the center of our unity. This government of reference is a trustee for the *whole*, and not for the parts.
>
> (Burke, 1968, p. 303)

Political trust, for Burke, is not reducible to transactions or deals between voters and their particular representative. He argued that *unelected* kings, lords and judges are 'representatives of the people' and 'trustees for the people,' as are the elected members of the House of Commons (Burke, 1981a, p. 292). His view of government as 'trusteeship' means 'an elite caring for others' (Pitkin, 1967, p. 172).

> [Burke] does not essentially challenge the principle of oligarchy, for the representative system he defends is not government by the people but government for the people by the qualified few. Yet it earns its authority only by acting for the whole people.
>
> (Bromwich, 2014, p. 159)

Those who have 'no connexion with the interest of the people [. . . nor] with the sentiments and opinions of the people' are not fit to be 'put forward into the great trusts of the State' (Burke, 1981a, pp. 279–280).

Nonetheless, in denouncing the refusal of the House of Commons to accept the election of John Wilkes to the seat of Middlesex (and its seating the runner-up in his stead), Burke asserted that the effect of the right of election 'is to give to the people, that man, and *that man only*, whom by their voices, actually, not constructively given, they declare that they know, esteem, love, and trust'; further, that only a form of despotism could hold that a 'power of discretionary disqualification [of Wilkes] is vested in hands that they may trust.'

> The people are satisfied to trust themselves with the exercise of their own privileges, and do not desire this kind of intervention of the House of Commons to free them of the burthen. They ought not to trust the House of Commons with a power over their franchises.
>
> (Burke, 1981a, pp. 301–302)

Once rightfully elected, however, the member should use his judgement to act for the good government of the nation as a whole – and *not* as the individual trustee of a particular constituency or interest-group with its partial wishes. The interests of communities can be judged objectively (on their behalf) by representatives through parliamentary deliberations (Pitkin, 1967). The Burkean representative is not 'an Agent and Advocate, against other Agents and Advocates,' all elected to the same parliament by diverse communities with competing interests. 'Parliament is a *deliberative* Assembly of *one* Nation, with *one* Interest, that of the whole.'

The member of parliament should not sacrifice his or her better judgement to the partial opinions and preferences of constituents. In his oft-cited 'Speech to the Electors of Bristol' of 1774, Burke uses the word 'trust' only once, to assert that the representative's 'unbiassed opinion, his mature judgement, his enlightened conscience . . . are a trust from Providence, for the abuse of which he is deeply answerable' (Burke, 1996, p. 69) – hence answerable to God more than to fellow human beings. The 'forms' of government and those who administer it all derive from 'the people,' but government is 'an institution of Divine authority' (Burke, 1981a, p. 292). Among his uses of *trust* overall, the abstract noun stands out (compared with Hobbes's preference for verbs), signifying a divine calling and a profound public duty to the well-being of all, incumbent upon those who exercise any power over others.

The taxation of the American colonies (without their 'actual representation' in the British parliament) was addressed in his 'Speech on Conciliation with America' in 1775. In favour of the liberties and privileges of the American colonists, Burke began by saying:

> I found myself a partaker in a very high trust; and having no sort of reason to rely on the strength of my natural abilities for the proper execution of that trust, I was obliged to take more than common pains, to instruct myself in everything which relates to our Colonies.
>
> (Burke, 1996, p. 106)

A conscientious elected representative is entrusted with the faculty of reason and the capacity to form judgements independently. The 'high trust' incumbent upon him as a member of the House of Commons, governing a vast empire, is incumbent upon all its members, and, at the end of the speech, he exhorts:

> We ought to elevate our minds to the greatness of that trust to which the order of Providence has called us.
>
> (Burke, 1996, p. 166)

This trust imposes the highest accountability upon the representative and the assembly. They properly execute their 'high trust' if and only if they act in the objective interests of the people whom they govern, no matter how distant they may be. The parliament, through the law, may impose subordinate or 'derivative' trusts (as duties and responsibilities) on other public or commercial bodies. And electors should vote for a person they trust. But the basis of political trust is not to be found solely or primarily in the relationship between electors and their elected representatives; it is originally a divine calling and duty.

John Stuart Mill: political trust comes of age

In Mill's *Considerations on Representative Government*, we find a range of uses of trust in political contexts. Like Burke, he frequently uses 'trust' in its abstract-noun form, meaning public duties and responsibilities, often in the context of defined offices, but without reference to God. So, for example, Mill notes that Roman Senators 'were not permitted even to leave Italy except in the discharge of some public trust' (Mill, 1991, p. 288). In Mill's own time, the principles of 'public trusts' apply to career administrators and inspectors at the local level (Mill, 1991, p. 419), as well as public servants whose duties are above the merely routine and 'to whom functions of particular trust, and requiring special capacity, are confided' (Mill, 1991, p. 409). Elsewhere, he refers to 'situations of trust' to which people are appointed by governors (Mill, 1991, pp. 238, 463).

Parliamentarians acquire an especially onerous 'trust' once elected, and Mill was concerned that they should be adequately mentally equipped. A parliamentary assembly that lacks members 'of mental competency sufficient for its own proper work, that of superintendence and check,' could inappropriately withdraw their support from those members of the executive 'who endeavour to fulfil their trust conscientiously' while overlooking 'abuses of trust' committed by others (Mill, 1991, p. 292).

Mill expands particularly on the trust entailed in representative democracy for voter and representative. The elected representative has a trust, in the sense of a duty or responsibility, and the electors 'are the judges of the manner in which he fulfils his trust' (Mill, 1991, p. 376). Mill devotes close attention to the franchise itself as a trust, arguing against the notion that it is instead a right. The franchise confers a political power on the voter, and Mill argues that no one can have a *right* to power over others, except in circumstances defined in law. Any power over others – be it the power of those elected to pass laws, or the power of the voters to decide whom shall represent them – 'is morally, in the fullest force of the term, a trust' (Mill, 1991, p. 353). So, the voters wield a political power over the candidates for election, as a trust, a public duty or responsibility.

When looking at how Mill uses the verb *to trust*, we find considerable variety. So, for instance, a people who are as yet 'unfit for liberty' may unwisely 'trust [a ruler] with powers which enable him to subvert their institutions' (Mill, 1991, p. 209). Or, if people share the opinions of Plato, they may agree 'that the proper person to be entrusted with power is the person most unwilling to accept it' (Mill, 1991, p. 348). This concerns political power in general.

The extent to which voters trust the particular representatives whom they elect raises again the question of whether the representative is a trustee or a delegate of the people. Mill endorses an electoral system in which the voter chooses a candidate 'whom he most willingly trusts to think for him' (Mill, 1991, p. 311). Constituents should seek talented individuals 'whom they can trust to carry on public affairs according to their unfettered judgment; to whom it would be an affront to require that they should give up that judgment at the behest of their inferiors in knowledge' (Mill, 1991, p. 380). They should search for 'a representative of such calibre as to be entrusted with full power of obeying the dictates of his own judgment' (Mill, 1991, p. 382). A conscientious representative need not be bound by prior pledges, nor by promises to consult constituents on every new matter that arises between elections. This is akin to Burke's claim that the representative 'owes you, not his industry only, but his judgement.' But there is the significant difference that, for Burke, the 'trust' entailed in the representative's faculty of reason comes 'from Providence,' whereas for Mill, the *relationship* of political trust is eminently human, between the electors and their representative, and it relies upon the latter's intelligence and conscience. Mill's aim was that the less-educated majority should choose representatives from among their superiors, the educated minority, and then 'defer to their opinions,' thus saving the country from 'class legislation' and from 'political ignorance' (Mill, 1991, p. 383).

Mill also uses the verb *to trust* with an institution as either subject or object. For example, he discusses the extent of powers 'entrusted to the executive' by the sovereign assembly, and he argues that 'there is no fear that the assembly will not be willing to trust its own ministers with any amount of power really desirable,' provided that the assembly has the constitutional powers 'to turn them out of office' (Mill, 1991, p. 285). In another direction, he considers 'how far the local authorities ought to be trusted with discretionary power, free from any superintendence or control of the State' (Mill, 1991, p. 422). Furthermore, he applies the adjective *trustworthy* not to persons and their statements, but to a proposed 'machinery' or 'system of general examination' for determining whether people have sufficient knowledge to act as electors (Mill, 1991, pp. 331, 336). Hence, a governmental body or system may trust or be trusted, and not only a person or persons. The verb *to trust* floats free of any personal subject and object to represent the actions and responsibilities of *impersonal* organized systems. In this, Mill goes further than Locke, as it is not always clear who or what is trusting, especially due to his frequent use of the passive voice. He often uses a phrase such as 'entrusted with powers' without naming by whom. On one occasion he writes generally of 'trust in constitutions' (Mill, 1991, p. 326).

So, Locke opens the door to the political notion of trust in government, and Burke thinks of trust as a public duty, while Mill also imagines an impersonal trust, a trust in and between institutions, or an abstract moral duty appurtenant to public office. For Mill, moreover, trust is secular and has effective force without appeal to natural or divine law. Instead, there is only accountability to oneself and others, including a wider public. Mill's political trust can also apply to institutions, as in some contemporary meanings.

This is not to say that Mill entirely ignores questions of trust between private individuals.[5] Here we turn to his depictions of everyday commerce in *Principles of Political Economy*. As a general observation, he remarks that 'the economical well-being of a people, and of mankind, depends in an especial manner upon their being able to trust each other's engagements' (Mill, 1994, p. 288), and many contemporary authors would fully concur. In spite of the small minority of 'rogues and swindlers,' he adds, 'people will go on trusting each other's promises.' A sole trader or person starting a business is often unwilling to deny someone credit, and will take the risk, but it is pointless to insist 'that he ought to make proper inquiries, and ascertain the character of those to whom he supplies goods on trust,' as fraudsters can often provide good references (Mill, 1994, p. 293). In addition to these interpersonal forms of trust, Mill was also aware of the wider systemic role of trust in an economy. So, for example, when a number of firms found that they could not renew their credit and stopped payments, 'their failure involved more or less deeply many other firms which had trusted them; and, as usual in such cases, the general distrust, commonly called a panic, began to set in' (Mill, 1965).

What we gain from reading Mill is a fuller comprehension of the modern uses of trust, including its economic and political contexts. He sees representation as a form of trust, but also upholds an abstract trust as a duty to the public of those in elected or appointed positions. Mill's uses of trust are both interpersonal and institutional in scope; they encompass particular transactions, such as voting or lending, as well as the broader social obligations of political power.

Conclusion

Although the examination of the uses of trust in key works of four prominent English philosophers may not include all possible meanings, we can at least track, from Hobbes to Locke, how trust shifted beyond its interpersonal significance to the realm of the political. Later, for Burke, trust signifies a profound politico-religious duty to the common good with accountability to God. And then, in J.S. Mill, we can see meanings that agree with many contemporary social-scientific understandings. We can virtually see, through these authors, the emergence of Nietzsche's promissory animal (see Chapter 6). The fully fledged modern subject of trust, especially *political* trust, is a product of historical transformations, as observable 'in writing.'

From these four great thinkers, it is clear, moreover, that the model of 'A trusts B to do X' is too simplistic and one-dimensional to comprehend trust's actual political uses. To begin with, trust is a relational quality that depends upon *reciprocated* actions. Moreover, it involves many different kinds of actions and obligations. And the foregoing has provided us with many instances of the varied *politics* of trust. Here are a few practical illustrations:

- A gives goods to B; B returns later with due payment; A's verbally stated price has not changed in the meantime.
- Two parties have a disagreement about land-tenure, and they ask a third person to decide for them how to settle the matter fairly; an agreement is soon concluded.
- The conqueror grants a vanquished soldier his liberty, and the soldier pledges loyalty and obedience to the new ruler.
- A petitioner honours the superior status of the local chief and gives him a gift.
- The people choose one among them to act on their behalf and in their interests; that individual refrains from misappropriating their common funds.
- A group of friends or neighbours share interests in common, and they act in unison when the need arises.
- One person states that he/she knows what is right and good for the community, and others unquestioningly follow that person's advice.
- A person refrains from exploiting an opportunity to act selfishly, and others praise that person for his/her good judgement.

- One person in a community has always shown courage and concern for others, and so he/she is chosen to lead the community in time of danger.
- A civic leader is encumbered with a morally difficult decision that affects many people and so attends church to seek guidance from the Creator.
- The adult population elects a small minority of their fellow citizens to pass laws and to govern the country, and then the elected representatives have to negotiate a viable coalition.

Going by all that we have observed in this chapter, any of the above may be deemed 'trust' in the sense of mutual or shared obligations that are being observed in practice. The next chapter will look at the consequences of this modern concept of a political trust, contrasting the Hobbesian and Lockean approaches, considering them in their historical contexts, and showing that, in some senses, contemporary debate about trust retains the contradiction between these two past thinkers. This will lead us towards an appreciation of further transformations of trust in the social and political thought of the twentieth century.

Notes

1 If, on the other hand, the prisoner of war is kept in captivity, and 'is not trusted with the liberty of his body; he cannot be understood to be bound by covenant to subjection; and therefore may, if he can, make his escape by any means whatsoever' (Hobbes, 1998, p. 147, XXI.22). See also Baumgold (2013).
2 'The Hobbesian thought is that promises are always made for fear of the consequences of not making them, and that fearing imminent death is just a particularly vivid instance of the much more general phenomenon' (Brooke, 2017, p. xxviii). As Walzer points out, the alternative, but equally unpalatable, view is that no morally or legally binding agreements are possible during warfare as no-one is 'morally bound to fulfill a contract or commitment he was coerced into making' (Walzer, 1969, p. 778). Locke differs from Hobbes, as 'promises extorted by force, without right . . . bind not at all' (1980, p. 97, §186). See also Chwang (2011).
3 'For, having once established this tenet, That there are innate principles, it put their followers upon a necessity of receiving some doctrines as such; which was to take them off from the use of their own reason and judgement, and put them on believing and taking them upon trust, without further examination: in which posture of blind credulity, they might be more easily governed by, and made useful to some sort of men, who had the skill and office to principle and guide them. Nor is it a small power it gives one man over another, to have the authority to be the dictator of principles, and teacher of unquestionable truths; and to make a man swallow that for an innate principle, which may serve to his purpose, who teacheth them' (Locke, 1975, pp. 101–102).
4 'Thus it was easy, and almost natural for children, by a tacit, and scarce avoidable consent, to make way for the father's authority and government. They had been accustomed in their childhood to follow his direction, and to refer their little differences to him, and when they were men, who fitter to rule them? . . . The government they had been under, during it [their childhood], continued still to be more their protection than restraint; and they could nowhere find a greater security to their peace, liberties, and fortunes, than in the rule of a father' (Locke, 1980, p. 41, §75).
5 A vivid illustration of distrust, due to unequal power and cultural differences, is provided in Mill's discussion of colonial rule. He regards colonial rule by 'a free people

over a barbarous or semibarbarous one' as a matter of 'the highest moral trust' (Mill, 1991, p. 454), but nevertheless he also realizes that there is an underlying conflict and distrust.

> The laws, the customs, the social relations, for which they [the colonial governors] have to legislate, instead of being familiar to them from childhood, are all strange to them. For most of their detailed knowledge they must depend on the information of natives; and it is difficult for them to know whom to trust. They are feared, suspected, probably disliked by the population; seldom sought by them except for interested purposes; and they are prone to think that the servilely submissive are the trustworthy. Their danger is of despising the natives; that of the natives is, of disbelieving that anything the strangers do can be intended for their good.
>
> (Mill, 1991, pp. 455–456)

Mill is notorious for his Eurocentric belief that colonized nations were 'barbarous' and not yet suited for liberty and democratic government. Yet he was evidently aware of the distrust between foreign rulers and indigenous peoples. This passage also reveals some awareness that different laws, customs and social relations – different cultures, in short – create difficulties in establishing relations of trust, and that imperial power-relations are based on misrecognition, taking servility to signify trustworthiness.

References

Austin, J. L. (1975). *How to do things with words.* Oxford: Clarendon.

Ball, T. (1985). Hobbes' linguistic turn. *Polity, 17*(4), 739–760.

Baumgold, D. (2013). 'Trust' in Hobbes's political thought. *Political Theory, 41*(6), 838–855.

Bromwich, D. (2014). *The intellectual life of Edmund Burke: From the sublime and beautiful to American independence.* Cambridge, MA: Belknap.

Brooke, C. (2017). Introduction. In T. Hobbes (Ed.), *Leviathan* (pp. ix–xxxvi). UK: Penguin.

Burke, E. (1968). *Reflections on the revolution in France.* London: Penguin.

Burke, E. (1981a). *The writings and speeches of Edmund Burke* (Vol. II). Oxford: Clarendon Press.

Burke, E. (1981b). *The writings and speeches of Edmund Burke* (Vol. V). Oxford: Clarendon Press.

Burke, E. (1996). *The writings and speeches of Edmund Burke* (Vol. III). Oxford: Clarendon Press.

Chwang, E. (2011). On coerced promises. In H. Sheinman (Ed.), *Promises and agreement: Philosophical essays* (pp. 156–182). Oxford: Oxford University Press.

Gert, B. (2010). *Hobbes.* Malden, MA: Polity Press.

Hobbes, T. (1994). The elements of law natural and politic. In T. Hobbes (Ed.), *Human nature and De Corpore politico* (pp. 1–182). Oxford: Oxford University Press.

Hobbes, T. (1998). *Leviathan.* Oxford: Oxford University Press.

Lloyd, S. (Ed.). (2013). *The Bloomsbury companion to Hobbes.* London: Bloomsbury.

Locke, J. (1975). *An essay concerning human understanding.* Oxford: Clarendon Press.

Locke, J. (1980). *Second treatise of government.* Indianapolis, IN: Hackett.

Mansbridge, J. (2003). Rethinking representation. *American Political Science Review*, *97*(4), 515–528.

Mill, J. S. (1965). *The collected works of John Stuart Mill, Volume III: The principles of political economy, Part II*. Retrieved November 21, 2017, from Online Library of Liberty: http://oll.libertyfund.org/titles/243#lf0223-03_footnote_nt_225_ref

Mill, J. S. (1991). *On liberty and other essays*. Oxford: Oxford University Press.

Mill, J. S. (1994). *Principles of political economy*. Oxford: Oxford University Press.

Pettit, P. (2008). *Made with words: Hobbes on language, mind, and politics*. Princeton, NJ: Princeton University Press.

Pitkin, H. F. (1967). *The concept of representation*. Berkeley, CA: University of California Press.

Urbinati, N., and Warren, M. E. (2008). The concept of representation in contemporary democratic theory. *Annual Review of Political Science*, *11*, 387–412.

Walzer, M. (1969). Prisoners of war: Does the fight continue after the battle? *The American Political Science Review*, *63*(3), 777–786.

Wittgenstein, L. (2009). *Philosophical investigations*. Chichester: Wiley-Blackwell.

4 Transformations of trust

The previous chapter's reading of Hobbes, Locke, Burke and Mill shows how trust emerged into English political philosophy, the various forms in which it was depicted, and how it evolved discursively from an interpersonal relational quality into an abstract political and economic factor. The present chapter considers the seventeenth-century social and political context in order to evoke the kinds of doubts that fuelled distrust and made it into a political-theoretical concern, and it then outlines further transformations up to the present. Hobbes and Locke use the word 'trust' in different ways, and they make quite different assumptions about what it would mean to trust others in a state of nature. But they both assume that trust exists naturally 'as is.' Our understandings and practices of trust have a history, however, and we will begin to see this more clearly in this chapter and the following two chapters. Trust re-emerged as a significant matter for theory and research across the social sciences in the last quarter of the twentieth century – along with the growth of complexity, technical know-how and risk. Theoretical developments, such as social capital and abstract trust, reflect this. The digital economy produces yet another 'restructuring' of relations of trust.

The historical context

The obvious historical and political context from which Hobbes's thought arises is the civil strife and revolution (and the later restoration) of mid-seventeenth-century England. The question of the institution of a sovereign figure or assembly that could provide protection had real salience for him and his native country. An immediate political problem that Hobbes addresses is the dilemma faced by ex-Royalists regarding their oaths of allegiance to the former king, Charles I, and hence to his exiled successor (Charles II), as against their obligations to the new conqueror, Oliver Cromwell, and to the Commonwealth (Hill, 1980; Thomas, 1993). As Hobbes would have it, 'covenants without the sword are but words and of no strength to secure a man at all' (Hobbes, 1998, p. 111, XVII.2), so logically the subject should submit to the authority of the ruler who provides real protection in the present. In *Leviathan*, the multitude do not evade the condition of war by placing *trust* in a sovereign, however. The sovereign is *authorized* by them. Trust features frequently in *Leviathan*, but it is largely depicted between subjects, and not often between the sovereign and any subject. The threat of lawful punishment is required to make people keep promises and be trustworthy – or, in effect, obedient. And his conception of trust is often closer to 'credit,' as it relates to commercial exchange. Trust in itself is not an essential ingredient of any solution to a civil war or a state of nature, therefore.

For Locke, the backdrop was the 'regime change' that occurred when William of Orange was invited by protestant nobility to invade England and the catholic King James II was deposed. William married Mary, James II's daughter, and they were jointly crowned. The subsequent Bill of Rights 1689 asserted parliament's freedoms and rights, as against royal prerogatives; the Act of Settlement 1701 ended the principle of the divine right of kings by making it clear that parliament can determine the succession (Davies, 1999). The idea that a monarch who attempts to rule arbitrarily, and who betrays the trust of the people, can and should be replaced by one who accepts a constitutional compromise with a free parliament is reflected in Locke's *Second Treatise*. As we have observed, though, Lockean trust originates in the intimacy of the family and the duties of parenthood.

Historical research has also revealed the extent to which the seventeenth-century economy relied upon social networks and credit, given the short supply of metallic forms of money. Economic communities 'consisted of masses of informal sales credit . . . in which trust was considered the crucial factor in buying and selling' (Muldrew, 1998, p. 124). The competitiveness and uncertainty, as well as the sociability, created by such close networks of economic exchange meant that sensitivity to reputation and creditworthiness was heightened, and fear of default and mistrust were ever-present. Because of the complexity and ubiquity of credit networks in English communities and industries, defaults could have 'knock-on' effects, leading to unexpected financial problems for others. Many debts were written off as 'desperate.' In spite of an increase in default, and the efforts people had to make to recover debts, however, 'trust in one's neighbours remained the foundation upon which the actual business of the world depended. People still had to be trusted, and had to attempt to be trustworthy' (Muldrew, 1998, p. 182). Without such trust, there would have been less trade, households would have lacked supplies, and markets would have collapsed. Even as it broke down so frequently, trust came to be 'emphasized more strongly, in order to stress its necessity because of the worry generated by its increasing unpredictability.' With the economy largely reliant upon the activities of households, and with weak institutions of state, interpersonal trust was 'the central institutional bond of society,' and it remained so until replaced by large state and private bureaucracies and banking institutions that could rely upon 'calculated utility' (Muldrew, 1998, p. 182). The notions of contract (or covenant), promising and honouring are central to Hobbes's argument, reflecting everyday commerce in his time. This social context also helps us to make sense of why Locke describes promises and oaths as 'bonds of human society' (Locke, 1948, p. 156). Reputations and social cohesion were a matter of close interpersonal bargains, contracts and credit.

Given the historical problems posed for trust in early-modern political theory, and the distinct approaches taken by Hobbes and Locke, we can consider how their thinking is reflected in contemporary theory. Although we now live in a completely different world from theirs, the ways in which the problems of trust are formulated in contemporary literature rehearse the basic differences between the Hobbesian and the Lockean problematics of political power.

The Hobbesian problem of trust

For Hobbes, coercive centralized power and trust in others are positively correlated. An absence or breakdown of effective 'common power' makes it unwise to trust others. One of the main advantages of a protective sovereign that punishes injustice is that people are more inclined to make and to keep promises. Regulation and sanctions are required to make people trustworthy, or to make it rational to trust others. The general Hobbesian view (that trust requires state power) recurs today, for example in research supporting the hypothesis 'that the state as enforcer of private agreements fosters interpersonal trust' (Herreros, 2012, p. 484; see also Robbins, 2011), or in those who conclude that highly capable public administration and a good quality of government 'generate social trust,' which in turn increases the production of public goods and fosters greater human well-being (Rothstein, 2015). It has been commented that 'almost no one other than anarchists disagrees with this [Hobbesian] view' that trust depends on effective government (Hardin, 1999, p. 22). Rule of law, enforcement of property rights and contracts and credible economic policy are regarded as basic preconditions for business confidence and investment. Without this governmental-regulatory background to everyday commerce, trust in business dealings would be harder to achieve.

The initial motive for Hobbes's concern with trust is the doubt instilled by human gullibility, however. People can be misled by unscrupulous merchants and lenders; they may trust blindly in preachers, sophists or pretenders to power, and believe false or unorthodox doctrines. In turn, established authorities – whose legitimate power should be combined with orthodox beliefs – may be dishonoured. At worst, then, justice will fail to be performed; debts will go unpaid and injuries uncompensated; men will be obliged to do whatever they must simply to preserve themselves. *Trust arises as a political problem due to doubts about people's abilities to judge what to believe, and in whom to believe.*

This is not dissimilar to the problems that have recently been termed 'post-truth politics.' Conspiracy theories and fake news circulate rapidly through online networks, extreme ideas and sentiments (from both the far-left and far-right) gain in currency, and an information war and physical street-violence erupt. Many people are taking their beliefs from 'false prophets' (who may preach, for example, that the Trump election was a corporate *coup d'état*, or that 'the white race' is under threat of extinction), and their trust or belief in liberal-democratic institutions – and indeed their fear of the powers of the state itself – may decline or even vanish, leading towards a Hobbesian 'condition of war.' In the internet age, a civil war would differ from those of the past, be it King versus Parliament or Union versus Confederates. But, apprehensively, one asks what it *would* look like (Ricks, 2017).

The Lockean problem of trust

Due to Locke's acknowledgement of *tacit* trust and consent, the trust given by the people to rulers or law-makers at any particular stage in history need not have been given expressly in a public speech-act, charter or ceremony. It may be an evolving unspoken and unwritten trust. In contrast, Hobbes depicts trust as spoken and enacted between persons. And in a further difference from Hobbes, Locke often writes of trust as some*thing* that is put or reposed or lodged in the legislators or executive, often as an adjunct to *power* that has fallen or was given into their hands (Locke, 1980). Power must then be used pursuant to that trust, as if trust were an aim or standard. Conversely, trust may be breached or acted against, as an object. So *trust* is nominalized or reified, and the granting of power is a gift of trust. Lockean trust in itself does not *depend* on the establishment of political power, however, because 'the faithful fulfilment of contracts . . . and the obligation to keep promises' are derived from the law of nature (Locke, 1965, p. 119). In a state of nature, there is already a duty to be trustworthy that is even more fundamental than moral conventions and civil laws, because, without trust, 'human society would not be possible at all' (Dunn, 1984, p. 287). But Locke shifts focus with insufficient justification from the trust that endures in family and friendship to the trust that is supposed to exist between rulers and the ruled. People in Locke's hypothetical state of nature, by definition, would not know of the latter political form of trust, even though they may have experienced the former. The leap from the interpersonal to the political, or from parental government to civil government, is taken without critical reflection.

For Locke, then, the problem of trust arises quite differently from the way it did for Hobbes. It begins with unspoken familial trust, embodied in 'nursing fathers tender and careful of the public weal' (Locke, 1980, p. 60, §110). When the scope of authority expands into a large established commonwealth, the bonds of family and friendship are absent, but the natural law still applies, as it is 'perpetual and universal' (Locke, 1965, p. 191). How can ruler and ruled be bound in mutual obligation when the 'natural' grounds for trust (family and friendship) are absent due to a profound 'political division of labour' (Dunn, 1988, p. 88)? Trust is a political problem because *bonds of obligation founded originally in natural law and in face-to-face sociability become strained once people place their trust in a select few to make law and to govern*, especially when those few are only seen at a distance, if at all, by the large majority of the people. We also find in Locke a grammatical usage of 'trust' that is not found in *Leviathan*. That is, Locke writes of a body of people trusting another body of people, especially 'the legislative' (see for instance Locke, 1980, p. 123, §240). Trust can thus be collective or institutional; it is not only interpersonal. This brings trust into its modern *political* discursive role. Whereas Hobbes problematizes interpersonal trust, Locke goes further, as he questions our trust in political trust itself.

Originally, according to Locke, the rule by a patriarch was 'tacitly submitted to . . . till time seemed to have confirmed it' (Locke, 1980, p. 59, §110); there was, at that stage, no explicit statement of the conditions of this trust. As historical experiences show, however, political trust is all too often broken or violated, and hence Locke implies that rulers (if left to themselves) *cannot* be trusted to act for the public good and the security of the people. Hence, the naïve or tacit trust that he supposed had originally established the right to govern must be brought to public attention (or re-presented) 'to examine more carefully' (Locke, 1980, p. 60, §111) – but only *after* (and indeed *because*) it was broken through excesses and abuses of power. A retrospectively conceived implicit trust becomes an explicit *political* concern due to its apparent violation. While trust observes a universal law of nature, found originally in the unconditional affectional bonds that govern the family, the trust that upholds *civil* government is remote and more readily betrayed, and hence it may call for critical examination and deliberate re-establishment.

Locke's social contract still makes sense to us today, but his refusal of toleration for the atheist is antiquated. 'Promises, covenants, and oaths, which are the bonds of human society, can have no hold upon an atheist' (Locke, 1948, p. 156). As atheists do not believe in God, they do not fear God's punishment, and they cannot be bound by their word. Without a common belief in God, according to Locke, self-interest would be our only guide, and a normative social order would be impossible (Numao, 2013; Spencer, 2018). Of the four thinkers examined in Chapter 3, it is Burke who places the greatest religious significance on political trust. For J.S. Mill, on the other hand, trust in a person in public life or commerce does not depend on her belief in God or membership of a particular congregation. And nowadays, atheists too are trusted; one need not inquire into a person's religious beliefs in order to assess her creditworthiness. An eternal guarantor may still be called upon (for instance, when 'swearing in'), but is not necessarily called *for* when making a binding promise or contract. Outside of the circle of attachment-based trust in friends and loved-ones, it is the insertion into a system of impersonal law or institutional regulation that enables us to trust others, regardless of their religious beliefs. Contemporary toleration and inclusion of atheists, and of followers of diverse religious creeds, requires seeing the individual as socially and legally accountable for promises, without having to invoke the fear of divine punishment. Locke's distrust of the atheist may no longer be relevant, but it exemplifies how trust has a history.

Reconstitution of political trust

In its distinctly Lockean wording, the United States Declaration of Independence (1776) announces a withdrawal of consent from the British monarch due to breaches of political trust, such as: 'He [the King] has kept among us, in times of peace, Standing Armies without the Consent of our legislatures.' With political trust broken, the Declaration absolves the colonies 'from all Allegiance to the British Crown.' The subsequent Constitution of the United States (1787) can be seen as a set of promises to limit, divide and regulate the executive and legislative powers, and so to protect liberties and prevent the kinds of abuses that the former colonies had suffered. It embodies a *transformed* political trust between law-makers and the people. But this trust had to be made explicit; it was reformulated, written down and adopted at a constitutional conference.

As the modern era progresses, global mobility, religious diversity and entrepreneurial risk become the norm, while political and economic liberalism promotes freedom of choice and individual autonomy. This is advanced by the growth of technologies that make risk more calculable and manageable. The individual then shoulders responsibility for choosing to trust or distrust particular politicians, commodities, business partners, employees, credit, investments, etc. (Baker and Simon, 2002; Bernstein, 1996). He or she must be flexible and mobile, placing less faith in religious dogma or ancient traditions, and instead being self-responsible and resilient in the face of disruption of occupations and customs due to competition and technological innovation. Choices of place, occupation and social participation widen. Investments and business partnerships require decisions to trust others, while facing an unpredictable future (Luhmann, 1988). Locke's concept of political trust reflects 'in embryo' this historically emergent and reflexive sense of freedom, choice and risk, alongside the need to provide security, so that social life and commerce can flourish in an uncertain world.

Lockean political trust works 'at a distance,' moreover. While the people, in a modern democracy, are trusted with the power to elect their representatives, individual electors rarely meet face-to-face those whom they elected. The latter are 'known' only in print or mass media formats; their work as representatives is conducted at a remove from the public, even when in a publicly accessible legislative chamber. Furthermore, policy-making and public services are complex matters handled largely by anonymous advisers and professionals. Hence, relations of political trust are now institutionalized and remote.

Locke's formulation of political trust opens the way towards some of our contemporary understandings. Social contract theory still informs debates, for instance, about the balance between state surveillance for the purpose of security and the individual's right to privacy. As the democratic franchise evolved, however, political trust expands beyond a generalized Lockean 'trade-off' of rights and security, to encompass the more particularized relations of representation as discussed by Mill.

Hume's alternative

Locke's social contract theory has never enjoyed universal approval, and so it is worth summarizing David Hume's theory as an important alternative. Hume rejects a social contract as the origin of government, and so Locke's idea of a trust 'given' to governors and legislators is rejected too. Hume nonetheless often refers to 'trust' and 'mutual trust' in his own work, but largely as consequences of promises. In restating the Lockean theory of social contract (in order to critique it) Hume talks of 'promise' where Locke uses 'trust.' That is, Hume's version of the social contract has it that the people are obliged to obey their governors and law-makers because (and only because) they promised to – which is not the same as saying that the people have given them their trust. For Hume, trust grows (or is later broken) only after a promise is made; the performance of a promise 'is requisite to *beget* mutual trust and confidence in the common offices of life' (Hume, 1969, p. 595, italics added). Conversely the failure to perform on one's promise can incur 'the penalty of never being trusted again' (Hume, 1969, p. 574). Unlike Locke, he says that the keeping of promises is not an injunction of the universal law of nature; it arises from human convention and from speech. For Hume, moreover, the obligations to keep promises and to obey government are quite distinct. The former is necessary for mutual trust, the latter for public order and harmony.

The origins of government are found, according to Hume, in the growth of social conventions that preserve one person's interests in the protection or promotion of others' interests, or 'a general sense of common interest; which sense all members of the society express to one another, and which induces them to regulate their conduct by certain rules' (Hume, 1969, p. 541). This comes about from 'a convention of agreement betwixt us, tho' without the interposition of a promise.'

> Two men, who pull the oars of a boat, do it by an agreement or convention, tho' they have never given promises to each other. Nor is the rule concerning the stability of possession [of property] the less deriv'd from human conventions, that it arises gradually, and acquires force by a slow progression, and by our repeated experience of the inconveniences of transgressing it.
>
> (Hume, 1969, p. 542)

One might counter-argue that the cooperation of the two men in the boat signifies that they trust one another to share the task. Hume's assertion that no promise is interposed may not be a problem for social-contract theory if *tacit* trust does not require a spoken promise. One can be trusted implicitly without any speech-act promising to do something. Hume sees *interests* as the building-blocks of society, however, and trust as a beneficial *consequence* of social convention and law. This reflects a shift, during the eighteenth century, away from the problem of credit and reputation within social relations and towards the pre-eminence of the self as a locus of interests in pursuit of happiness and prosperity. As institutions of finance, business and state became more established and bureaucratic, and as techniques of statistics, probability and book-keeping became more sophisticated, economic success became increasingly calculable, across greater expanses of time and space, enabling collaboration with strangers as well as acquaintances. Commerce could be regarded in more impersonal and abstract terms. The entrepreneur had to make self-interested decisions, based on risk, and was less bound to close interpersonal relations in which trust is paramount and resonant; success depended upon understanding the subjective needs of others, and providing goods and services in accord with that, rather than abiding by time-honoured oaths, customs and loyalties. As Adam Smith later argued, relations with others are governed by 'sympathy,' or the capacity to perceive all others (neighbours or strangers) as essentially like oneself, experiencing feelings and desires, seeking happiness and avoiding pain. In a competitive market, traders would learn to be trustworthy. They must cater to others' interests or lose business to those who do.

Towards a contemporary political trust

We can observe, then, significant historical changes in political and economic institutions and social norms reflected in discursive shifts in the meanings and uses of trust in the texts of political theorists. And we can observe some continuity too. The role of governmental powers in making trust possible, compared with the role of a 'natural' human sociability – the difference between Hobbes and Locke – is a dilemma that is still with us today. To what extent do law and public administration enable us to trust one another, and at what point does the overuse or misuse of governmental powers undermine voluntary cooperation and association? Moreover, the rise to prominence of individualism and subjective interests – *contra* Burke – is observable in those contemporary definitions of trust (see Chapter 2) that are based on a reflexive compatibility with the interests of the one who trusts.

For Locke, the people had placed their trust in princes and law-makers since the earliest governments. Burke rejected the idea of a social contract but, like Locke, he regarded all political power as a trust. As a member of parliament, Burke's view of trust also encompasses political representation. This involves two struggles: between parliamentarians and court, and between individual members and their electors. The Burkean representative is 'answerable to but not mimicking the suffrage of the people; serving to refine the policies and improve the knowledge of the executive, yet sometimes acting as a barrier against monarchical power' (Bromwich, 2014, p. 415). He sees the MP, and the House collectively, as representing the whole nation, thus making a claim against the court and its favourites. Opposing this, 'the king sought to keep the members of Parliament in their place by arguing that each spoke only for his own separate community; they did not collectively "represent" the realm' (Pitkin, 1967, p. 252). Burke had also to defend his independent stance – as a trustee of the whole nation – against the partial opinions and demands of the electors of Bristol who, in 1780, dismissed him from that seat. Burke's pleas for a higher 'trust,' to act on behalf of the people, for which he should be accountable ultimately to God, were successful electorally only until voters lost patience with his policies and his remoteness.

Mill's version has one side in common with Burke, and another with the contemporary model. His model of voters' trust in representatives does not, however, amount to the contemporary 'trust in government' which is seen as a ratio between public perception of governmental performance and public expectations of government (Hetherington, 2005). Rather, for Mill, individual representatives use their good judgement to act in the interests of the people. They are in 'a situation of trust,' with significant public duties, and they should be trusted to know best. This ideal of a popular trust in the conscience and judgement of the representative, inherited from Burke, 'continued to prevail throughout the first half of the nineteenth century' (Manin, 1997, p. 203). As the male franchise was widening, however, and as he and others argued for the participation of women, Mill was concerned that the rule of the majority could lead to mediocrity in politics and to ill-informed or class-based legislation.[1] He proposed redesigning the electoral system so that all voters would have at least one representative they trusted, and a minority (those of more 'cultivated' minds) would be more likely to be returned.

Mill's understandings of trust thus form part of an historical 'bridge' to the twentieth century. Today's trust in representatives is vested more in political parties and governments, however, not only in individuals. But, even if most people today tell surveyors that they do not trust politicians, they are (regardless of whether or not they voted) implicitly trusting political parties and leaders, as representatives, to use their judgement to address complex policy problems and events on behalf of all. In part this may be justified by the representatives having access to more information than voters.

To continue this historical analysis of trust, we next consider more recent theories: the tragedy of the commons, social capital and abstract trust. We must also take account of how the digital online world is re-forming the ways and means by which people are called upon to trust.

From state of nature to tragedy of the commons

What kinds of doubts re-evoked theoretical interest in trust in the latter decades of the twentieth century? As technological change and space exploration in the 1960s made it possible to imagine a 'global village,' debates about the environment and the planet itself became more urgent, and the Cold-War nuclear threat put the survival of our species into question. Biopolitical concerns about public health grew in the face of a global 'population explosion.'[2] In his influential essay on the tragedy of the commons, Garrett Hardin argued that the problem of population admitted of 'no technical solutions,' and it required 'a fundamental extension in morality.'

> Individuals locked into the logic of the commons are free only to bring on universal ruin; once they see the necessity of mutual coercion, they become free to pursue other goals. . . . The only way we can preserve and nurture other and more precious freedoms is by relinquishing the freedom to breed, and that very soon.
>
> (Hardin, 1968, p. 1248)

Hardin did not address the complexity of global social and environmental problems, and, like Thomas Malthus before him, probably overstated the imminence of 'universal ruin.'[3] Moreover, it was realized that high-risk, complex or 'wicked' problems do not respond readily to moral, political or technical solutions. By their very characteristics, the most important public-policy problems lack defin-able boundaries, let alone solutions (Rittel and Webber, 1973). But a growing understanding of unsustainable resource use and the risk of collapse of human and ecological systems led to critiques of 'the growth model' of economics (Meadows, Meadows, Randers, and Behrens, 1972; Daly, 1974, 2015). Moral, legal and political thought and international cooperation are required to address concerns such as over-fishing and climate change. Regulation at a global scale is needed to prevent ecosystem collapse, and yet political will and force of law at that level have been weak. Many states have now accepted responsibility for reducing car-bon emissions, for instance, but insufficient supra-governmental powers exist to enforce compliance, and huge industrial-capitalist interests still stand in the way.

The neoliberal turn of the 1980s heightened policy-makers' commitments to growth, deregulation and resource extraction, however. The 'tragedy of the com-mons' was re-deployed to argue that public ownership only leads to inefficiency and degradation of resources, due to free-riders, as it is 'little more than a regu-lated commons.' Free markets mean efficient resource-allocation, while private ownership provides the incentive to invest in the long-term value of assets and to manage resources on 'a sustained-yield basis' (Smith, 1981, pp. 457, 468).

The problem of political trust is also a problem of the commons. In fact, it is a meta-problem, as collective or cooperative actions to resolve any problem of the commons depend upon trust, and markets benefit from trust too. But how well does trust fare if defined as a private good – or as others acting in one's own interests? If a person's choice to nurture trust (or not) is based on the costs and benefits that she herself will experience, then rationally there is little incentive to invest in 'building' trust within a community, as the 'asset' accrues only 'in the commons' and cannot be privately appropriated. Social capital and trust are regarded as valuable common 'resources,' but, in a competitive world, the first to trust is the first to lose. How, then, can we sustain our 'stocks' of trust?

Rational-choice theory considers 'collective action problems,' as it recognizes 'the potential for choices made by individuals to have an adverse societal effect when there is an absence of trust, obligation or other incentives to cooperate' (Cairney, 2012, p. 134). The tragedy of the commons thus performs a role rather like the state of nature in social-contract theory. It implies that some freedoms may have to be curtailed, or collective action may be needed, in order to continue to enjoy 'other and more precious freedoms,' at least where free markets fail. And trust is a necessary precondition for effective collective action. So, the method-ological individualism of rational-choice theory led to conclusions that put trust on the neoliberal policy agenda, under the rubric of 'social capital,' due to the fear that unregulated markets 'kill the goose that laid the golden egg' of social cohesion and progress.

Trust and social capital

> The concept of social capital boils down to networks, norms, and trust.
>
> (Farr, 2004, p. 8)

In the tradition that extends from de Tocqueville to Putnam, a high level of trust in others is seen as a quality of civil society, enabling citizens to freely associate independently of centralized powers. Entrusting a portion of our liberties to an authority may serve our common interests, up to a point, but the machinery of government may override our 'natural' inclinations to achieve things on trust. At best, a benevolent government might interfere with the 'spontaneous' social networks that rely upon and deepen trust; at worst, a corrupt government will engender open distrust. Gellner goes so far as to say that 'effective' government 'destroys trust,' while 'the absence of any strong central authority' engenders it (Gellner, 1988, p. 143). Locke would not have gone that far, although he did warn that governments have abused the trust placed in them. But, by this logic, we arrive at a fundamental 'collective action problem,' as no other collective problems can be effectively addressed (whether it be by voluntary association or by centralized government) without the common good of political trust. And yet, in an atomized competitive marketplace, there could be little or no incentive for actors to 'invest' in trust-building. Even if one thinks of economic life as embedded within social relations, such as long-term business relationships and social reputation, the trust that develops with closer association also brings 'enhanced opportunity for malfeasance' (Granovetter, 1985, p. 491). In an unfettered market, it may be hard to establish trust. Government regulation may help, but that too is of limited benefit. Appealing to the law is a costly last resort in cases of gross betrayal, and ill-conceived public policy can sometimes diminish trust even further.

Such concerns rely, however, on a false premise (addressed in Chapter 2) that haunts trust literature: the spectre of 'a world without trust,' and the corollary that 'trust is a *precondition* for social cohesion and economic prosperity.' Trust, however, as argued above, is not a 'condition' that social groups can intelligibly be 'without.' Of course, we can observe that trust, economic productivity and social cohesion do go together when things are working well. Indeed, successful social and economic interactions *exemplify* the observation of trust. And, when they fail, they fail 'as a whole.' One is not a 'precondition' for the other; they are simply different ways of describing events. But, for the time being, let us follow the logic of social capital in its own terms.

So, how is trust positioned and conceptualized within the theory of social capital? James Coleman's famous example was the wholesale diamond market in New York City. What made it possible for one merchant to trust another with a bag of stones for private inspection was the tightly knit intermarried Jewish community to which they belonged.

> The strength of these [family, community, and religious] ties makes possible transactions in which *trustworthiness is taken for granted* and trade can occur with ease. In the absence of these ties, elaborate and expensive bonding and insurance devices would be necessary – or else the transactions could not take place.
>
> (Coleman, 1988, pp. 98–99, italics added)

Social capital is thus a productive resource that makes our goals achievable; without it, business ventures may be impractical or too costly. But social capital is not a tangible or countable resource like money; 'social capital inheres in the structure of relations between actors and among actors [in a social setting]' (1988, p. 98). Coleman concludes that social capital is not a private good: its benefits cannot be appropriated by the individual, and any individual's contribution to social capital is, by its very nature, shared by others. By this rational-choice logic, there will be an under-investment in social capital as each individual prefers to invest in goods the benefits of which he or she can privately appropriate, even though the very prosperity that each individual is pursuing is dependent upon shared 'stocks' of social capital.

During the 1990s – as if to compensate for the individualism of neoliberal ideology – interest in social capital increased. Robert Putnam's leading ideas spring from an analysis of the development of new regional governments implemented throughout Italy from 1970. He concluded that the factor which most strongly correlated with the emergence of good government was 'strong traditions of civic engagement' (1993, p. 36) – such as high voter turn-out, strong newspaper readership, membership in cultural, religious and other community organizations and participation in social activities. Putnam goes on to claim that 'the social capital embodied in norms and networks of civic engagement seems to be *a precondition for economic development*, as well as for effective *government*' (1993, p. 37, italics added), and hence policies 'should be vetted for their indirect effects on social capital' (1993, p. 41).

In *Trust: The Social Virtues and the Creation of Prosperity*, Francis Fukuyama surveys a number of European, North American and East Asian countries (with the notable absence of any Scandinavian examples), and analyzes the interrelatedness of social organization, cultural values and material prosperity. He argues that economic development is dependent on social cooperation and the degree of trust inherent in the society.

> [A] nation's well-being, as well as its ability to compete, is conditioned by a single, pervasive cultural characteristic: the level of trust inherent in the society.
>
> (Fukuyama, 1995, p. 7)

> Property rights, contracts, and commercial law are all indispensable institutions for creating a modern market-oriented economic system, but it is possible to economize substantially on transaction costs if such institutions are supplemented by social capital and trust. Trust, in turn, is the product of preexisting communities of shared moral norms or values.
>
> (1995, p. 336)

In this view, the development of a vibrant and prosperous economy requires stable family life, but not of a kind which engenders such strict loyalty that it holds back those transactions with non-kin which are essential in impersonal organizations and business dealings. Hence, without attention to the fostering of appropriate customs and values of *civic* life, private economic prosperity will also be in jeopardy.

Going by the above, trust is a taken-for-granted, inherent and pervasive feature of social networks and relationships. Putnam's definitions of social capital appear to let trust slide, however, from being one of social capital's core defining features (along with social networks and norms), to being a quality that only '*arises from*' the defining features of social capital, which are restricted now to social networks and relationships (Hooghe and Stolle, 2003). A similar ambiguity is noticeable in Fukuyama who states that trust is one condition of well-being and economic competitiveness, which gives it a foundational role, and yet that it is 'the *product of pre-existing* communities of shared moral norms or values' (Fukuyama, 1995, p. 336) which seems to reduce the foundational role of trust. Trust is further distinguished from social capital *per se* by Field, who concludes that trust 'is almost certainly best treated as an independent factor, which is generally a consequence rather than an integral component of social capital' (Field, 2008, p. 72).

Hence, by definition, social capital refers to strong social networks and relationships that share norms, and trust is one of the beneficial features produced by such networks and relationships. This tends to reify trust as a factor – 'the civic lubricant of thriving societies' (Delhey, Newton, and Welzel, 2011, p. 787) – and as a variable to be measured and correlated with other variables in order to generate theories about trust (and diverse forms thereof) as a cause or consequence of other social factors (Newton, 2008).

There is a basic 'structure of belief' about trust within social-capital theories. First, social networks with shared norms 'produce' trust, as a beneficial effect. Secondly, it is in our interests to trust, for our own and/or mutual benefit. Thirdly, other important matters are contingent upon trust: for example, the ease and extent of voluntary social collaboration or of doing business. At a purely utilitarian level, trust is considered to be a socially shared *economic* resource, as it means people can collaborate without costly legal contracts and performance monitoring, and this reduces transaction costs.[4] But trust arises from religious or other traditional cultural sources that are '*not* the consequence of rational calculation' (Fukuyama, 1995, p. 352, italics added). The problem posed for trust is thus a tragedy of the commons: unregulated exploitation of a shared resource will degrade that resource.

Like other contemporary theories of trust, social capital is concerned about 'a world with declining trust,' and it regards trust in terms of how it serves our interests, private or shared. Trust is seen as a resource perpetually 'at risk,' rather than a culturally contingent ethical quality of social life. Social-capital theory addresses an impersonal, *systemic* form of trust, distributed and reciprocated between and among networks. To expand on the systems approach, we turn, in the next section, to abstract trust, and then, in the next chapter, we consider money as a distributed impersonal form of trust 'in action.'

Abstract trust

The scope and complexity of governmental institutions and public policy have increased greatly since Locke's time. Similarly, the objective risks of modern life, from nuclear war to climate change, and the production of new knowledge about forms of risk, and hence risk-perception itself, have all increased along with the rapid evolution of science and technology. Consequently, the theory of trust must keep pace. Luhmann placed a much greater emphasis than Locke on uncertainty, or the role of trust in 'the reduction of complexity.' But Giddens' account of 'abstract trust' in systems was another step forward.

> Trust may be defined as confidence in the reliability of a person *or system*, regarding a given set of outcomes or events, where that confidence expresses a faith in the probity or love of another, or in the correctness of *abstract principles.*
>
> (Giddens, 1990, p. 34, italics added)

'Trust as confidence' is common in dictionary definitions. You can't trust someone without having some confidence in him/her; you can have confidence in a person's ability or punctuality without really trusting that person. So, trust is a 'subset' of confidence. But, to qualify as 'trust,' our confidence needs to be an expression of 'faith.' And here Giddens may be guilty of circularity, basing the definition of one abstract noun (trust) on another ill-defined abstract noun (faith), even though they overlap in usage. He elaborates, however, on how trust in others involves ontological security; it is 'a psychological need of a persistent and recurrent kind' (Giddens, 1990, p. 97). We cannot do without this faith. Aside, however, from faith in other persons, Giddens acknowledges the ways in which the modern subject must also trust in 'systems' and the 'abstract principles' that guide them. The latter are products of human thought and activity – the work of countless anonymous persons. One cannot possibly avow a trust in each and all of the persons who design and manage institutions and complex systems such as airlines, banks and police forces. The individual may only encounter a few such persons as 'access points' to those systems.

So, given the complexity of modern organizations and systems, 'why do most people, most of the time, trust in practices and social mechanisms about which their own technical knowledge is slight or non-existent?' At school, we learn about science, but more importantly, we acquire 'respect for technical knowledge of all kinds,' and hence 'trust is only demanded where there is ignorance' (Giddens, 1990, pp. 88–89). As we are necessarily ignorant about so many things that affect our lives, the trust that is supposedly 'demanded' must be profound. We have no choice but to 'trust' the financial system, the armed forces and the many global industries that supply us with goods, services and social media. We do not (and cannot) know all about what they do, why they do it, and what the consequences may be; yet participation in everyday life requires or assumes a trust in them, like it or not. The regulated activity of these systems and institutions creates a sense of security that we rely upon for our daily existence; they also do the risk–benefit calculation on our behalf, foreclosing the need for us to express doubts. But the activity and innovation of these systems are altering the very universe of events in which risk is perceived and calculated. Today, for example, social media have created surveillance of our everyday lives and thoughts, and the information is sold to advertisers without our knowledge. These same systems, from which we benefit and in which we trust, also produce new sources of risk and insecurity, and hence new causes for distrust or cynicism. In spite of this, 'no-one can completely opt out of the abstract systems involved in modern institutions' (Giddens, 1990, p. 84). Trusting in these systems becomes routine; it is 'to a large extent enforced by the intrinsic circumstances of daily life'; rather than a choice or commitment, such trust is a 'tacit acceptance'; 'alternatives are largely foreclosed' (Giddens, 1990, p. 90).

So, is Giddens calling 'trust' that which political theory, notably Hobbes, traditionally called 'obedience'? Are the students and teacher in a classroom *trusting* the textbooks of science and the institutions of education, or are they obeying state-mandated technical authority?[5] Do people 'trust' the big banks and corporations? We would be unable to live a 'normal' social life if we refused to participate in these complex systems – and, as Hobbes put it, we owe obedience in as much as our survival depends on it (see Chapter 3). Moreover, Giddens sees no 'opt out' clause in case of a breach of trust, as in Locke's withdrawal of consent. After the global financial crisis of 2008, for instance, individuals and governments had little choice but to continue to deal with the very banks that had breached their supposed 'trust.' We are forced 'to trust' as we cannot opt out of institutions that we necessarily depend upon.

Abstract trust is a conceptual step forward, but Giddens' reliance on ignorance and faith to help explain it makes trust look like obedience. And a trust based on ignorance is exactly the kind that Hobbes warned us against. But Hobbes did not have to consider the complex, technically advanced systems that Giddens was dealing with in the late twentieth century. The structure of the 'forced choice' helps to comprehend this dilemma for modern political trust, and this will be explained (in the next chapter) in relation to money. Moreover, Giddens' 'abstract trust' was introduced only at the dawn of the internet age, and things have evolved since then.

Trust at the click of a mouse

At the beginning of this chapter, I cited historical accounts of the importance of trust, credit and reputation in the day-to-day commerce of seventeenth-century England. Given the shortage of coined money, households mostly made purchases and did business face-to-face on credit, often relying upon formal promises and oaths, or on written records of goods exchanged on a *quid pro quo* basis (Muldrew, 1998). The internet has now profoundly changed the ways in which people form relationships and do business. We need to comprehend this as a further shift in what it is that we mean and do when we say we trust.

Like it or not, we are being rated online. You can find out, for example, how I rate as an academic author based on citations h-index. Peer-to-peer online systems in transport, accommodation and second-hand goods all encourage buyers and sellers to rate one another after each transaction. This conditions us to an extra effort of civility and responsiveness, in order to get a good review and to keep up our reputation-ratings. A poor record may lead to difficulties getting customers or the best service.[6] For example, using machine-learning technology, a company called Trooly developed an automated online system for screening and predicting trustworthy relationships at high speed and low cost. Called, apparently without irony, 'Instant Trust™,' this service was 'designed to fill a "trust gap" caused by the speed of modern commerce and community, which requires instant evaluation of potential reward and risk – without the trust-building interaction history and feedback loops that people use to evaluate relationships offline.'[7] In mid-2017, Trooly was acquired by Airbnb in order to protect guests and hosts from scams.

The Chinese government is planning to take this kind of rating model a big *political* step further, however, by developing, in association with Alibaba, a comprehensive 'social credit' rating for all its citizens, to become compulsory in 2020. This involves gathering a wide range of information, including consumer choices, bill-payment records, and social-media comments. Local CCTV foot-age and facial recognition may also track individuals' movements. The aim is to evaluate and enhance 'trustworthiness' and 'sincerity' – although an unstated but strategic effect will be to enhance obedience. As payment of fines may take minor misdemeanours off the person's negative scores, this is a disciplinary political technology. Individuals will modify their conduct, knowing it to be under obser-vation and 'counting' towards their social credit-rating, as a good rating will gain privileged access to services, while a poor rating could result in denial of services. As the actions of one's online friends can also 'count,' individuals will engage in mutual surveillance, thus socially 'building in' the means and principles of con-trol and subjection. And people will be under pressure to share their ratings with new acquaintances and in online dating profiles (Botsman, 2017). While Western governments are not apparently planning anything so overtly disciplinary, massive digital data-capture is known to occur (Greenwald, 2014), commercial surveil-lance through Google, or 'surveillance capitalism,' is in place (Zuboff, 2015), and political uses and abuses of Facebook data have been alleged (Cadwalladr, 2017). We are thus witnessing a new stage in the evolution of political trust, with technologies that reshape and exploit relations of trust and distrust.

The genius of Jeremy Bentham's ideal prison, the Panopticon, was that direct surveillance did not need to occur at all times (Bentham, 1995). Without infliction of bodily pain, the inmate would internalize the principles of correction through the awareness that, at any moment, he *might* be under observation. Today's 'free' individual will increasingly be subject to a similar kind of self-awareness. Rather than being observed, or potentially observed, from a central space, however, the subject of the digital world feels and acts *as if* observable from all angles, at all times, even while mobile. This means weightless surveillance and accumulation for the big data companies, and an 'inside-out' panopticism to normalize the actions of the free and mobile. The smartphone and the ankle-bracelet perform similar tracking functions, but the former is much more informative.

Conclusion

We have considered so far how trust entered into the lexicon of English political philosophy in the seventeenth century, and the legacy particularly of Hobbes, Locke, Burke and J.S. Mill. Contemporary theory of trust reflects that heritage, especially Locke's; it also advances it, notably through the work of Luhmann and Giddens. No single general definition of trust can capture the varied forms of interactions, ethics and power-dynamics involved in trust, however, especially when we take account of the historical, technical and cultural changes through which trust is manifested.

I return, then, to a key question posed in the introduction: What doubts troubled philosophers sufficiently to make them write about trust at all? Setting aside the well-known historical-political upheavals of their times: for Hobbes, the basic doubt was about the gullibility of men who believe in false doctrines and trust pretenders, leading them into civil strife; whereas for Locke it was the problem of entrusting political powers to others whom one cannot know directly and who may become inclined to abuse that trust. Hobbes assumed that we may trust one another in a state of nature – although of course we wouldn't be as reckless as to do so. Locke says that we can and we ought to trust others, even in a state of nature, as it conforms to natural law and makes a community and a commonwealth possible.

The legacy of this theory of trust persists, or has been revived, but we now live in a world of massive, complex, global institutions, networks and systems, and the very meanings of trust, and the ways in which we find ourselves establishing trust, evolve accordingly. Trust is not a static or natural trait or ability; it has a history and it undergoes transformations. The constant redistribution of relations of trust that is occurring in the internet age need not surprise us, however, as a similar historical process has already come into effect through a medium that we all know well – money.

Notes

1 'Mill's theory dilutes universal suffrage by denying the right to vote to persons who cannot read, write, or do simple arithmetic, who pay no taxes, or who receive welfare (parish relief)' (Thompson, 1976, p. 98).
2 As Foucault wrote, referring to the threat of nuclear war, 'the power to expose a whole population to death is the underside of the power to guarantee an individual's continued existence' (Foucault, 1990, p. 137).
3 Between 1968, when Hardin's essay was published, and 2015, world population more or less doubled. For many human beings, moreover, the most precious freedom may be 'the freedom to breed.'
4 '[C]ertain societies can save substantially on transaction costs because economic agents trust one another in their interactions and therefore can be more efficient than low-trust societies, which require detailed contracts and enforcement mechanisms' (Fukuyama, 1995, p. 352).

5 Both Hobbes and Locke warned us not to take so much on trust. But, in their time, it was plausible that one could learn and master a science oneself, rather than rely on experts.
6 Financial credit rating is certainly not a new practice, however. It pre-dates the internet by several decades.
7 See Trooly's LinkedIn profile: www.linkedin.com/company/3718162 (last accessed, 20 November 2017).

References

Baker, T., and Simon, J. (2002). *Embracing risk: The changing culture of insurance and responsibility*. Chicago, IL: University of Chicago Press.

Bentham, J. (1995). *The panopticon writings*. London: Verso.

Bernstein, P. L. (1996). *Against the gods: The remarkable story of risk*. New York, NY: John Wiley.

Botsman, R. (2017). *Who can you trust?: How technology brought us together and why it might drive us apart*. New York, NY: Public Affairs.

Bromwich, D. (2014). *The intellectual life of Edmund Burke: From the sublime and beautiful to American independence*. Cambridge, MA: Belknap.

Cadwalladr, C. (2017, May 7). *The great British Brexit robbery: How our democracy was hijacked*. Retrieved December 18, 2017, from The Guardian: www.theguardian.com/technology/2017/may/07/the-great-british-brexit-robbery-hijacked-democracy

Cairney, P. (2012). *Understanding public policy: Theories and issues*. Houndmills: Palgrave Macmillan.

Coleman, J. (1988). Social capital in the creation of human capital. *American Journal of Sociology, 94*(Supplement), S95–S120.

Daly, H. E. (1974). Steady-state economics versus growthmania: A critique of the orthodox conceptions of growth, wants, scarcity, and efficiency. *Policy Sciences, 5*(2), 149–167.

Daly, H. E. (2015). *From uneconomic growth to a steady-state economy*. Cheltenham: Edward Elgar.

Davies, N. (1999). *The Isles: A history*. London: Macmillan.

Delhey, J., Newton, K., and Welzel, C. (2011). How general is trust in 'most people'? Solving the radius of trust problem. *American Sociological Review, 76*(5), 786–807.

Dunn, J. (1984). The concept of 'trust' in the politics of John Locke. In R. Rorty, J. Schneewind, and Q. Skinner (Eds.), *Philosophy in history: Essays on the historiography of philosophy* (pp. 279–301). Cambridge: Cambridge University Press.

Dunn, J. (1988). Trust and political agency. In D. Gambetta (Ed.), *Trust: Making and breaking cooperative relations* (pp. 73–93). Oxford: Basil Blackwell.

Farr, J. (2004). Social capital: A conceptual history. *Political Theory, 32*(6), 6–33.

Field, J. (2008). *Social capital* (2nd ed.). Abingdon: Routledge.

Foucault, M. (1990). *The history of sexuality. Volume 1: An introduction*. New York, NY: Vintage.

Fukuyama, F. (1995). *Trust: The social virtues and the creation of prosperity*. New York, NY: Free Press.

Gellner, E. (1988). Trust, cohesion, and the social order. In D. Gambetta (Ed.), *Trust: The making and breaking of cooperative relations* (pp. 142–157). Oxford: Basil Blackwell.

Giddens, A. (1990). *The consequences of modernity*. Stanford, CA: Stanford University Press.

Granovetter, M. (1985). Economic action and social structure: The problem of embeddedness. *American Journal of Sociology, 91*(3), 481–510.

Greenwald, G. (2014). *No place to hide: Edward Snowden, the NSA, and the U.S. surveillance state.* New York, NY: Metropolitan Books.

Hardin, G. (1968). The tragedy of the commons. *Science, 162*(3859), 1243–1248.

Hardin, R. (1999). Do we want trust in government? In M. E. Warren (Ed.), *Democracy and trust* (pp. 22–41). Cambridge: Cambridge University Press.

Herreros, F. (2012). The state counts: State efficacy and the development of trust. *Rationality and Society, 24,* 483–509.

Hetherington, M. J. (2005). *Why trust matters: Declining political trust and the demise of American liberalism.* Princeton, NJ: Princeton University Press.

Hill, C. (1980). *The century of revolution: 1603–1714.* London: Routledge.

Hobbes, T. (1998). *Leviathan.* Oxford: Oxford University Press.

Hooghe, M., and Stolle, D. (2003). *Generating social capital: Civil society and institutions in comparative perspective.* New York, NY: Palgrave Macmillan.

Hume, D. (1969). *A treatise of human nature.* London: Penguin.

Locke, J. (1948). *The second treatise of civil government and a letter concerning toleration.* Oxford: Basil Blackwell.

Locke, J. (1965). *Essays on the law of nature.* Oxford: Clarendon Press.

Locke, J. (1980). *Second treatise of government.* Indianapolis, IN: Hackett.

Luhmann, N. (1988). Familiarity, confidence, trust: Problems and alternatives. In D. Gambetta (Ed.), *Trust: Making and breaking cooperative relations* (pp. 94–107). Oxford: Basil Blackwell.

Manin, B. (1997). *The principles of representative government.* Cambridge: Cambridge University Press.

Meadows, D. H., Meadows, D. L., Randers, J., and Behrens, W. W. (1972). *The limits to growth.* New York, NY: Universe Books.

Muldrew, C. (1998). *The economy of obligation.* Houndmills: Macmillan.

Newton, K. (2008). Trust and politics. In D. Castiglione, J. W. van Deth, and G. Wolleb (Eds.), *The handbook of social capital* (pp. 241–272). Oxford: Oxford University Press.

Numao, J. (2013). Locke on atheism. *History of Political Thought, 34*(2), 252–272.

Pitkin, H. F. (1967). *The concept of representation.* Berkeley, CA: University of California Press.

Putnam, R. (1993). The prosperous community: Social capital and public life. *The American Prospect, 13,* 35–42.

Ricks, T. E. (2017, October 10). *What a new U.S. Civil War might look like.* Retrieved December 7, 2017, from Foreign Policy: http://foreignpolicy.com/2017/10/10/what-a-new-u-s-civil-war-might-look-like/

Rittel, H. W., and Webber, M. M. (1973). Dilemmas in a general theory of planning. *Policy Sciences, 4*(2), 155–169.

Robbins, B. G. (2011). Neither government nor community alone: A test of state-centered models of generalized trust. *Rationality and Society, 23*(3), 304–346.

Rothstein, B. (2015). Guity as charged? Human well-being and the unsung relevance of political science. In G. Stoker, B. G. Peters, and J. Pierre (Eds.), *The relevance of political science* (pp. 84–103). London: Palgrave.

Smith, R. J. (1981). Resolving the tragedy of the commons by creating private property rights in wildlife. *Cato Journal, 1*(2), 439–468.

Spencer, V. A. (2018). Human fallibility and Locke's doctrine of toleration. In V. A. Spencer (Ed.), *Toleration in comparative perspective* (pp. 41–60). Lanham, MA: Lexington.

Thomas, K. (1993). Cases of conscience in seventeenth-century England. In J. Morrill, P. Slack, and D. Woolf (Eds.), *Public duty and private conscience in seventeenth-century England* (pp. 29–56). Oxford: Clarendon Press.

Thompson, D. F. (1976). *John Stuart Mill and representative government*. Princeton, NJ: Princeton University Press.

Zuboff, S. (2015). Big other: Surveillance capitalism and the prospects of an information civilization. *Journal of Information Technology, 30*(1), 75–89.

5 Money
Trust in action?

A symbolically rich, yet very common, activity among friends is to meet for coffee. The tastes and aromas, the stimulant effects, the varieties of coffee and the aesthetics of café design, taken all together, form opportunities or pretexts to meet others, to see strangers, and to be seen, and this produces experiences of cultural and symbolic importance, as well as trade and employment – or a rich mixture of things, values, contracts and people (Mauss, 2002, p. 33). If two people meet for coffee, there are numerous factors that contribute to deciding who pays, such as the depth of friendship, whether it is a date, or the frequency of such meetings. But, as Mauss would have it, there is no such thing as a 'free gift' – no act of giving operates without somehow establishing or developing mutual ties and mutual obligations, consolidating or changing the meaning and structure of social bonds: 'the gift necessarily entails the notion of credit' (2002, p. 46). The appropriate observance of giving, receiving and reciprocating creates and discharges 'credit' – it makes persons and their social bonds believable; it gives them structure – and so it consolidates mutual esteem and *trust*.

If I pay for coffee for a friend, then it may be in return for an earlier favour, or it may assume that the gift will be reciprocated in some way in future. Trust entails such gestures, mostly on an unspoken basis. Moreover, having supplied us with the coffee, we were trusted by the café to pay before we leave. The simplest commercial transactions entail trust. Breaches of personal trust, such as failure to reciprocate a gift, may lead to the informal sanction of a reluctance to advance a friendship; while the trust inherent in everyday commerce (to deliver goods and to pay for them) is backed also by law. The state enforces its monopoly to declare a currency by fiat; it bans counterfeit currency; it requires creditors to accept legal tender in payment of debts; in turn, the state will always accept its own currency in payment of taxes. In the café, I may pay with notes and coins, or by an electronic transfer which may be either an immediate debit, or a charge against my credit account. The café-owner and I have no need to inquire into one another's creditworthiness. But can it properly be said that, in concluding the sale, we are *trusting* the currency or the system of electronic payments?

Historically, it took people a long time to accept paper money. The practice originated in China, and the Mongol rulers of the thirteenth century enforced, on pain of death, an obligation to accept paper notes and a ban on counterfeit.

When Marco Polo reported on paper money to his readers in Europe, there was disbelief. And for several centuries after that in Europe, coinage remained 'the only acceptable and trusted form of money,' in spite of its repeated debasement by rulers (Davies, 2002, p. 180). Today, we have come to accept (with little resistance) immaterial electronic representations of money, but our apparent 'trust' in money, in financial systems and in electronic systems of payments must still be backed by force of law, although with penalties less severe than death. That 'trust' may be shaken from time to time by major financial crises, such as in 2008, but 'distrust' does not, paradoxically, stop us from using the currency and electronic payments. We have little choice, in spite of the rise of alternative cryptocurrencies such as Bitcoin.

Notions of trust have been relied upon frequently in contemporary theories of money, to explain its liquidity, acceptability and stability.[1] But, are trust and money inter-related in a conceptually robust way? This chapter examines how trust came to be integrated into understandings of money, and questions the role of trust in this context. Trust is treated here as integral to relations of mutual recognition in which the parties regard one another as free agents who undertake to exchange things, or willingly to reciprocate actions that respect and benefit one another. Trust may be a factor in relations ranging from polite conversation to the deepest intimacy, but, in the present chapter we are looking at exchanges of goods. Trust has also been conceived of as a quality of social systems and our attitudes thereto, or as 'abstract trust' (Giddens, 1990), and this is pertinent to financial systems.

Money or credit? Back to Locke

To show that trust and money were once treated separately, as concepts, and how they later came to be closely integrated, we may consider three significant historical 'signposts.' The first is provided by John Locke and Charles Davenant in the seventeenth century; the second by Georg Simmel at the end of the nineteenth; the third by Niklas Luhmann in the late twentieth.

Although Locke's social contract is founded upon trust, in Chapter V of the *Second Treatise* he expounds a 'metallist' theory of the origin of money, but without a single use of the word 'trust' (Locke, 1980). In his essay 'Some Considerations of the Consequences of the Lowering of Interest, and Raising the Value of Money' (1692), the word 'trust' is used only three times (in more than 40,000 words), and one of those is in the sense of secretive associations or conspiracies (Locke, 1991). Locke was aiming to discourage the imposition of a maximum interest-rate, and he addresses the general question of money-supply, where 'money' is regarded solely in its metallic forms. He ponders how much 'money' should be in circulation in order to meet the needs of the various classes, including labourers. The latter, he says, live 'from hand to mouth,' and so they and their employers must hold certain sums of ready cash at all times. Labourers cannot be expected to 'live upon Trust till next Pay Day.' 'This the Farmer and Tradesman could not well bear, were it every Labourer's Case, and every one to be trusted' (Locke, 1991, p. 236).

For 'living upon trust,' we might today prefer to say 'living on credit' – but, in the absence of today's institutionalized credit facilities, this would have been a local and informal understanding of credit. In sixteenth- and seventeenth-century England, most gold and silver coin was held by the wealthy or in the royal treasury. At the neighbourhood or village level, informal tokens made of various materials were common, or people simply used their credit. Market transactions in towns and villages occurred between friends and acquaintances who could estimate one another's reputation or 'credit' – a term which had not yet separated into financial and social meanings. Friends and business acquaintances could, from time to time, reckon up their exchanges, and the debtor could then pay the balance, as transactions could be valued in the accepted monetary unit. So, while people were largely making cashless transactions – in kind, *quid pro quo* – they applied a monetary unit of account in order to keep balances. Moreover, the closely networked social atmosphere of towns and villages pushed people into observing codes of behaviour in order to maintain their reputation within 'emotionally resonant economic bonds of trust and dependence' (Muldrew, 1993, p. 183). As credit-relations became legally complicated, such customary uses of debt also became 'discredited,' however, due to the frequency of informal disputes and formal litigation (Graeber, 2014). So, although Locke believed firmly in the foundational socio-political role of trust (Dunn, 1984), in his writing on money, trust plays no role. 'Money' is metallic coin and this does not entail trust. In contrast, credit basically *is* trust. Money and credit (or trust) are treated as quite different.

Charles Davenant (1656–1714), a contemporary of Locke, gives us a further example of the correlation of credit and trust in a piece entitled 'On Credit, and the Means and Methods by which it may be restored' (1697). We give up 'trusting the public, or private persons,' he points out, when they are guilty of fraud or bad faith, or when they are at risk of defaulting on their debts. But, if the problems are only accidental, and the parties (be they private persons or the government) can provide assurances of sufficient funds, then 'men's minds will become quiet and appeased' and they will be inclined to trade and cooperate. The prosperity of a nation is not simply a matter of the stock of goods at its disposal; helping others and relying upon credit is essential, as no-one succeeds independently. Hence, 'trust and confidence in each other, are as necessary to link and hold a people together, as obedience, love, friendship, or the intercourse of speech' (Davenant, 1967, pp. 151–152). This statement is about economic prosperity as much as social cohesion. For Davenant, trust and credit are seen in personal terms as well as in the context of the public treasury and national economy. His perspective switches from one to the other with ease. Credit is quite distinct from the metallic money-commodity, however.

Locke and Davenant were both writing about money with public audiences and policy aims in mind, but the relevant points for the present are: first, that these two authors separate *money* (as coinage) from social relations of *credit*; secondly, credit is based on trust, but money is not. Indeed, credit is a practice of trust itself.

Fast-forwarding to the second theoretical 'signpost,' Georg Simmel argued (contrary to Locke) that money, the measure of value, need not have any intrinsic value in itself. Money represents value in its abstracted form, as an expression of the relativity of things of value. By the nineteenth century, going by his account, credit had become the norm of the wealthy, signifying the buyer's social distinction as gentleman. Credit demands that the debtor be trusted, and so it reinforces the social distance between classes. It is 'the common man' who uses cash. Simmel's monumental text on money does not rely heavily on the concept trust, but, on the occasions when he does use the word *Vertrauen*, he argues that trust is inherent to all forms of money, *including* metallic coin, unlike Locke and Davenant. He breaks down the supposed opposition between coin and credit. Metallic coin involves credit in two ways. First, its use requires 'public confidence [*Vertrauen*] in the issuing government,' or a trusted third party. Secondly, the stability and acceptability of any coinage requires 'confidence [*Vertrauen*] in the ability of an economic community to ensure that the value given in exchange for an interim value, a coin, will be replaced without loss' (Simmel, 2004, p. 178). Simmel saw the continuity between coin and credit, both relying upon trust and confidence.

In the late twentieth century, as our third 'signpost,' Niklas Luhmann expounded the sociological significance of trust [*Vertrauen*] underpinning money.

> Generalized trust in the institution of money, then, replaces, through one all-inclusive act, the countless individual, difficult demonstrations of trust which would be necessary to provide a sure foundation for life in a co-operative society.
> (Luhmann, 1979, p. 51)

Were it not for money, a shopkeeper would have to run a credit-check on, and extract a promise from, every new customer. This recasts Simmel's views about money as a factor that transforms social relations. But, for Luhmann, money necessitates and creates a new kind of trust *per se* – a 'generalized' institutional trust. These three historical and theoretical 'signposts,' represented by Locke, Simmel and Luhmann, show that trust has not always been assumed to play a part in the social institution of money, but the two have 'grown together' in the history of the theory of money. A further summary of theories of money will help to put this in context.

Three theories of money

Monetary theory has long been concerned with how money originated and evolved, and explanations differ depending on whether one looks primarily at the material commodity of money (traditionally, gold and silver), or the centralized state and financial institutions (the chartalist theory), or the creditor–debtor relationship.

The most well-known approach is the commodity theory, and again we can appeal to Locke for an explanation. He asks us to imagine a primitive economy that lacks an agreed medium of exchange such as coins, and that has few commodities and only a rudimentary level of specialization of labour. It is assumed that the only way to give effect to economic exchange under such conditions is direct barter, a quantity of one commodity for another. If one has a surplus of plums, for example, one would be willing to exchange some of them, before they perish and are wasted, for a supply of nuts. Ultimately, traders in such an economy will begin tacitly to agree upon one or two metallic commodities as common means of payment. Gold and silver are especially suited to this role for a number of reasons: they do not corrode; they are scarce and highly desirable, and hence economically valuable in themselves; they are malleable and easily struck into units of equal weight; they are readily stored and transported. Such coins can be hoarded without spoilage and without harm to anyone else's rights, and exchanged at will for the perishable goods that we need (Locke, 1980). All of this could have evolved, it is thought, prior to, or outside of, the social contract. It is the cumulative work of many traders, not the issue or edict of the sovereign. When civil government is instituted, its job is to protect property rights and to standardize and guarantee the value of the currency. Eventually, as banking and trade become more specialized and undertaken over long distances and time-spans, systematized practices of credit emerge, initially through such instruments as bills of exchange. So, the basic evolution is from barter, to metallic money, to 'paper' money and credit. This emergence-from-barter theory appeared first in the work of the Italian banker Bernardo Davanzati (1529–1606) (Graeber, 2014, p. 403), and Locke gave it another push. In Adam Smith's *The Wealth of Nations* (Smith, 1999; first published 1776), it found a place as a standard dogma within the discipline of economics, and it remains so today.

Influenced by Hegel, Marx took a dialectical approach, relating money and value to alienated labour and the social relations of production; but nonetheless, he too adopts an emergence-from-barter theory – or, a theory of the money-commodity (Nelson, 2001). According to Marx, money is a special commodity removed from the system of relative values of all other commodities, to become a 'universal equivalent.' This particular commodity – gold – is used to signify all exchange-values in a market by being *excluded* as a commodity. The natural properties of gold make it more effective in this role than any other commodity, even though, in theory, any commodity, such as linen, could perform the same function. Hence, 'money is by nature gold and silver' (Marx, 1990, p. 183). The arrival of a universal equivalent eliminates the problems posed by barter. From that base, Marx accounts for the transformation into capital, and then complex forms of credit and 'fictitious capital' (Jessop, 2013).

Crude commodity theories, such as Locke's, assume that, without money in the form of coins, or similar durable medium of exchange, people must have had to barter all the time. And yet there is no historical or ethnographic evidence that this was ever the case, either in general or in any particular society; no historian, explorer or anthropologist ever found the mythical society of barterers (Graeber, 2014). Moreover, the earliest coins appear to have been too valuable and too scarce for use in everyday commerce (Wray, 1998). The story of how money replaced barter lacks evidence.

If commodities are 'objects produced for sale on the market,' then money is not a commodity; it is 'a token of purchasing power which, as a rule, is not produced at all, but comes into being through the mechanism of banking or state finance'

(Polanyi, 2001, pp. 75–76). Commodity theories may have served a function of 'naturalizing' money in a material thing, thus shoring up people's willingness to use it. But today's currencies are 'self-referential.' Gold is now a commodity valued in dollars, rather than the dollar being pegged to a gold standard. Most of our transactions are conducted electronically, often automatically, and the abstract immateriality of money is plain to see.

The chartalist theory, by contrast with the commodity theory, is often seen as 'heterodox.' It argues that a centralized authority had to declare an abstract monetary unit of account and a means of payment to represent it. The state declares the unit and the 'thing' that stands for it; those who agree to a contract can then confidently denominate the value of goods in terms of that unit and use the 'money-thing' to discharge their debts. This theory points, for historical backing, to the hierarchical structures of ancient civilizations and their customary payments of rents, tithes, taxes and fines to royal palaces and temples (Wray, 2002). These obligations would originally have been discharged in basic commodities, especially grains, or in labour, but the central authority could also specify unit-weights of precious metals as equivalents. Minted coins began to be issued by rulers (but only many centuries after the first appearance of money-of-account) in order to facilitate the payment of taxes and fines into the ruler's own treasury. Coins may also have rewarded soldiers or other servants of the state who did not produce agricultural goods (Peacock, 2003). But, whatever form money took, its validity 'is secured by its acceptance by the state as payment of taxes and in payment by the state for the goods and services of its citizens' (Ingham, 2004, p. 55). Currency, whatever its material or immaterial basis, *is* the currency because the state imposes a tax in order to purchase military or other public services, or to accumulate a basic commodity such as grain. It issues a monetary token as evidence of its debt, and then accepts it back from its subjects in payment of taxes or penalties. Subjects can trade in coins (or whatever else represents money) among themselves in order to earn more of these tokens and to meet their tax obligations to the treasury, thus participating in a monetized market that was created by the actions of rulers – and not in a 'free' market. The institution and evolution of monetary systems are seen then to progressively rationalize and transform economic behaviours and social interactions over the course of history.[2]

Another version of chartalist theory links the appearance of monetary rationality to the ancient Germanic legal codes based on *wergild* (Grierson, 1978). These compensatory codes set the 'price' of a man's life, depending on rank, extrapolated to include lesser damages such as injury, insult or other kinds of harm or loss (Hough, 2006). They could be denominated in terms of commodities, such as cattle or furs, in the absence of coin. These codes turned private feuds – which bear the risk of ongoing retaliation – into enforceable obligations that discharged a 'debt' to the victim. They may have been the source of shared rationality based on abstract units of value, or they may have supported the idea of money in an age when coinage itself was in short supply (Peacock, 2003). Hence, money may have evolved through practices such as 'blood money' (or *diya* in Islamic law) and 'bride price' – 'a unit of account to measure debts for the purpose of paying fines in compensation' (Wray, 2013, p. 84). Rulers regulated payments in order to settle disputes or damages between subjects, in the common interests of peace and social cohesion. Duelling, looting and robbery were long considered to be legitimate and honourable for nomadic societies and conquerors,[3] but systems such as *wergild* regulate litigation and compensation with things of equivalent values, governing reciprocity collectively and subjecting all actors to the same monetized system, while *in*equality of status is recognized and preserved. Chartalist theory holds that money does not arise originally from the initiative of mutually respectful traders who needed to overcome the 'inconvenience' or the 'transaction costs' of barter. Instead, the origins of money are in state coercion, including penalties, taxes, tributes and restitution. Hence, 'a system of legal compensation for personal injuries, at once inviting mutual comparison and affecting every member of the community' is likely to lie behind most notions of money as 'a general measure of value' (Grierson, 1978, p. 19).

Credit theories of money begin, in contrast, from the point of view of interpersonal relations of mutual obligation and exchange – although they do overlap with chartalism, as they eventually appeal to the state, or other central authority.[4] Credit theory assumes that any exchange of goods creates a credit, which immediately implies a debt. Not even a gift comes free of some such obligation, as Mauss observed. Often, the debt may be formalized in a promise to return something of equivalent value. A socially or legally valid debt-obligation may be recognized, and an expectation of repayment created, in a variety of gestures – be it a handshake, an IOU, a pawned object, the offer of a gold coin or credit card. A good or benefit is offered, and a promise to reciprocate, or to repay with something of an equivalent value, is made in reply. Many different forms of exchanges may create such debts or obligations, in the broader sense, but not all debts are *monetary* in nature. Money as legal tender has a special role or force, because, whenever sufficient legal tender is offered, the debt is discharged 'on the spot.' For debt to be regarded as money, however, 'it must be able to circulate at a constant nominal value among the members of an economic community' (Bjerg, 2016, p. 64).

Social life involves many promises and obligations, but only some of our promises require money in fulfilment. Money represents the promise to pay, and also fulfils it. This self-fulfilling promise is accepted due to our confident expectation that all others in the same economic community will readily accept it too, at the same face-value. And, as users today of electronic payment systems, we know that money need not appear in the physical forms of notes and coins. It is basically immaterial. The 'monetary circuit' approach accepts that private credit–debt relations appear prior to commonly accepted currencies and monetary policies. It is critical of the commodity theory of money, as this 'confuses the material support of money [such as coins and notes] with money itself' (Parguez and Seccareccia, 2000, p. 106). And it introduces an important third party into the account of credit-relations: the banks, including a central bank. The banks are constantly creating and destroying money, in the form of debts that are issued freely and *ex nihilo* to firms and individuals who spend these debts in order to meet their needs for resources. These agents are then committed to repaying the loans through their own efforts to produce goods and services or to sell their assets, thereby cancelling their debts towards the banks as well as the debts that the banks 'issued on themselves to finance the loans' (Parguez and Seccareccia, 2000, p. 103). Credit theory blends into the chartalist theory in that the acceptability of money (in whatever form it takes) is ultimately protected and enforced by the state. Even when people trade goods and services 'on credit,' they are most likely nonetheless to reckon up the balance using the state's monetary unit-of-account.

The evolving role of trust

Looking back, then, to Locke's theory of money, we can observe a significant shift in the discursive relationship between trust and money. For Locke, money is coined precious metal; it is not reliant upon trust, as it is inherently valuable. 'Living on trust,' or credit, is treated differently. Although the commodity theory of money persists today, especially in the erroneous notion that money overcame the 'inconvenience' of barter, more complex theories that view money in the context of social relations and state power emerged in the twentieth century. Simmel saw all 'moneys' as forms of credit, and hence broke down the Lockean distinction between the two. Consequently, trust has become an important theme for many theorists of money, as an explanatory device and as a social 'good' that underlies monetary policies and stable currencies. For example, Ingham states: 'Money is a promise, and the production of a promise involves trust' (2004, p. 74). Historically, however, enforcement and the threat of punishment must have preceded any such 'trust' in currencies (Ingham, 2004, pp. 55, 65; see also Wray, 1998). In order to accept – indeed to trust – money, someone initially had to inflict pain, or to beat and burn it into us.[5] Ingham further hypothesizes a transformation in the relations of trust when (initially purely private) credit-based exchanges are incorporated into the state and extended beyond the 'closed circuits' of *interpersonal* trust, to be accepted by a whole community.

> The creation of extensive monetary spaces requires social and political relations that necessarily exist independently of any networks of exchange transactions. The extension of monetary relations across time and space requires *impersonal trust and legitimacy*. Historically, this has been the work of states. . . . The essential monetary space for a genuinely impersonal sphere of exchange [in credit-money] was eventually provided by states.
> (Ingham, 2004, pp. 187, 122, original italics)

A similar idea, focused on 'financial institutions,' has it that:

> credit-related trust is transformed from a private and subjective into a social and objective relationship as a result of the practices of financial institutions. The capitalist credit system is a set of institutional mechanisms that turn trust into a formal, objective, measurable, and therefore social, relationship.
> (Lapavitsas, 2007, p. 418)

There could be no uniform means to achieve such a transformation from *inter*personal (private, subjective) into *im*personal (social, objective) trust, as it would be contingent upon historical circumstances, but it could not happen without legitimate forces of the state. In a similar vein, Luhmann had referred vaguely to 'one all-inclusive act' that 'replaces' trust at the level of individuals with a 'generalized trust' in money (1979, p. 51). Lascaux argues that society's 'collective agreement' on the acceptability of money depends upon a regulated hierarchical institutional structure, with state money enjoying the highest levels of trust, and hence political authority lends the system legitimacy (2012, p. 77). So, trust has become a core explanatory concept for theories of money, alongside the state.

Trust in money today

Modern commerce depends upon trade between complete strangers who may not even speak the same language, and cash makes such transactions convenient. The impersonal or abstract trust that appears to be 'generated' by modern money and monetary policies underpins the willingness to hold money, or the expectation that others will accept our money and that 'our claim on future goods will be met' (Ingham, 2000, p. 29). The use of cash in the fiat-currency system has some disadvantages, however. It is prone to being stolen, and it disguises criminal activity, money-laundering and tax-evasion. On the other hand, it facilitates trading in situations where the new electronic systems do not extend or are too expensive to install, such as casual second-hand trading. When cash passes hands, buyer and seller do not have to recognize or trust one another – and no credit-check is required – so long as both parties understand modern money. Cash 'homogenizes' the actors in an economic community, as it works the same way, and holds an equivalent value, for anyone in possession of it, impartially and impersonally, regardless of 'identity.' In spite of inequality of incomes and wealth, the cash-nexus produces a common rationality for the comparison of values. In cash, one's trust (according to the theory) is placed in the issuing authority, a state-sanctioned central bank, and in the economy as a whole. With electronic credit card transactions, one's trust is also an abstract trust in the system of payments.

The digital revolution again transforms the money–trust relation. For instance, Birch (2014) claims that 'identity is the new money.' Although identity is routinely verified by banks when someone opens an account or seeks credit, new technologies will automate such processes, bringing credit-checks into everyday transactions, including peer-to-peer electronic payments, mediated by online networks that automate personal recognition as well as payment.

> I wander up to the trader to buy a hot dog and through his Google Glasses my face is outlined in green, which means that the system recognizes me and that I have good credit. The trader winks at me, and a message pops up on my phone informing me that I am being charged £1. I press 'OK.'
>
> (Birch, 2014, 947/1609)

The trader would not have to recognize the buyer by face or by name as 'the system recognizes me.' The *system* automates the credit-check; the participants 'trust' the system. Trust-relations would thus change from an abstract trust in an impersonal monetary form (a note issued by a central bank) to a trust in algorithms that automatically identify persons by facial recognition and confirm (or deny) their creditworthiness.

> So what will link changing identities with changing money as these trends converge? In a word, trust. In *a world based on trust*, it will be reputation rather than regulation that will animate trust in economic exchange.
>
> (Birch, 2014, 173/1609, italics added)

To cite another example of the extraordinary reliance upon 'trust' as an explanatory factor:

> Trust obviates the need for money, and money without trust has no value. Perhaps it is trust [not money] that makes the world go round.
>
> (King, 2016, p. 83)

So, we often act on trust without the mediation of money, and indeed, it is partly because money is *not* exchanged that we call it 'trust.' Among family and friends, an offer of money in exchange for gifts or gestures of kindness, or money as a gift in itself, can cause bewilderment or give offence, and there are diverse customs and norms governing relations between money and gift (Zelizer, 1997). But, it seems, a society cannot sustain the value of its money without some form of trust – and so this 'trust in money' must be trust of a different *kind* than that which is observed between friends when, say, they share belongings or tasks. Trust, King implies, is somehow more fundamental than money – it is money's *sine qua non* – and yet we cannot quantify trust. It is simply 'there,' and it 'makes the world go round.'

Does trust help to *explain* money, as an economic institution and/or as social relations, or does it only obfuscate material inequality and political subjection? Going by the theorists reviewed so far, a level of impersonal trust is necessary if specially printed paper (for instance) is to achieve recognition and use as money; while at the same time modern money and its institutions are considered to transform trust itself from its basic interpersonal form into an impersonal, generalized or abstract form. There may be circular reasoning here: trust is necessary for, and yet subject to, evolving monetary institutions and practices.

One falls back upon vague and circular reasoning when appealing to faith, confidence or trust in currencies and payment systems in order to explain money's ubiquity, why people use it, and what prevents hyper-inflation or mass financial panics. Such vaguely defined theories evade questions of ideology and power (Ganßmann, 1988; Ingham, 2000). If trust and confidence are, in any sense, fundamental to money and to the banking system, then they could surely be called into question due to real-world financial crises, however (Dow, 2013; Kennedy, 2000).

The trust placed in 'trust' as an explanatory factor in this contemporary theory of money requires further critical thought.

It is appropriate to say that I trust a friend to repay me for a loan. But trust may have little to do with the institution of money itself. The singular 'all-inclusive act' or the 'transformation' that generates a supposed impersonal or social form of trust from its interpersonal or private foundations is merely presumed and not explained. One could as well say that we use money precisely because *we do not want to trust anyone*. We relinquish the burden of trusting the other for a common systemic estimation of values, or reliance upon 'what average opinion believes average opinion to be' (J.M. Keynes, quoted in Dostaler and Maris, 2000, p. 249). But this may not need to be characterized as a common or higher order of trust.[6]

Is money inimical to trust?

Contrary, then, to the claim that money is based in trust, one may argue that money can only debase, distort or confound the expression of the human capabilities and values that we demonstrate when we trust. In his 'Economic and Philosophical Manuscripts' (1844), Marx suggests that a rich coward can pay for a bodyguard, and hence be brave; a lonely person with cash can pay a prostitute, and hence be loved. But genuinely expressed courage and love elude them. Money produces qualities without our having to will or express or possess those qualities ourselves. It does so by universalizing and abstracting all values, but at the expense of debasing them and confounding them with their own negation. Money makes the customer welcome, and the transaction is 'trusted' without the buyer and seller needing to establish an interpersonal trust any deeper than a temporary civility. Money brings trust into an exchange, without the parties needing to be genuinely trust*worthy*. Conversely, money depends upon trust itself, but only in an abstract and universalized form, emptied of its human significance (Marx, 1992, pp. 377–379). As an externalization and alienation of the human function of exchange, money brings slavery to its 'climax'; it becomes 'a veritable God' (1992, p. 260). Credit, moreover, represents 'perfidy taken to its logical conclusion' (1992, p. 264). Even though credit might appear to return us to interpersonal trust as the basis of exchange, this is an illusion, due to 'the mistrustful reflection about whether to extend credit or not.' Thus credit cultivates distrust, due to competitiveness and the risk of default, and the person herself appears as 'the incarnation of capital and interest . . . transformed into money.' When the 'moral recognition' of the person takes the form of credit, especially in the 'state-dominated' banking system, 'the sheer depravity of this morality, no less than the hypocrisy and egoism contained in that confidence in the state, emerges clearly and shows its true colours' (1992, p. 265). Marx might argue that the automated credit-checking and transfer system envisaged by Birch (2014; see above) would *not* lead to 'a world based on trust.' It would instead be a world based on distrust.

Given the unscrupulous behaviours of bankers, investors and credit-rating agencies that led to the 2008 financial crisis, one could easily renew the 'early' Marx's condemnation of the credit system. The 'later' Marx of *Capital* (volume 3) provided further relevant analysis, observing the tendency of the capitalist mode of production to become dominated by finance, credit and 'fictitious capital,' as the few gamble in order to increase their profits from the labour of the many (Jessop, 2013).

Credit-based capitalism is not the first system in which the moral worth or honour of a person is represented in terms of economic potential, however. Ancient customs of plunder or potlatch also equated wealth accumulation (and even destruction) with social status. Moreover, Marx's utopian evocation of 'a true community' that both activates the 'essence' of humanity and arises out of its members' own activities (1992, p. 265) is somewhat romantic. His moral condemnation of credit as 'perfidy' is analogous to the Marxist epistemological critique of ideology as 'false consciousness,' as a veil over, or obstacle to, knowledge. As Foucault put it, Marxist analysis viewed ideology as a 'negative element' that clouds, obscures or violates the subject's relations of knowledge. Political-economic conditions that impose ideology leave a 'mark' or 'stigma' on the subject, in this Marxist view, and hence they impose conditions, from the outside, onto a subject of knowledge 'who rightfully should be open to the truth' (Foucault, 2000, p. 15). Marx's idea that money debases human relationships mirrors the idea that ideology 'distorts' the truth. Marxism poses a 'scientific' truth against bourgeois power, and authentic human relationships against debased relationships mediated through money and property.

Foucault instead saw power as productive of 'truth,' and not as a distortion thereof. Political and economic conditions are the very grounds on which subjects of knowledge and orders of truth are formed. Similarly, money may be seen as productive and transformative in the realization of values and of qualities of relationships, including forms of trust. Rather than corrupting or debasing a 'true' or 'natural' trust, monetary relations change *how* people may trust and distrust; they are productive of the ordering principles by which economic agents appear and interact.

Money seen as distortion or debasement of 'real' or 'authentic' human values and self-expression, as a source of a cheapened trust, will not suffice. Such a critique presumes – but cannot show us – a natural or authentic trust that is unspoiled by powers, conventions and economic imperatives. Marx's distrust of how people use money may have a fine pedigree: Aristotle regarded it as 'unnatural' to use money for the purpose of accumulating more money (effectively disapproving of 'capital,' in Marx's terms); the monotheistic religions all prohibit usury, to differing degrees. The relation between money and trust requires more nuanced critical examination, however. All the same, Marx's critique of money is worth considering, as it challenges any naïve assumption that money and trust go together naturally.

Does trust explain money?

Theories of money struggle to explain the near-universal acceptance of currencies and the standardization of credit-relations in advanced modern economies. Money's acceptance, moreover, needs to be accounted for as more than just a matter of utility, confidence or freedom to choose (Ganßmann, 1988). Another approach is to point out that money is also a symbol that is fetishized in and of itself ('the love of money'), as both Keynes and Freud observed (Dostaler and Maris, 2000). Mauss suggested the origins of money may be found in talismans. As objects invested symbolically with *mana*, talismans and such sacred items are attributed with magico-religious power and are considered desirable or valuable by members of a community. As gifts or tokens of exchange, they can perform socially significant functions, such as paying honour, confirming inheritance, discharging obligations or settling disputes. Hence, as objects invested with immense value, they could have begun to perform a money-like role, or they may have been the artefacts from which some money-forms evolved. The power inherent in owning or exchanging a talisman could thus become a form of purchasing power, or a medium with which to settle debts, according to Mauss (cited in Orléan, 2013). Again, this is a speculative historical and ethnological hypothesis. But it stimulates our thinking about money as both means of payment and object of fascination and symbolic power. Money should not be defined merely by what it does in economic exchange, but also 'in its capacity to gain the general assent of the group as the legitimate expression of value' (Orléan, 2013, p. 55). The notion of 'value' at work here could be considered more broadly, if we are to account for the 'power' of money, or the common desire for and fascination with it. Orléan states that 'money is a matter of social belief' (2013, p. 61), although this is not to imply that it is 'imaginary' and hence lacks power. Our recognition of a currency is due to its symbolic representation and our 'belief' therein, and it has efficacy as such, in addition to its obvious practical utility.

According to Luhmann, 'there has to be a *presumption* that money itself enjoys *trust* for the mechanism [of decentralized transactions] to be workable' (Luhmann, 1979, p. 50, italics added). He and others (cited above) often resort to trust as an explanatory concept, even though they do not account for how that belief or 'presumption' arises. An appeal to 'trust in money' cannot *explain* money adequately, as trust itself eludes definition, it is culturally contingent, and it struggles against the competitiveness and individualism of markets.

> One wonders how monetary systems, which by all appearances are based largely on trust (mostly in the state and the central bank as 'lender of last resort') can be as stable as they are. If – as experience would suggest – little occasion exists in market transactions for individuals, groups, or social classes to cooperate or trust each other, there have to be quite elaborate institutional safeguards if promises (to pay) are to be as good as gold.
>
> (Ganßmann, 1988, p. 310)

The modern social beliefs in forms of money that are increasingly immaterial in character (from metal to paper to data) always had to be backed by the authority of the state – which, in turn, had to sustain belief in its own authority. But state authority ultimately relies upon force, which is not the same as trust.

Giddens' 'abstract trust' may help us understand monetary systems, as it does address complexity and institutional norms (Giddens, 1990; see Chapter 4). Our trust in complex systems is largely forced upon us, he claims, and alternatives are impracticable, if not impossible. There is no walking away from relations of 'abstract trust' when one feels betrayed; there is no Lockean 'withdrawal of consent.' One may profess not to trust 'the big banks,' but one is obliged to use their credit nonetheless. One may hoard wads of notes in a mattress, but that would still imply an 'abstract trust' in the state and its flimsy 'money-thing.' So, the modern subject has little or no choice but to 'trust' in complex computerized credit and payment systems and/or notes and coins. This verges on conflating trust with obedience, however, or with a *lack* of choice.[7] In Locke's world, trust may be tacit, but it was 'given' to institutions of government, and it can be rescinded. For many contemporary theorists, moreover, trust is regarded as a rational choice or belief. It is risky, but it wagers that others will act in one's own interests (see Chapter 2). By these definitions, one could also choose not to trust and not to cooperate, if necessary. So, if trust is supposed to be chosen, then it makes no sense to propose a 'trust' in an institution from which we cannot exit. Trust appears to be a construct that is poorly equipped to account for the acceptability and stability of money. Does it properly apply, as a concept, to our participation in contemporary systems of payments? Has it been used by theorists of money as a 'soft landing' to account for things that they cannot rigorously account for? We can make better sense of money, however, through the logic of 'forced choice.'

Money as a forced choice

Suppose you go into a shop to buy milk, and there are two brands, A and B. You can buy A *or* B. Logically, this 'or' may be exclusive or inclusive. If you only can afford, or only want, one of the two, then you have a choice of either A or B, but not both. Choosing A, however, did not *deprive* you of the choice of B – until the purchase is made. If you want to cater for different tastes and have enough money for two units, there is a third inclusive option: buy both A and B. So far, so good, applying the logic of 'the free market.'

There is, however, an alienating form of 'or' which operates quite differently. Your options are: have neither A nor B; or choose B and be deprived of A. This is the logical structure of a *forced* choice. The armed robber's injunction 'Your money or your life' does not present you with a choice between saving either your money or your life, because, if you 'choose' to hold on to your money, then you will lose your money anyway, after losing your life. You end up with neither. So, keeping 'your money' is not really an option you can choose. The only 'choice' is to surrender your money in the hope of saving your life. This has been decided in advance. Another example of a forced choice is 'Your freedom or your life' (when that means 'slavery or death'). The captive who reasons that there is no 'life' worth living without freedom ends up with neither; the slave lives (Dolar, 1993; Lacan, 1977).[8]

The forced choice in the contemporary discourse of trust and money, however, is *not* the same as 'your money or your life' (lose your money and live, or lose your life *and* your money). Instead it is: '*Our* money or your life' (accept Our money, or renounce normal life). I capitalize 'Our' to signify that this (non-)subject pertains to the big Other. No person actually says it to you. But if you reject 'Our money,' then you can't have the kind of life that is normative and recognized; you will be couch-surfing and dumpster-diving, living in the wilderness, and/or acquiring cash-free means of production and exchange. A 'cash-free' person may be living on other people's incomes and assets anyway; indeed, all humans began life, and end it, 'cash-free.' For those who renounce cash, a 'loss of life' does not refer to life in its animal, biological sense, but rather in its normative civil-social sense. One abandons a style of 'life,' but lives by occupying an exceptional status and adopting extraordinary habits – a choice that may, in some senses, be liberating. Such social withdrawal or exile continues a long tradition of ascetics, mendicants and renouncers such as Franciscans and Jainists. The forced 'life-choice' for the rest of us, however, is to accept 'Our money.' It is decided in advance that one will adopt the common monetary rationality in general, and a national currency in particular. This is a part of the process of emerging from the primary dependence on the family (the realm of gift-exchange) and participating in 'civil society' (in Hegel's sense) as a self-interested actor conscious of one's own freedom – a transformation made possible by the state.

The 'trust' that is attributed to those (almost all) of us who participate in monetary economies is a forced choice. It is like the injunction to trust and honour one's parents, given that one didn't choose them. The frequent use of the word 'trust' serves only a 'soft' explanatory purpose for theory of money. It masks the 'obedience,' or the forced choice, as if it were an authentically 'free' choice. It re-presents and naturalizes a contingent, yet almost inescapable, socio-economic order as a system in which we *choose* to participate. The ranges of products and brands, each with a price, produce a 'freedom to choose' – one may even say 'imperative to choose.' Money, perhaps more powerfully than any other social institution, constitutes the logic and the vector of choice itself. Money is said to give us choices; without money, we have fewer choices in life. But our 'acceptance' of money itself is a forced choice. Money is the product of force and it is a productive force in itself; to be universally 'acceptable,' it needs the force of law and, as a last resort, the force of arms. It is a rare and exceptional person who chooses not to use money.

The Bitcoin effect

The institutions of money that have become normative in national economies have, it is often said, transformed the interpersonal trust or credit required for individual acts of exchange into a collectivized or generalized trust. The state-sanctioned 'trusted third party' issues the currency – in metallic form or by fiat as a 'promissory note' on special paper – and law-enforcement agents police its use. The problem with the 'trusted third party' and its subsidiary 'trustees' (the banks) is that they deduct taxes and fees, and the banks have to be secured against rob-bers and hackers. A bank is vaulted and its ledger is not transparent to its users. Given this institutional power, 'trust' is invoked (unconvincingly, I argue) as the necessary foundation, asset and function of the business of banking.[9]

It is often claimed that the cryptocurrency Bitcoin eliminates the need for a state-sanctioned 'trusted third party' to intermediate between a multitude of strangers, and hence is 'trustless.' The ledger is public and the technology works by consensus, regardless of the trustworthiness of individual users. Nonetheless, Bitcoin is also premised upon trust – in this case, a trust in the inviolability of the code of the computer-programme that governs it, among other things (Qureshi, 2017). Cryptocurrencies 'substitute trust in a government money-issuer with trust in a computerized algorithm' (Vigna and Casey, 2015, p. 21). Independent computers on the Bitcoin network are constantly confirming transactions and maintaining the common transparent ledger. Exchanges are not centralized, however, and so the trust in the currency emerges from the common incentive to participate in the process of confirming information about transactions. The criti-cal factor is the blockchain. Although I have questioned the validity of attributing the acceptability of money to a vaguely specified 'trust,' Bitcoin is not able to be distinguished altogether from conventional national currencies on the grounds that it is supposedly 'trustless.' In as much as trust is seen as relevant or even essential to money, Bitcoin too relies on a further transformation of the structure of trust. It 'rearranges the rules of trust around which society manages exchanges of value' (Vigna and Casey, 2015, p. 27). All the same, state regulators have moved in to set rules around Bitcoin, which could culminate in cryptocurrencies coming under a 'trusted third party' model. Others have called for Bitcoin simply to be outlawed. Not everyone trusts in Bitcoin, and the force of law looms over it.

Conclusion

Materially, socially and conceptually, money and trust evolve, with a shared and complex history, as products of shifting social relations and technological innova-tion, and not as creatures of nature. They were not always spoken of in the same breath. In the seventeenth century, money was not regarded as founded upon trust. Today, by contrast, in spite of the extent of fraud, conflict and xenophobia in the world, it is possible for authors on money to envisage 'a world based on trust' – mediated via the internet – or to say 'trust makes the world go round.' So, just as trust is sometimes poorly 'explained' by reference to 'faith' – putting one intangible construct at the behest of another intangible construct – assertions that money relies upon (or simply *is*) trust are equally unsound. The tendency of some contemporary theories of money to fall back upon trust as an explanatory factor has to be critically examined; it may be stretching the uses and meaning of the word too far. If we find ourselves saying 'we have no choice but to trust in money,' then we should ask if we have imported the wrong concept.

Going back to the benign café scene that opened this chapter, one may observe different types of relationships characterized by trust, for different purposes and with variable depth and duration. But trust *describes* qualities of relationships and the interactions of people; it is not an explanation thereof. We should not rely on an abstract notion of trust as a conversation-stopper. In contrast, the fetishization of monetary objects is observably a social-psychological factor in common monetary practices. This fascination is engendered by an empty, self-referential signifier (sovereign, pound, dollar, etc.). It is backed up by the threat of retaliation for broken promises, the force of law, and the powers of the state – precisely because we prefer *not* to trust. With money, we can act as if people are *un*trustworthy, so long as we assume that the state's currency is, by force, sound legal tender.

If I pay someone for something with a banknote – rather than make a verbal promise to reciprocate in some way at a later time – then I need not be fully recognized or trusted. It is the banknote (not me) that is recognized by the vendor; I am simply a customer through whom the vendor's economic objective is met. There is no trust required, beyond a basic civility between strangers. The state's central bank, as issuer of the banknote, is not authentically a *trusted* third party, because the banknote's acceptability (as legal tender and non-counterfeit) is enforced by law. No-one really needs to be trusted, if it is a forced choice. The Bank of England's ten-pound note states, 'I promise to pay the bearer on demand the sum of ten pounds.' If you take the note back to the Bank of England, they can only give you another (a new polymer one) in return, and so the 'promise' is always already fulfilled. (Is such a self-fulfilling utterance effectively even a *promise*?). Outside of the Bank, in the marketplace, you are 'free' to use the note to purchase a wide range of things, but a vendor is not (strictly speaking) free to refuse it. The most one may say is that money represents a (largely taken-for-granted) expectation of acceptability and stability. All the same, the institutionalization and virtual universalization of money and credit in modern financial systems have altered or 'restructured' our practices of reciprocity in everyday social and economic relations, such as promising, giving and repaying. Transformations of monetary institutions, practices and rationalities mean transformations also in the ways in which people will trust or distrust one another. Using money in shops means we do not need to trust one another very much at all. Using money in friendships, on the other hand, may undermine trust. Holding cash instils distrust due to the fear of being robbed – and hence banks are useful. And, regardless of how much I may declare a distrust in government, central banks, commercial banks and bankers, I still use money and have a bank account.

Appealing to trust as an *explanation* or necessary condition for money is akin to pantheism: it invokes an immanent influence that is supposedly both ineffable and shared in common. Trust itself is frequently defined in terms of faith. Such a 'faith-based' explanation is conceptually weak and does not account for things that people actually do. The observable, almost-universal acceptability and use of money may better be accounted for by our preference for trusting no one to compensate us for taking possession of our goods – other than those closest to us (and, even then . . .). These conclusions about dis/trust are paradoxical. To encompass paradoxes, we should turn to dialectical theories, rather than the traditionally essentialist and 'univocal' approaches of liberal political-economic thought.

Notes

1 'Trust in money can exist in three principal dimensions: that the monetary promises will be kept and debts will be repaid on time and in a previously agreed form and amount (this condition can be termed "the liquidity of money"); that money will be widely accepted as a legal means of payment in discharging private and public obligations (the acceptability of money); and that the value of money relative to other goods and services will remain constant or, at least, vary only within predictable limits (the stability of money)' (Lascaux, 2012, p. 75).

2 Wray (1998) provides some documented historical evidence of this process from colonial governments.

3 It is disagreeable to 'the strong and autonomous personality' to have to 'efface himself' through subordination to the objective norms of a system of payment in exchange (Simmel, 2004, p. 97). See also Gellner (1988) for an account of trust and social cohesion among nomadic raiding parties.

4 Some treat chartalist and credit theories as distinct (Bjerg, 2016), others do not (Graeber, 2014).

5 This resembles the Nietzschean view that the capability to promise and hence to trust (in this case, in currencies) arises from the exercise or threat of state violence (Nietzsche, 1998).

6 Lapavitsas (2007) begins to address this problem when he reasons that, the more 'objective and social' trust becomes, the weaker its *moral* force, as it has to be specified more in writing and enforced by law.

7 An early example of the mutual implication of trust and obedience is in Hobbes's discussion of the treatment of prisoners of war following conquest and the acquisition of sovereignty. The vanquished may be 'trusted with his corporal liberty' provided he promises to obey or to pay his ransom, as that was his only way to preserve his life (Hobbes, 1998, p. 135). See Chapter 3.

8 As Hobbes would have had it, one is not really 'free' to choose death, as the law of nature compels us to preserve ourselves.

9 Lanchester (2013) asserts that banking 'is based on trust – on credit in more than just the economic sense. Trust is the banks' most important intangible asset: if it were lacking, none of us would ever use them for anything, ever. In a sense, trust is what banks do.'

References

Birch, D. (2014). *Identity is the new money*. London: Mondon Publishing Partnership (Kindle version).

Bjerg, O. (2016). How is bitcoin money? *Theory, Culture & Society, 33*(1), 53–72.

Davenant, C. (1967). On credit, and the means and methods by which it may be restored. In C. Whitworth (Ed.), *The political and commercial works of that celebrated writer Charles D'Avenant, LL.D.* (Vol. 1, pp. 150–167). Farnborough: Gregg Press.

Davies, G. (2002). *A history of money from ancient times to the present day*. Cardiff: University of Wales Press.

Dolar, M. (1993). Beyond interpellation. *Qui Parle? 6*(2), 75–96.

Dostaler, G., and Maris, B. (2000). Dr Freud and Mr Keynes on money and capitalism. In J. Smithin (Ed.), *What is money?* (pp. 235–256). London: Routledge.

Dow, S. C. (2013). The real (social) experience of monetary policy. In J. Pixley, and G. Harcourt (Eds.), *Financial crises and the nature of capitalist money: Mutual developments from the work of Geoffrey Ingham* (pp. 178–195). Houndmills: Palgrave Macmillan.

Dunn, J. (1984). The concept of 'trust' in the politics of John Locke. In R. Rorty, J. Schneewind, and Q. Skinner (Eds.), *Philosophy in history: Essays on the historiography of philosophy* (pp. 279–301). Cambridge: Cambridge University Press.

Foucault, M. (2000). *Power: Essential works of Foucault 1954–1984.* London: Penguin.

Ganßmann, H. (1988). Money – A symbolically generalized medium of communication? On the concept of money in recent sociology. *Economy and Society, 17*(3), 285–316.

Gellner, E. (1988). Trust, cohesion, and the social order. In D. Gambetta (Ed.), *Trust: The making and breaking of cooperative relations* (pp. 142–157). Oxford: Basil Blackwell.

Giddens, A. (1990). *The consequences of modernity.* Stanford, CA: Stanford University Press.

Graeber, D. (2014). *Debt: The first 5,000 years.* Brooklyn, NY: Melville House.

Grierson, P. (1978). The origins of money. *Research in Economic Anthropology, 1*(1), 1–35.

Hobbes, T. (1998). *Leviathan.* Oxford: Oxford University Press.

Hough, C. (2006). Wergild. In M. Schaus (Ed.), *Women and gender in medieval Europe: An encyclopedia* (pp. 831–832). New York, NY: Routledge.

Ingham, G. (2000). 'Babylonian madness': On the historical and sociological origins of money. In J. Smithin (Ed.), *What is money?* (pp. 16–41). London: Routledge.

Ingham, G. (2004). *The nature of money.* Cambridge: Polity Press.

Jessop, B. (2013). Credit money, fiat money and currency pyramids: Reflections on the financial crisis and sovereign debt. In J. Pixley, and G. Harcourt (Eds.), *Financial crises and the nature of capitalist money: Mutual developments from the work of Geoffrey Ingham* (pp. 248–272). Houndmills: Palgrave Macmillan.

Kennedy, P. (2000). A Marxist account of the relationship between commodity money and symbolic money in the context of contemporary capitalist development. In J. Smithin (Ed.), *What is money?* (pp. 194–216). London: Routledge.

King, M. (2016). *The end of alchemy: Money, banking, and the future of the global economy.* New York, NY: W.W. Norton.

Lacan, J. (1977). *The four fundamental concepts of psycho-analysis.* Harmondsworth: Penguin.

Lanchester, J. (2013, July 4). *Are we having fun yet?* Retrieved March 27, 2016, from London Review of Books: www.lrb.co.uk/v35/n13/john-lanchester/are-we-having-fun-yet

Lapavitsas, C. (2007). Information and trust as social aspects of credit. *Economy & Society, 36*(3), 416–436.

Lascaux, A. (2012). Money, trust and hierarchies: Understanding the foundations for placing confidence in complex economic institutions. *Journal of Economic Issues, 46*(1), 75–99.

Locke, J. (1980). *Second treatise of government.* Indianapolis, IN: Hackett.

Locke, J. (1991). Some considerations of the consequences of the lowering of interest, and raising the value of money, 1692. In P. H. Kelly (Ed.), *Locke on money* (Vol. 1, pp. 205–342). Oxford: Clarendon Press.

Luhmann, N. (1979). *Trust and power.* Chichester: Wiley.

Marx, K. (1990). *Capital* (Vol. 1). London: Penguin.

Marx, K. (1992). *Early writings.* London: Penguin.

Mauss, M. (2002). *The gift: The form and reason for exchange in archaic societies.* London: Routledge.

Muldrew, C. (1993). Interpreting the market: The ethics of credit and community relations in early modern England. *Social History, 18*(2), 163–183.

Nelson, A. (2001). Marx's theory of the money commodity. *History of Economics Review, 33*(1), 44–63.

Nietzsche, F. (1998). *On the genealogy of morals.* Oxford: Oxford University Press.

Orléan, A. (2013). Money: Instrument of exchange or social institution of value? In J. Pixley, and C. Harcourt (Eds.), *Financial crises and the nature of capitalist money: Mutual developments from the work of Geoffrey Ingham* (pp. 46–69). Houdmills: Palgrave Macmillan.

Parguez, A., and Seccareccia, M. (2000). The credit theory of money: The monetary circuit approach. In J. Smithin (Ed.), *What is money?* (pp. 101–123). London: Routledge.

Peacock, M. (2003). State, money, catallaxy: Underlaboring for a chartalist theory of money. *Journal of Post Keynesian Economics, 26*(2), 205–225.

Polanyi, K. (2001). *The great transformation: The political and economic origins of our time.* Boston, MA: Beacon Press.

Qureshi, H. (2017, December 18). *Why Bitcoin is not trustless.* Retrieved January 10, 2018, from Hackernoon: https://hackernoon.com/bitcoin-is-not-trustless-350ba0060fc9

Simmel, G. (2004). *The philosophy of money.* London: Routledge.

Smith, A. (1999). *The wealth of nations, books I–III.* London: Penguin.

Vigna, P., and Casey, M. J. (2015). *The age of cryptocurrency: How Bitcoin and digital money are challenging the global economic order.* New York, NY: St. Martin's Press.

Wray, L. R. (1998). *Understanding modern money.* Cheltenham: Edward Elgar.

Wray, L. R. (2002). State money. *International Journal of Political Economy, 32*(3), 23–40.

Wray, L. R. (2013). A new meme for money. In J. Pixley, and G. Harcourt (Eds.), *Financial crises and the nature of capitalist money: Mutual developments from the work of Geoffrey Ingham* (pp. 79–100). Houndmills: Palgrave Macmillan.

Zelizer, V. A. R. (1997). *The social meaning of money.* Princeton, NJ: Princeton University Press.

6 Hegel and Nietzsche

Analyzing the theory of money in the previous chapter has brought our thoughts about trust into the realm of political economy, to ask how it may or may not be 'at work' within complex global financial systems. This has problematized the presumed role for trust in distributed systems of payments, as the acceptance and use of money are a forced choice, bordering on obedience and structured in ways that are decided in advance. In as much as trust has a discursive role in monetary practices, this has a genealogy; trust and money have had to be brought together conceptually, in order to normalize money. Moreover, trust and distrust are mutually involved, rather than mutually exclusive. An electronic system of payments is clearly preferable to trusting every *un*trustworthy stranger who walks into our shop wanting something. Similarly, placing our trust in political representatives, in a democratic constitution, is conditioned and limited by a prudent *dis*trust in people's propensity to abuse power. This chapter will deepen the understanding of trust's historicity, and it will also expand upon a dialectical approach that encompasses these paradoxes more readily.

Having reread Hobbes and Locke (in Chapter 3) for a history of the political idea of trust, we may observe that, although they treated subjectivity differently, they both assumed that the subject is static and identified, already a given, regardless of history, and by nature already capable of trusting. The idea of trust as a *natural* and inherited capability is supported in recent times by evolutionary theories that see a natural selection advantage in social cooperation and moral reasoning (Nowak and Sigmund, 2005; Wilson and Wilson, 2007). As outlined in Chapter 2, many contemporary authors define trust as an affective or cognitive predisposition towards cooperation with others, based upon one's assessment of the other's likelihood of acting in one's own interests (A trusts B to do X, where X is in A's interests). This model supposes that there is a univocal subject (A) with definable and known interests who makes a bet as to whom will act in those interests.

Today, however, we cannot pretend that a history of the subject *per se* has not been thoroughly and critically addressed, disrupting the received modern traditions. Foucault noted that philosophers used to presuppose a fixed Cartesian 'subject of representation as the point of origin from which knowledge is possible and truth appears.' But the subject is not 'definitively given'; it 'constitutes itself within history and is constantly established and reestablished by history'

(Foucault, 2000, p. 3). In this passage, though, Foucault evokes the subject that knows and in other lectures he discusses truth-telling (Foucault, 2014). The present chapter will instead open the subject that *trusts* to critique 'in history.' This means turning towards a tradition of political theory quite different from that which commenced in seventeenth-century England; one that would not leave the historical emergence of trust's subjectivity unexamined; a kind of theory for which trust is not a natural or pre-programmed inner state, but in which it undergoes a series of formations, made possible or forged only under certain strenuous conditions. For this, I turn to G.W.F. Hegel and Friedrich Nietzsche, nineteenth-century German philosophers. Hegel rejects the idea of a 'naturally free' subject founded within, or traceable back to, a state of nature or a perpetual law. There is an alternative approach to trust that we can infer from Hegel's concepts of 'mutual recognition' and 'ethical life.' Changes in the formalism of right, in different historical epochs, correspond with 'different stages in the development of the concept of freedom' (Hegel, 1991, p. 59, §30); similarly trust, being a recognition of others' freedom, must also go through stages. Nietzsche's genealogy of morals traces the development of 'an animal allowed to promise,' and also throws light on the historicity of trust (Nietzsche, 1998). The chapter ends with Foucault and hence with a critical examination of a politics of trust that may be apprehended within a human science.

Before proceeding, however, a digression to consider translation is called for. In Chapter 3, we considered in detail four English authors' uses of the word 'trust,' revealing considerable variety and historical progression. The present chapter is concerned mainly with two authors who wrote in German, and we should not assume that complex terms such as *trust* and *confidence* can be translated without problems. In German, the most common translation of 'trust' is *Vertrauen* (as discussed in Chapter 1). Luhmann's distinction between trust and confidence is translated from *Vertrauen* and *Zutrauen* respectively (Luhmann, 1988). In the English translations of Hegel and Nietzsche quoted below, I insert the original terms appearing in the German texts. Translation is not trivial, as trust arises through interactional and inter-subjective practices, and there is no discoverable pre-discursive form or origin. Translators have no common 'object' to point to; there is no referent that is specifiable without the variability of cultural norms. The historicity and diversity of trust, in speech and action, across languages and cultures, need to be acknowledged as an interpretative paradox that both advances and confounds our theoretical work.

Hegel

We may contrast Hegel's view of the state with the social contract tradition, which he rejects. For Hegel, the formation and legitimacy of the state cannot properly be regarded as any kind of contract, no matter whether we think of an agreement of all with all, or one between citizens and the governors in whom they supposedly trust. Belonging to a state is not a matter of arbitrary will or consent; it is instead a necessity. There are no 'natural' individual rights that exist without, or prior to, belonging to a state; membership of the state is instead the vehicle by which rights and duties are developed and acquired. In its turn, the public authority's right to administer justice (which is also its duty) 'is not in the least dependent on whether individuals choose to entrust [*beauftragen*] it to an authority or not.' Right in the form of law is 'self-sufficient' (Hegel, 1991, p. 252, §219). Membership of the state does not, therefore, involve the relinquishment by individuals of certain liberties and 'natural rights' (such as the right to execute justice) in return for security and protection; it represents instead the very possibility of achieving one's right through the consciousness and recognition of one's own freedom. My individual, immediate, abstract right, which I only realize through interaction with others, acquires 'a new significance when its existence is recognized as part of the existent universal will and knowledge' (Hegel, 1991, p. 249, §217), or in the concrete freedom that is actualized by the state. And recognition of individual right arises through participation in civil society and interaction with others who also pursue their own ends and make their own claims. It is only thus, under the rationality of the law of the modern state, that a fully free and personal self-realization and fulfilment are possible.[1]

This interaction between the personal subjective will and the unifying work of the state is not a singular or one-dimensional trade-off or authorization, as suggested by social-contract theories. It is rather an outcome of a perpetual dialectical process, the product of continual work by individuals, by communities, and by the state, and it reveals an historically developing spirit. For Hegel, the culmination of this long historical development was supposed to be an inner comprehension of the spirit of objective freedom, the willing adoption of duties within a framework of constitutional law, and a civil society in which the political disposition is characterized by an underlying sense of security, confidence or trust.

Like other political theorists, freedom for Hegel does not mean a licence to do whatever one wishes. Indeed, one only exercises freedom through a commitment to a finite and determinate course of action. Rights and duties arise together, enlarging one another, and so it is through the adoption of duty that one achieves a universally recognized liberty. 'In duty, the individual liberates himself so as to attain substantial freedom' (Hegel, 1991, p. 192, §149). The actual practice of our duties towards others implies a mutual recognition of our freedom as persons, *and* our willingness to realize such freedom through commitments to finite courses of action. In trusting someone, then, I am assuming that he or she will be guided and limited by obligations towards me and vice versa. In mutually recognizing subjective freedom, parties to a relation of trust enlarge one another's objective freedom.

In terms of the Hegelian struggle for recognition, then, relations of trust supersede the master–slave relation. Trust does not involve coercion or control over others' actions, nor treating the person as prisoner or tool. The freedom and unpredictability – and the right to non-interference – of all actors is recognized, while their actions are nonetheless governed through ethical norms of mutual obligation. Relations of trust are as important between equals as they are between those who may be unequal in terms of age, authority, wealth, etc. This ethical 'government' between individuals is observed (and observable) in common forms of conduct, such as promising (and promise-keeping), forgiving, trading, sharing and abstaining. The significance of promising will be taken up by Nietzsche, and the ways in which such complex interactive forms of conduct reproduce immanent and distributed power-relations are best comprehended through Foucault.

Trusting assumes the free *and good* will of others. But mutual recognition involves more than this. In the moment of basic self-awareness, I only become self-aware in as much as I am aware of others who are self-aware, like me, *and* I am aware that *they* are aware of me as such (Hegel, 1977). Trust that is unequal or one-sided (such as my trusting someone who does not recognize me as trust-worthy) is a form of misrecognition, and this imbalance in a relationship is unlikely to endure for long without force. But when trust is mutually well-founded and enduring, it involves at least two parties who willingly limit their subjective free-dom in relation to one another – accepting obligations and foregoing immediate advantages – in order to realize a greater freedom that arises through the enjoy-ment of companionship and cooperation.

For Hegel, civil society is not a collection of individuals who *relinquish* some of their freedom to enjoy the advantages of a collective existence; it is an organ-ism of interdependent persons who *discover* freedom through mutual recognition with other individuals outside of the realm of the family. The concrete concept of freedom is found also in the form of feeling in relations of friendship and love – relations involving trust – in which

> we are not one-sidedly within ourselves, but willingly limit ourselves with reference to an other, even while knowing ourselves in this limitation as our-selves. In this determinacy, the human being should not feel determined; on the contrary, he attains his self-awareness only by regarding the other as other. Thus, freedom lies neither in indeterminacy nor in determinacy, but is both at once.
>
> (Hegel, 1991, p. 42, §7)

We can only claim the right to be trusted, or be recognized as trustworthy, in as much as we adopt the obligation to trust others; we can only practise the duties of a trustworthy person in as much as we also claim the right to take things on trust with others.

> Hegelian recognition is about the constant effort, on the individual level, to establish and maintain relationships of reciprocity that are freely given and freely accepted. On the larger social/political level, recognition is about the effort (and often, but not *necessarily*, the struggle) to establish conditions that are conducive to relationships of reciprocity.
>
> (Monahan, 2006, p. 413)

In trusting someone, I recognize that person, in and for herself, as a being as independent and free as myself, and not merely as a conduit to my private inter-ests, and the other recognizes this self-consciousness reciprocally in me. Trust must be much more than a wager or belief that the other will act in my interests, as it involves a mutual and inter-subjective acknowledgement between self-aware persons, known to one another as such. In as much as it may involve one another's private interests, this means mutual recognition as persons with needs and rights, and not one isolated individual's calculation about others' motives. Both parties trust, and recognize one another's actions or gestures of trust, not necessarily consciously, but as an active quality of their relations – and in doing so they put into practice and enlarge the scope of their mutual duty and liberty. The practice of trust determines and yet refines their substantial freedom. Freedom lies within this contradiction between the determinacy of obligations to be trustworthy, on one hand, and the potential to realize personal aims, on the other hand, with reference to and cooperation with others.

A Hegelian account of freedom opens up a more dynamic inter-subjective view of trust. It views trust beyond the individual – as more than the trait, belief or choice of an individual – and sees it as an emergent and yet concrete feature of relationships that accompanies the development of self-awareness and personal fulfilment. Hegel does not neglect the private desires, needs or interests of the individual – he regards them as developing in consciousness and finding their fulfilment within the complex reciprocal and ethical interactions of civil society. He is also helpful in addressing the systemic or abstract trust that is socially shared and barely noticed (see Chapter 4). The state is seen as an organism that produces, preserves and regulates itself through its differentiated powers and functions, involving all of its particular institutions and individuals, all of whom rely upon the state for their security and their duties *and* for the free pursuit of their aims, and none of whom can voluntarily opt out. These latter aspects of the state, as they actually function, give the political disposition its particular contents. The state 'is not a mechanism but the rational life of self-conscious freedom and the system of the ethical world,' and so the disposition of its citizens, or their consciousness of this disposition in principles, 'is an essential moment in the actual state' (Hegel, 1991, p. 297, §270).

People are inclined and entitled, of course, to criticize the state and its actions. Subjective opinion is varied and often distrustful of public figures and agencies of the state. And yet people's behaviour in public spaces indicates a sense of security or confidence in the actual institutions of state and their rationality. This is 'the basic sense of order that everyone possesses' and that holds the state together (Hegel, 1991, p. 289, §268); it is a 'political disposition' or an everyday patriotism that is based upon on 'a volition which has become *habitual* . . . and is a consequence of the institutions within the state . . . in which rationality is *actually* present.'

> This disposition is in general one of *trust* [*das Zutrauen*] (which may pass over into more or less educated insight), or the consciousness that my substantial and particular interest is preserved and contained in the interest and end of an other (in this case, the state), and in the latter's relation to me as an individual. As a result, this other immediately ceases to be an other for me, and in my consciousness of this, I am free.
>
> (Hegel, 1991, p. 288, § 268)

Ordinary and habitual patriotism is that disposition which 'knows that the community is the substantial basis and end' – and it is grounded objectively, in truth, and not in subjective representations and thoughts. We should distinguish (an often distrustful) public opinion from 'what they genuinely will':

> They trust [*Das Zutrauen haben die Menschen*] that the state will continue to exist and that particular interests can be fulfilled within it alone; but habit blinds us to the basis of our entire existence.
>
> (Hegel, 1991, p. 289, §268)[2]

For Hegel, our membership, participation and cooperation within the state is not the result of a risk-taking choice. It is a necessity, and the only realistic 'opt-out' is to become a member of another state. There is normally a confident expectation, to which we hardly give any thought, 'that the state will continue to exist.' Hegel does not give us illustrations of trust at work in activities such as commerce (as Hobbes does) or an elaboration of the role of trust in the formation of a political society (as Locke does). Hegel does, however, provide a framework within which we may rethink trust inter-subjectively and collectively, beginning as a form of mutual recognition, and progressing to a sense of common identity, 'to the degree that the members of a community recognize their commonality' (Buchwalter, 2012, p. 2).

Parties to relations of trust acknowledge one another as self-aware beings and as free agents; they abide by limitations to their freedom of choice; moreover, they develop their consciousness of themselves as free, even as they limit their actions in pursuit of determinate goals. Trust recognizes and fulfils freedom, and yet 'conditions' it through our obligations to one another. Thereby we know ourselves as free, and we obtain an objective freedom as participants in civil society. Trust, then, is an immanent quality of relationships that is characteristic of civil society, and that develops as the subject emerges from the unreflective belonging to and identification with the family. While trust, in a Hegelian sense, does have a place in our understanding of the stable order institutionalized by the state, it is not something 'given' to legislators or governors. Instead it emerges – for each individual as well as in its cultural-historical forms – as a characteristic of the ethical life we live, with its framework of rights and obligations, customs and laws. This can encompass a moment in which trust extends beyond the interpersonal realm and becomes a quality of social institutions and of the state and its law and administration. For Hegel, though, such a political trust is not a matter for consent; it is a necessity, but also a public right and duty; it is a relational quality of customary ethical life. It involves and perpetuates our particular interests, but it is not for the sake of private interests that trust arises. Instead, we trust because we want and need the continuation of a community that is the basis and the substantial end of our existence. In as much as the law sometimes steps in to protect our personal interests, it is not over-riding or crowding out a 'natural' propensity for trust; the law is instead expanding the scope of trust through awareness of formalized obligations entailed in exchanges or relationships.

Paradoxically, a relation of trust both limits and recognizes the parties as free agents, and hence it expands our self-awareness from a freedom that is untrammelled in its mere self-interestedness to a freedom that is bound by obligations and yet enhanced by the possibilities of social cooperation. At certain moments, these advantages require the sanction of law in order to recognize some instances of trust as having a public significance, and hence a value to the community and the state.

Nietzsche

Quite unlike Hegel, Nietzsche holds that the state is the product of violent usurpation, subjugation and/or appropriation, born of the will to power, not reason. Foundational theories of this kind do not seem, at first sight, to be conducive to thoughts about trust. Moreover, there is scholarly controversy over Nietzsche's contribution (if any) to political thought, and his dismissive attitude to democracy (Hunt, 1985; Siemens and Shapiro, 2008). But his oft-cited passages in *On the Genealogy of Morals* are relevant to one of the key elements of trust. The hypothesis about 'the promissory animal' suggests that the practices of trust are the product of social forces and power struggles, and that they are reliant upon a belief-structure that has no rational foundation.

While there is debate about what Nietzsche meant exactly by 'will to power,' his 'genealogical hypotheses' reveal how power is 'an inherent, but denied component of moral values, institutions and practices' (Saar, 2008, p. 461) – and in this we may include the morally significant practices by which we trust one another. Power is about more than just physical strength or force, and more than the compelling effects of law or religious doctrine. The subject itself is a product of power-relations (not a party thereto), and hence the practices entailed in trusting one another (including promising and forgiving) are an outcome of complex and multi-valent uses of power (Saar, 2008).

Nietzsche seeks to reconstruct a genealogy of 'the task of breeding an animal which is entitled to make promises' (Nietzsche, 1998, p. 40). The key to this task is memory, or more exactly the overcoming of forgetfulness. It is always easier to forget than to remember, especially when in debt. But, to make promises, the debtor needs to remember, 'to instill trust [*Vertrauen*] for his promise of repayment' (Nietzsche, 1998, p. 45). Only a speaking subject can make a promise, and, having done so, the promise only succeeds if remembered. Having promised, one should neither forget nor be distracted by other aims or wishes.

At the root of all such capabilities to promise, and so to trust and be trusted, Nietzsche sees the commercial relations of buyer and seller, and hence debtor and creditor. The expansion of trade means that exchange cannot be limited to the immediate moment. Traders have to allow time for delivery. As 'the most powerful aid to memory was pain,' the debtor pledged that 'the creditor could subject the body of the debtor,' in order to guarantee against the failure to perform as promised. That is, 'instead of a direct compensation for the damage, the pleasure of violation [or] an entitlement and right to cruelty.' The entitlement of the aggrieved debtor to inflict suffering or bodily harm or pain onto the defaulting creditor is the crucible in which the ability to promise (and hence to trust) is formed. Nietzsche holds that there is no 'law of nature' that connects infliction of suffering with compensation for a debt. Belief in the 'equivalence' of suffering and debt, which we now take for granted, has had to be acquired. He asks sceptically, 'to what extent can suffering compensate for "debt"?' Our belief in this equivalence is also a disbelief. After all, how often does the plaintiff say, even in court, that nothing can compensate for certain losses? So, this equivalence requires our willing suspension of disbelief. One may try the counter-argument that it is somehow 'natural' to seek revenge and inflict pain on a debtor who reneges on a promise. Even an animal will use tooth or claw to avenge itself. But Nietzsche forestalls this explanation, 'for revenge itself leads back to the same problem: "How can inflicting pain provide satisfaction?"' (Nietzsche, 1998, pp. 43–47). And, as a speech-act, there is nothing 'natural' about a promise.

Entwined within the origins of our abilities to promise, to trust and to be trusted is thus a suspension of disbelief in equivalences between wrongs done and suffering in return. Through practices such as *wergild* and *diya* (see Chapter 5), direct infliction of pain onto wrongdoers was transformed and regulated by lawful penalties or compensation. At the core of criminal and civil law lies the acquired idea of an equivalence between crime and punishment, or injury and compensation, and this constitutes the legal subject *per se*, Nietzsche argues. Further, this derives from the relation of creditor and debtor 'which points back in turn to the fundamental forms of buying, selling, exchange, wheeling and dealing' (Nietzsche, 1998, p. 45). At the heart of trust, then, we can discover trade, and hence the capacities to remember and to equate signifiers, such as three thousand ducats 'for an equal pound of your fair flesh' (*Merchant of Venice* I,3), and 'the fiduciary phenomenon of credit or faith (*Glauben*)' (Derrida, 2014, p. 152). Promising and trusting as signifying practices, and the very idea of the legal subject, emerge within historically evolving and contingent relations, in the struggles for gain and for justice to which commercial relations have given rise. But this requires belief in a barely believable equation of suffering with debt.

There are some greater social and historical consequences of this. Although, for Nietzsche, the *origins* of the state were violent, 'the community stands in the same important fundamental relationship to its members as the creditor does to his debtors . . . because one lives protected, looked after, in peace and trust [*im Frieden und Vertrauen*]' (Nietzsche, 1998, p. 52). Punishment follows for those who break their 'pledge' or promise to the community. Hence, culturally and historically contingent inter-subjective practices of trust emerge from and govern relations between those who trade as equals, between 'unequals' (powerful and weak, creditor and debtor), and between the individual and the community.

The security that the individual achieves through belonging in a social group entails trust, as it creates a debt and a promise to obey, but not in the manner of Locke's conditional 'gift' of trust. Nietzsche holds that the violent and cruel subjugation of a docile majority that formed the earliest states also gave rise, through sheer pain, to the capacity for making and keeping promises. No 'law of nature' enjoins us to keep our promises. Trust is a fortunate outcome of the original violence. Those who are cruelly preyed upon learn to internalize and memorize the supposed promise that underwrote the debt to their masters. Usurpation of power and the struggle between debtors and creditors form unwittingly the anvil upon which the entitlement or permission to promise is forged. For Nietzsche, trust is *not* a precondition for the formation of society (as suggested by Locke) but a product of the forces that shaped it, and that thereby form subjectivity and inter-subjective bonds or bargains. Because Locke refuses to tolerate those who do not believe in and cannot swear before God, his rational subject, cognizant of 'natural law,' is not yet the Nietzschean 'sovereign individual.' The latter can vouch fully for himself without reference to God; the Lockean subject cannot be trusted *unless* he believes in God.

Nietzsche's hypothesis about the promissory animal also differs from the Hobbesian account which assumes that the ability to promise or to trust is an *a priori* human faculty, but that one would prudently not trust others in a state of nature. In contrast, Nietzsche argues that the emergence of *the ability* to promise is only due to subjection and to cruelties that were formalized into lawful punishments. There is nothing 'natural' or *a priori* about it at all; it has a genealogy. The animal that has acquired the permission to issue promises, as an autonomous being – eventually without accounting to God – has acquired this talent by 'unnatural,' artificial, sometimes violent contradictions and subjection.

In his genealogy of the promise, however, Nietzsche has not given as clear a depiction of the other speech-act entailed in trust: forgiveness. As Hannah Arendt (1958) would later describe it, to forgive someone releases her from the consequences of what she has done and means that she is not perpetually the victim of her past. Nietzsche does observe, however, that mercy is a sign of a highly developed culture, to the extent that he imagines a society of sufficient cultural strength such that punishments are no longer needed.

> The justice which began with: 'Everything can be paid off, everything must be paid off,' ends with a look the other way as those who are unable to pay are allowed to run free.
>
> (Nietzsche, 1998, p. 54)

And he acknowledges the historical Christian realization of universal redemption.

> God as the sole figure who can redeem on man's behalf that which has become irredeemable for man himself – the creditor sacrificing himself for his debtor, out of love (are we supposed to believe this? –).
>
> (Nietzsche, 1998, p. 72)

Compare, for instance, the radically different forms of the injunctions to forgive in Leviticus 25 and Matthew 18. Leviticus contains a divine injunction on the Israelites to be trustworthy – or not to take advantage of one another – when buying and selling land. Land prices would drop in accordance with the number of years left until the Jubilee (once every fifty years) at which time any land that had been 'sold' was returned to its original owner. Hence, debts were forgiven and indentured labourers released to return to their ancestral lands.[3] Such forgiveness is regulated externally, by law, so that no family can be held in perpetual servitude, alienation or poverty. God imposes a structure that engenders trust in others through their confidence in socially sanctioned forgiveness. In Matthew 18, the parable of the unmerciful servant suggests quite a different regimen of debt-forgiveness and redemption. Because the servant failed to show forgiveness to a fellow servant in the same way that his master had forgiven him for a large debt, the servant is condemned 'to be tortured, until he should pay back all he owed.' Given that the servant's debt to the master was far more than any labourer could earn in a lifetime, the 'torture' may have lasted until death. But Jesus tells Peter, 'This is how my heavenly Father will treat each of you unless you forgive your brother or sister from your heart.' To earn God's forgiveness one must do much more than simply await the ordained day of redemption. One must forgive others, again and again, from the heart; not to do so means eternal punishment. In creating an ideal that we can never meet, Nietzsche argues, humanity is thus *un*forgiven, or 'beyond the possibility of atonement' and subject to a punishment beyond proportion to the actual culpability. Far from being a source of redemption, he argues, the Christian era breeds 'absolute unworthiness' and self-torture (Nietzsche, 1998, p. 73).

For the present purposes, Nietzsche's genealogy proposes that the speech-acts that give effect to trust – promise and forgiveness – are products of a painful history involving subjection, slavery, punishment and debt, as well as forgiveness, and also commerce as free subjects. As he sees it, however, we have yet to acquire the strength to liberate the will and to redeem ourselves from the consequences of the Judeo-Christian ideals. Trust is not yet fully formed.

What do Hegel and Nietzsche offer us?

Neither Hegel nor Nietzsche gives us a comprehensive theory of trust. The term does not serve a central purpose for either of them. Their thinking does inspire, however, an approach that is more historically dynamic, that sees trust as forged from the dialectics of social antagonism, state-formation and commerce. It helps us to place the individualism and essentialism of contemporary research and theory on trust into perspective.

As a counter to individualism, trust is neither located as an aptitude or propensity in the individual nor based on discrete decisions made by individuals. The formation of trust is found in neither the 'truster' nor the 'trusted'; it begins with conditions that forge the requirements of our being-with-others. Nor is trust best captured by the aggregation of survey respondents' opinions. Public opinion on trust (in others, or in government) may not reflect the actual social 'climate' of trust and the necessity of acting *as if* we trust. This may help us to understand the paradox by which large sectors of a voting population may express low levels of trust in political leaders, parties and the electoral system itself ('the system is rigged'), and hence vote for candidates who promise to disrupt the system, all the while 'trusting' that the electoral system will work lawfully to achieve some changes *and* that the apparatuses of the state on which they rely will continue undisturbed. Those who abstain from voting are (voicelessly) the *most* trusting, as they leave the decisions to others, while expecting public services to continue. An aggregated record of individuals' consciously expressed replies to survey questions about political trust may bear little resemblance to the implicit trust revealed through their actions in lived contexts.

As an alternative to the essentialist idea that trust is 'innate' or 'hard-wired,' Hegel and Nietzsche give us a view of trust that is historically and culturally contingent; or a trust that emerges and is transformed in its possibilities and structures. This can be contrasted with the unquestioning adoption of an *a priori* trust by Hobbes and Locke and with the essentialism of evolutionary biology. The Darwinian vision that natural selection and economic competition promote selfish behaviours has been overlaid with a theory that genetic 'programming' for altruism and reciprocity ultimately serves the 'selfish' needs of survival and reproduction (Nowak and Sigmund, 2000, 2005), or that selection can operate on a group level that confers the advantage to altruism (Wilson and Wilson, 2007). Cooperation and trust, through natural selection, improve the chances of survival. But, without denying the fossil record that attests to evolution, retrospective socio-biological explanations fall into a trap already identified by Hegel and Nietzsche: that of seeking to 'explain' presently observable human behaviour by reference to unobservable primordial 'origins,' as if the relation between the two is linear, without intervening transformations or reversals in underlying function or economy. The natural selection account gives us 'Just So' stories about prehistoric humans and their struggle for survival, supposedly to explain how trust (as we now know it) 'must have evolved.' Undoubtedly, the earliest human groups did collaborate, but trust leaves no fossil record. The particular human genetic code is necessary for our capacity to learn to speak, and hence to promise; but genetics provide no *sufficient* explanation for trust. To claim that trust must be 'genetically programmed' and hence 'hard-wired' – because we observe its present benefits – tells us little about trust in practice and in history, let alone pre-history. Such efforts to 'naturalize' trust can be taken too far.

These critiques of individualism and essentialism do not preclude us from thinking either that a person might at times consciously *choose* individually to trust others or *judge* that some people are basically untrustworthy. We may still observe that the human propensity to trust serves an advantageous 'survival' function for individuals and communities. Species or groups whose members can trust one another, and hence cooperate and share, do reap the benefits. The insights of the Hegelian and Nietzschean perspectives mean that we are no longer bound by the limitations of individualism and essentialism when observing such things. The individual actor still matters; trust, however, is basically inter-subjective and integral to the ethical life of the community. Trust has indeed evolved, but that evolution did not suddenly cease *before* history in Paleolithic times, nor is it 'genetically programmed.' Trust's norms and practices evolve *in* history, as one can observe in contemporary experiences with online trading and payment systems. The capability or permission to trust that human interaction perpetually calls for has been forged through social pressures and antagonisms, as well as through love and belonging in family and friendship. But just as Nietzsche denied us the comfort of believing that 'nature' must have endowed us with the faculties to know the truth – rather than a propensity to thrive on lies and fictions – so we should not assume that 'nature' has endowed us with a preference for trust and altruism as survival strategies – as compared with cruelty and domination. There is nothing in nature that makes us trustworthy rather than deceitful, and a genealogy of trust may well be 'unnatural,' founded in the threat to inflict pain for a failure to keep a promise, actions that only a speaking animal can perform. Natural selection and evolution cannot account for the trust and altruism that we observe.

From Nietzsche to Foucault

Nietzsche's approach to power and knowledge inspired Foucault, as discussed in the first lecture of 'Truth and Juridical Forms' (Foucault, 2000). The question of trust takes us down a rather different pathway, however. Being seen to speak the truth does often matter if one is to be trusted; but sometimes it requires abstaining from speaking the truth. Trust is more about acting 'true to one's word.' Foucault himself tells us little about trust, although his critique of the human sciences and the disciplinary society does have a bearing on social-scientific methods in the study of trust. As discussed in Chapter 2, laboratory experiments and opinion surveys are not ways to discover and investigate a pre-discursive state, trait or capability of trust. They are discursive practices that 'systematically form the objects of which they speak' (Foucault, 1972, p. 49); they are not observing a 'thing of nature.' The experimental methods of game-theory and the individualized and aggregated queries of social surveys are technologies that rely upon and advance a trust that is only *presupposed* to be the belief or decision of the individual. The techniques and their 'object' emerge together and constitute one another within the co-ordinates of a discursive formation.

We can see the discursivity of trust when we view it as a modality of power-relations. Power, according to Foucault, is neither a possession nor a physical strength. It is instead relational and immanent, and hence effective in all social settings as domination, submission, resistance and so on (Foucault, 1990). If the exercise of power is viewed 'as a mode of action upon the actions of others,' and, if these actions are characterized by 'the government of men by other men,' then power is exercised 'only over free subjects.' In other words, freedom appears 'as the condition for the exercise of power.' To extrapolate, then, trust may be regarded as an exercise of power, in that it presupposes the freedom of subjects, and it both limits and enables actions. Trust 'governs' in the sense that it works 'to structure the possible field of action of others' (Foucault, 1982, p. 790).

Viewed as a form of governmentality, trust assumes that the subject is both free (uncoerced) and responsible or obliged to others, and that the mutual obligations of the state and of markets (as in taxes, debts and payments) operate for the security and prosperity of a population, often (but not always) calculated on a rationality of utility. That is, by conventional rational-choice logic, we are said to trust because it is in our interests to do so, as it makes a moral-social life possible and economic transactions more efficient. But this conventional view of trust regards the relational qualities of trust as conceptually secondary to the individualized acts of judging or decision-making. In order to regard trust as dialectical and relational in the contexts of power-relations, the role of individual choice needs to be seen as secondary, or as a retrospective rationalization. Trust is not in itself primarily or objectively a choice; liberal political-economic rationality submits it to the *logic* of choice.

Liberalism avows a principle of the self-limitation of government, implying that power is largely an emanation from the state and a necessary evil to be 'fended off,' reduced or replaced. A liberal (or neoliberal) form of government relies upon trust as means by which 'to structure the possible field of action of others,' coupled with a distrust in the propensity to abuse powers. Trust emerges, for instance, to govern relations between voters and their representatives. (See the discussion of Burke and Mill in Chapter 3). It is no coincidence, moreover, that a surge of social-scientific interest in trust occurred during the renewal of liberal governance in the late twentieth century (Chapter 4). Trust serves the purposes of classical liberal governance as a means towards the self-limitation of the 'governmentalization' of the state; it further meets the purposes of *neo*liberal governance when rationalized through the principles of individual choice and efficiency that challenged late twentieth-century 'big' government.

Hence, I do not go in search of a primary or basic psychological or pre-discursive trust that can be observed, counted or measured, as if it were a rare species in need of a breeding programme. As speaking subjects, it is already too late for a naturalistic inquiry that purportedly investigates a being 'prior to itself,' imagined by the same speaking subject that inquires. It is common to recognize an unspoken or implicit trust, and yet we cannot speak reflexively of such trust without reforming and changing it: at the very least, it is no longer 'unspoken.' Speech betrays trust, and so talking about trust reformulates and renegotiates it. The need to speak and write about trust arises due to betrayal of trust, and then 'committing it to writing' irrevocably changes our relations of trust. The capability to imagine ourselves, and to act as if we were, autonomous and free persons (who make judgements or calculations about others' motives and actions and how they affect us) is a capability that has had to be forged within dialectical and conflictual social relations over the course of history, and that develops uniquely within each individual. The notion of trust as a belief or choice is thus an understanding that depends upon history, language and customs; it is a product of a particular grammar (A trusts B); it is not the defining 'essence' of trust itself.

We should aim instead to ask what made it possible for trust to be formulated as an 'object' of a discourse that concerns 'the political,' and what conditions made this comprehensible, self-evident or necessary. So, what are the practices that govern an order into which trust fits as a significant object of concern? We can observe textual practices in English political philosophy, from the seventeenth century onwards, that have systematically reformulated 'trust' (see Chapter 3). We can observe the transformation of trust from inter-subjective practices (that define or order relations of obligation and authority) into an object given or bestowed as a 'commodity' in the transactions of complex institutional power-relations. And then, in the late twentieth century, this object is comprehended as a trait or belief of the individual – an *individual* that is modelled for the purposes and professions of public and commercial life, as a locus of perceptions, interests, beliefs, opinions or preferences (see Chapter 4). The propensity to trust is also linked to the efficient conduct of business, the stability of financial institutions, and the acceptability of our money (see Chapter 5). Our will to trust must nowadays encompass others whom we cannot see and hear and who contribute to complex organized systems, and this 'trustworthy person' – the Nietzschean 'promissory animal' – takes centre-stage as a key figure in a global political economy.

Conclusion

That trust and distrust are mutually constitutive within complex social systems need no longer perplex us. A dialectical approach is not limited by the logical principle of non-contradiction; indeed, it seeks out the contradiction as the momentum of historical transformation. Trust and distrust may be lexical opposites, but they are, in practice, cooperative. We may speak, then, of dis/trust, and we will be able to explore this further through the two French thinkers discussed in the next chapter. The main lesson that we may take from Hegel and Nietzsche concerns the vital role of mutual recognition and struggle (between masters and slaves, debtors and creditors and so on) in the emergence and historical transformations of trust. This gives us a sound theoretical understanding of the relational, dialectical and historical character of trust.

Notes

1 The modern state 'allows the principle of subjectivity to attain fulfilment in the *self-sufficient extreme* of personal particularity, while at the same time *bringing it back to substantial unity* and so preserving this unity in the principle of subjectivity itself' (Hegel, 1991, p. 282, §260).
2 Although the translator has chosen 'trust' for this passage, such a blind and habitual expectation of the continuance of an orderly state would be given instead as 'confidence' in the distinction made by Luhmann (1988).
3 The people are regarded, in Leviticus, as God's tenants, and so a 'sale' of land is a temporary transfer of tenancy. Similarly, enslavement of fellow Israelites is outlawed, and one who becomes an indentured labourer due to poverty is to be released from this debt in the year of Jubilee. They may be redeemed earlier than that by paying the equivalent of a labourer's wage that would be payable up until the Jubilee.

References

Arendt, H. (1958). *The human condition*. Chicago, IL: University of Chicago Press.
Buchwalter, A. (2012). *Hegel and global justice*. Dordrecht: Springer.

Derrida, J. (2014). *The death penalty* (Vol. I). Chicago, IL: University of Chicago Press.

Foucault, M. (1972). *The archaeology of knowledge and the discourse on language.* New York, NY: Pantheon Books.

Foucault, M. (1982). The subject and power. *Critical Inquiry, 8*(4), 777–795.

Foucault, M. (1990). *The history of sexuality. Volume 1: An introduction.* New York, NY: Vintage.

Foucault, M. (2000). *Power: Essential works of Foucault 1954–1984.* London: Penguin.

Foucault, M. (2014). *Wrong-doing, truth-telling: The function of avowal in justice.* Chicago, IL: University of Chicago Press.

Hegel, G. (1977). *Phenomenology of spirit.* Oxford: Clarendon Press.

Hegel, G. (1991). *Elements of the philosophy of right.* Cambridge: Cambridge University Press.

Hunt, L. H. (1985). Politics and anti-politics: Nietzsche's view of the state. *History of Philosophy Quarterly, 2*(4), 453–468.

Luhmann, N. (1988). Familiarity, confidence, trust: Problems and alternatives. In D. Gambetta (Ed.), *Trust: Making and breaking cooperative relations* (pp. 94–107). Oxford: Basil Blackwell.

Monahan, M. J. (2006). Recognition beyond struggle: On a liberatory account of Hegelian recognition. *Social Theory and Practice, 32*(3), 389–414.

Nietzsche, F. (1998). *On the genealogy of morals.* Oxford: Oxford University Press.

Nowak, M. A., and Sigmund, K. (2000). Shrewd investments. *Science, 288*(5467), 819.

Nowak, M. A., and Sigmund, K. (2005). Evolution of indirect reciprocity. *Nature, 437*(27), 1291–1298.

Saar, M. (2008). Forces and powers in Nietzsche's genealogy of morals. In V. Roodt, and H. Siemens (Eds.), *Nietzsche, power and politics: Rethinking Nietzsche's legacy for political thought* (pp. 453–469). Berlin: Walter de Gruyter.

Siemens, H., and Shapiro, G. (2008). What does Nietzsche mean for contemporary politics and political thought? *Journal of Nietzsche Studies, 35–36*, 3–8.

Wilson, D. S., and Wilson, E. O. (2007). Rethinking the theoretical foundation of sociobiology. *Quarterly Review of Biology, 82*(4), 327–348.

7 Trust with or without conditions

In 2017, there were threats of a trade war between the USA and China. And rising between these two super-powers – like a return of the repressed from a conflict unresolved since 1953 – North Korea tested long-range missiles and detonated nuclear weapons. The collocation of 'trade' and 'war' aptly captured the instability of trans-Pacific east–west relations, with tension between actions that signify trust and actions that signify distrust. It encapsulated an age-old theme of rivalry between human groups. When tribes cross great distances and meet, do they celebrate and trade goods, or do they fight and plunder? As Marcel Mauss put it, 'one trusts completely, or one mistrusts completely. To trade, the first condition was to be able to lay aside the spear' (1990, pp. 104–105). No matter how rational or irrational we may believe the North Korean leader's actions to have been, his threatening displays of 'the spear' were eminently human. At the same time, alternative forms of contest and exchange that mitigate hostilities and give effect to trust, were also close to hand: for example, sports tournaments, tourism, trade and cultural exchanges.

In US–China relations, 'the economic' and 'the militaristic' are inextricably entangled, especially around the islands and sea-lanes of the disputed South China Sea, one of the busiest trade-routes on the globe, showing the embeddedness of 'the economy' in a wider transnational context of politics and conflict. War is the continuation of politics (or policy) by other means, as Carl von Clausewitz put it; hence also the continuation of *economic* policy by other means. We observe, therefore, an unstable boundary between warlike, hostile exchanges that lack or deter customary actions of trust, and peaceful, hospitable exchanges that rely upon and build trust.

'The economy' is always a *political* and a *moral* economy. And in order to expand upon the moral, political and economic significance of trust, it is necessary to re-examine the idea of 'the economy' that dominates contemporary media and policy debates. The orthodox model views 'the economy' abstracted from non-material values and cultural or religious norms. It is seen as a domain of action in its own right, separable from 'social' concerns and dominated by a corporate-business and political élite. Economic policy-making is treated as technical value-free problem-solving; the individual is regarded as a rational utility-maximizer; markets are ideally self-regulating and not 'distorted' by subsidies or political 'interference'; 'the economy' is represented in aggregated statistical terms such as gross domestic product. The phrase 'good for the economy' issues readily from the mouths of political and business leaders as if a single definable 'good' were applicable to all participants.

Here we can be guided by the notion of 'moral economy' which reinstates characteristics of human action that are neglected by neo-classical economic rationalism. Real-world economic behaviour is not reducible to 'laws' of supply and demand, external incentives and revealed preference. Cultural norms, traditions and political ideas shape or normalize actual economic activity, for example, by 'popular consensus,' indigenous customs, or shared understandings of fairness (Hann, 2010; Thompson, 1971). Cultural and moral norms may give cause to collective actions or protests that, from a rational-economic viewpoint, seem to be contrary to self-interest or utility-maximization, but that serve commonly valued purposes that are of over-riding significance to many people. This may include protests against inequality or 'unfair' prices, resistance to economic development that threatens traditional land-rights or environmental values, or even movements that support a populist leader's call for protectionist policies. Dis/trust can be seen as a part of such political-economic action and reaction among social groups. We have already looked at money (in Chapter 5), observing the complex co-involvement of this factor of economic activity with shifting meanings of trust. But there is more work to do, as the economic activities of trading, exchanging, delivering on promises, and forgiving debts – examples also of what we mean when we say that people are trusting one another – need to be brought together into a comprehensive understanding. The idea of 'moral economy' assists this.

The contemporary social-scientific interest in trust (for instance in social capital theory) has already helped to break down artificial intellectual barriers between the economic and the social. I push this further, however, by contrasting two French thinkers, Marcel Mauss and Jacques Derrida, and hence, respectively, an approach to trust that is 'conditional' or dependent upon reciprocity, and an 'unconditional' view of giving and forgiving. This will lead to a better appreciation of the role of doubt in relations of trust, or the dialectic of trust and distrust, necessary for advancing a political theory of trust.

The disembedded economy

The best-known critique of the trend towards 'disembedding' the economic from the social, political and environmental realms was made by Karl Polanyi (2001; first published 1944). He cites, for examples of embeddedness, the ethnography of Malinowski in the Trobriand Islands and the comments on economics in Aristotle's *Politics*. From the former, Polanyi comments on practices of reciprocity ('today's giving will be recompensed by tomorrow's taking') and redistribution ('an intermediary in the person of the headman or other prominent member of the group receives and distributes the supplies, especially if they need to be stored') (Polanyi, 2001, p. 53). Goods that are given 'are valuable only because they symbolize the social relationship they create by causing a debt to circulate endlessly between the partners' (Caillé, 2010, p. 182), thus sustaining the solidarity of the social group, as well as its rivalries. From Aristotle, Polanyi takes the example of the patriarchal household-estate – noting that the Greek roots of the word *economy* refer originally to the regulation of the household. Aristotle regarded the production of goods for use by the household, and the exchange of surpluses with others for mutual benefit, as 'natural.' This contrasted with the 'unnatural' practices of production and exchange purely for the sake of financial gain. Such 'unnatural' economic activity was sufficiently common in his time that Aristotle found it necessary to condemn it. And similar disapproval of usury and commodification is reflected in the laws laid down by the holy books of the three great monotheistic religions. The Books of Leviticus and Numbers, for instance, contain religious edicts regarding interest, labour, tithes, inheritances and debts, and the recognition of the various tribes as well as immigrants. Obedience to the laws of the Lord brings economic and social prosperity, it is said.

For most of human history – and pre-history – economic production and exchange have been subordinated to and regulated within structures of kinship, social groups, political hierarchies and religious institutions, helping to sustain them. It is only relatively recently, especially since the Industrial Revolution, that we witness the rise of the idea of a self-regulating market, unshackled from social and political obligations, subject only to laws that protect property rights and contracts, and driven by acquisitive and competitive urges conditioned by the price mechanism (supply and demand). Along with this, the 'free' individual emerges as an economic actor and politico-legal subject, enabled to make autonomous choices, while legally accountable, and regarded distinctly from any social group to which he or she belongs. Far from being 'natural,' such a form of freedom is the product of a conflictual history of civil wars, revolutions and state interventions. The creation of 'free' and mobile workforces and the enclosure and privatization of lands required law-reform, enforcement of laws, state violence and colonization. Along with this historical process, the ways in which people could analyse and even 'manage' the domain known as 'the economy' also underwent radical change.

Foucault traced changing meanings of 'economy' from the regulation of the family and household, to royal households and treasuries, and thence to its meaning as a national domain and an object of 'government' by the state, or a properly *political* economy. Beginning in the eighteenth century in Europe, 'the economy' was thus emerging as a distinct level of reality and as a field of intervention for the art of government. At the same time, 'the market' evolved from its feudal meaning as a site of exchange regulated by local laws and customs, into a principle that transcends the local and that spontaneously obeys certain 'natural' laws. The idea of a market economy governed by supply and demand was consolidated in the economic theories of the twentieth century. Although Foucault died (in 1984) before the historical implications of American neoliberalism were played out in real economic policies, his observations about its theory are pertinent. He correctly characterizes American neoliberalism as an extension of economic rationality into domains that had traditionally been considered to be non-economic, such as crime and marriage. The classical liberalism of the nineteenth century had acted as a principle of 'the self-limitation of government,' in favour of a *laissez-faire* (or hands-off) policy, to respect the freedom of 'the market.' American neoliberalism turns this principle of self-limitation back upon itself, such that the disciplines of the 'free' market have the reverse effect of 'regulating' government (Foucault, 2007, 2008). Governments are constrained by the potential for negative reactions in 'the markets'; global competition discourages worker-friendly legislation or higher taxes; *laissez-faire* is 'turned round' and the market becomes 'a sort of permanent economic tribunal confronting government' (Foucault, 2008, p. 247).

Hence, we may imagine – in rough outline – three broad historical conceptualizations of that aspect of human activities that we call 'the economy.' There are pre-literate and ancient communities and states in which economic activity is 'embedded,' or contained and governed within traditional structures, such that it respects and reinforces status, honour, religious rites, etc. Second, with the advent of the Industrial Revolution, we observe the emergence of an economy 'disembedded' from the community – or, a market, an economy and a discipline of political economy imagined as separate from the private or natural life of the family and the voluntary activities of communities, and also from the public realm of government. This abstraction of the economy is made possible by the techniques of statistics. But, according to Polanyi, such a radical distinction between economy and society is artificial, and efforts to detach 'the market' from the moral and political norms of societies is a utopian ideal destined to collapse upon itself as people react against it and seek social protection through regulation (Polanyi, 2001). Third, then, there is a neoliberal turn that goes further and seeks to 'colonize' the social and the moral with the individualistic and competitive rationality of the discursive form of 'the market.' Domains of life that once were thought of as non-economic – or even as 'sacrosanct,' and hence protected from economic rationalization – are submitted to the logic of utility-maximization, supply and demand, and contract law. Marriage is treated as a contract for services and reallocation of property rights; crime-rates are analysed in terms of supply and demand; public servants are assumed to be self-interested utility-maximizers; social protections are wound back.

A neoliberal view of 'the economy' does not do justice to our lived experiences, however, as we spend our days working in paid or unpaid capacities and meeting our needs. An active economic community serves human aims that, through the ages, have been understood in ethical-political terms, such as well-being, happiness, fairness and godliness. The effect of a market-based society, however, is to disembed people's economic activities from the social sources of their belonging and fulfilment. As Polanyi put it, referring to the *laissez-faire* policies of the nineteenth century:

> To separate labor from other activities of life and to subject it to the laws of the market was to annihilate all organic forms of existence and to replace them by a different type of organization, an atomistic and individualist one.
>
> (Polanyi, 2001, p. 171)

These words, first published in 1944, ring even truer today after the advance of free-market capitalism and the retreat of state regulation since the 1980s. But economic exchanges are still suffused with moral norms, even in the most impersonal free-market transactions. And these norms are derived from the communities in which the transactions occur, while the dominant practices of economic activity in turn reshape social norms. As the transformations in the structures and styles of trust reveal (see Chapters 4 and 5), the most advanced capitalist societies are not denuded of shared ethical expectations and mutual obligations. The 'disembedded' economy still relies upon, and in turn inculcates, a moral order of some kind, such that 'contrary to Polanyi-type arguments, all economies, including the near-to-pervasive market economies, are moral economies, embedded in the (ethical) framework of their communities' (Booth, 1994, p. 662).

Even the most scientific approaches to economics are value-laden, not value-free (Heilbroner, 1973). And the calls for 'individualism' and 'self-reliance' that accompanied economic reforms of the neoliberal era were moralistic in character. The rise of interest in trust and social capital in sociology, politics and political economy that coincides with the neoliberal turn represents a 'correction' to the methodological individualism of orthodox economics and to the utopian vision of consumers enjoying unlimited freedom of choice in deregulated competitive markets. Neoliberal rationality required a social 'glue' that would sustain consumers in responsibly raising families and coexisting as communities. Political and social theory sought to reveal how the ethically charged dispositions and activities that are entailed in what we call generically 'trust' are essential to the smooth functioning of markets and of communities, including voluntary contribution, civic engagement and social cohesion (Fukuyama, 1995; Uslaner, 2002).

Moral economy

In order to look beyond the orthodox technocratic and mathematical theories of economics, we may assume that every economy (every social system that produces and exchanges goods and services) is a *moral* economy. Even the simplest monetary purchase resonates with rights and equity and is governed by both written laws and customary assumptions about fairness. One may become indignant, for example, with the unfairness of a slot machine that takes one's money but fails to deliver the 'promised' snack. The most impersonal transactions are fraught with affective responses and ethical meaning, most noticeably when they fail. One may morally protest on discovering that the many songs and books in one's iTunes and Kindle libraries are not property that can legally be bequeathed in one's will, as the customer pays for access only, and not ownership of any 'thing.' The issue is technically about law and economics, but there is a moral dimension, especially in the emotionally significant context of inheritance. The digital revolution has redrawn customary boundaries of the gift.

It aids our reimagining of 'the economy' as a 'moral economy' if we cut across the dividing line between activities that are 'counted' for national economic-statistical purposes and those that are 'not counted.' The 'production boundary' that official statistics adopt in order to account for countries' GDP is rational for its purposes, but nonetheless arbitrary. It excludes unpaid domestic services, for instance.[1] But, for present purposes, we should not omit non-market and domestic transactions or gift-exchange. These create, reinforce or discharge morally significant obligations that are not normally monetized, but nonetheless form a vital aspect of a wider 'moral economy.' As a practical example, cooking a meal for the family is as much an 'economic' activity as buying the groceries from the supermarket. Reading the children bed-time stories is no less 'valued' morally – and is more time-consuming – than purchasing their books. From the point of view of a 'whole' theory of trust, moreover, both sets of actions and exchanges, on both sides of the official production boundary, are significant. 'The economy' is that which the people are doing and exchanging in real time and is not limited to the official statistical version that accounts for marketable production.

So, the production boundary between economic exchanges that are counted officially and those that are not counted – or 'excluded' – is porous and artificial. In actual human activity and day-to-day experience these two large sets of exchanges compose a continuous field of activity, interaction and social organization. Economy and society are integrated in fact, although discursively divided intellectually; norms of economic conduct are also moral norms, and all may be described in terms of trust.

In many transactions, such as an exchange of second-hand goods, in order to be trusted, or mitigate distrust and avoid conflict, the normative offer of cash instantly discharges the obligation. Both parties can walk away satisfied and with respect for one another. If invited to a friend's home for dinner, in contrast, the implicit obligation can only be discharged after a suitable time has elapsed, most likely through a reciprocal invitation. An offer of cash to discharge the debt 'on the spot' would cause bewilderment and offence. On the other hand, to return the favour at a later date would be a sign of the mutual trust that characterizes friendship. The two forms of exchange are evidently quite different, but each entails an ethic, or a sense of 'right' and 'rights,' and of what is owed by one person to another as a matter of mutual recognition and obligation.

Any exchange, then, entails the question of fairness and the recognition of belonging and status; each performance of exchange puts those relational balances at risk. A gift creates, expresses, fulfils and/or discharges obligations between people, and hence it recognizes reciprocity and the social bonding and ritualistic dimensions of giving. According to Marcel Mauss, no gift is ever 'pure' or 'free' in either an ethical or material sense. As Mary Douglas observes (in her foreword to Mauss's *The Gift*), 'Refusing requital puts the act of giving outside any mutual ties. A gift that does nothing to enhance solidarity is a contradiction' (in Mauss, 1990, p. vii). In a 'gift economy,' exchanges of valued goods are regulated by shared memories of past gifts or debts; they produce lasting bonds through expectations of future exchanges and the perpetuation of mutual obligations. In turn, *forgiving* is a way of foreclosing reciprocity when it becomes too burdensome. Debts can be annulled and wrongs forgotten, possibly in return for a minimal or token recognition in making amends. Forgiveness means that a full reckoning of obligations will not be carried out to its logical conclusion. Taken to an extreme, the act of forgiveness may involve deliberate wastage or loss of wealth, and hence become a conspicuous show of honour and status. Alternatives to such giving and forgiving are conflict, punishment, ostracism and debt-bondage – or even slavery.

Contemporary ideas about trust range across the spectrum of moral economy. We find a transactional model in those contemporary social-science approaches to trust of the kind, 'A trusts B to do X, in A's interests'; I choose to trust you so long as you act in my interests, reciprocate my goodwill, or care enough not to hurt me, or so long as I judge you to be trustworthy and you endeavour to cooperate (Gambetta, 1988; Hardin, 2006; Misztal, 1996). A rational-economic analysis sees trust as beneficial due to the reduction of 'transaction costs' of doing business. Put simply, 'trust works as a money-saving device' (Offe, 1999, p. 53); or conversely, 'absence of trust leads to economic inefficiency' (King, 2016, p. 81). Trust is regarded as a risk, but the alternatives are avoidance of others or coercion, or costly contracting and monitoring. This 'middle way' of trust is said to facilitate cooperation and to enable more complex social organization. Hence it has been described (in a mixed metaphor) as both the 'glue' of social cohesion and the 'lubricant' of democratic policy-making (van der Meer and Zmerli, 2017, p. 1). In this culturally depleted model of reciprocity, trust is regarded as a deal. A world without it would be unbearable; business and politics would suffer. In order to live well and to do the things we want to do, we need to trust others. So, trust pays – but not all of the time. To deal with this predicament, regulatory rules need to be designed to 'incentivize' trustworthiness.

Other studies of trust cut across disciplines and recombine intellectual interests in the interpersonal, the social, the political and the economic. Fukuyama (1995), for example, discusses firms, markets, cultures and family-structures, correcting the narrow economic rationalism of the neoliberal era. Giddens' 'abstract trust' encompasses political economy and networked systems, and this too bridges artificial distinctions between economy and society – between the material, the psychological and the cultural (Giddens, 1990). Social-network theories emphasize the shared nature of trust created within a group, rather than seeing it as emerging only from the subjective self-interest of each member of a group. It is not that the individual 'decides' to take a risk, and hence to partake or invest in a social group's shared 'resource' of trust. Instead, mutual obligations and reciprocal practices make the difference. For example, we can observe the emotional labour of caring or relationship-building that eludes economic valuation but is vital to organized cooperative activity and productivity. In a contemporary business context, 'it is the gift that creates networks and it is the reproduction of those networks that inspires trust' (Caillé, 2010, p. 183). Organizational life is dependent upon things that members give voluntarily, and that sustain trust, and not only on what they gain as individuals. Organizations that lack these shared relational qualities are sometimes described as 'toxic.'

So, transactional theories of trust range from some rich and varied accounts, especially in Mauss's social anthropology, to starkly utilitarian business-oriented accounts that aim to maximize efficiency and minimize fraud. In its most denuded form, trust and altruism are regarded as chosen tactics in a game between strangers, each of whom seeks to gain either materially or psychologically.

Adopting the idea of moral economy, however, helps us to rethink trust in the context of a wider scope of ethical reason than subjective 'interests.' By further regarding trust in dialectical – rather than individualistic – terms, as in Chapter 6, we can also observe how trust has been transformed in history, conceptually and in practice. Trust is not a static trait or 'hard-wired' capacity of the human being; it is a term by which we describe, express and perform historically contingent and customary forms of mutual obligations. The anthropological concept of reciprocity can advance our understanding, as it describes relations and cycles of giving, receiving, forgiving, repaying, etc., embedded in rich and varied cultural contexts.

Impossibility of trust

Let me contrast, then, the above transactional views with what I will describe as an 'unconditional' view of trust. One matter that is commonly agreed about trust is its relation to uncertainty, particularly about future events, unforeseen circumstances and consequences, and the unknown motives or future actions of others. In trusting, we are acting *as if* a range of possible actions will not be taken by those around us. Certain possible future turns of events and circumstances are thus removed from our thoughts, and many troubling questions about others' options for future conduct need not preoccupy us. We presume others to be free agents, and hence unpredictable, and yet we also presume that there are mutual obligations (like implicit promises) that keep everyone's actions within certain predictable constraints. People we trust may surprise us, but within limits – while the kinds of surprises that would hurt us as betrayals are ruled out of our expectations.

If trusting is built upon actions or events such as giving, forgiving and promising, it cannot be built upon that which was predictable. As a speech-act, a promise is in itself unpredicted, and it holds up the unpredictable as its gift. To promise that which was predictable or self-evident (e.g., 'I promise to wake up once I've finished my nap') is performatively ineffective or inauthentic. A genuine and effective promise is one that creates an obligation to do something that would not otherwise have happened and that its recipient was not already guaranteed or entitled to expect. Similarly, giving and forgiving, as meaningful events, need to defy or pre-empt predictions. 'A predicted event is not an event. The event falls on me because I don't see it coming' (Derrida, 2007, p. 451).

Derrida expands on this with regard to giving. The gift can have no expectations of reciprocity at all, not even an expression of gratitude or recognition of the act of giving, in any form whatsoever, 'symbolically, materially, or physically.' There must be no consciousness even of the gift, in either the giver or the receiver, as 'the mere consciousness of giving annuls the gift.' To be possible, giving must 'appear impossible.' Hence, the gift, rather than facilitating the cycle of regulated economic exchanges, is an unexpected and 'impossible' event that 'disrupts' such transactions. Forgiving is treated in a similar manner, as it is 'a form of giving':

> I can no more say, 'I forgive' than 'I give.' These are impossible statements. I can always make them, but in doing so, I betray what I mean to say.
>
> (Derrida, 2007, pp. 449–450)

If forgiveness is sought through negotiations and 'calculated transactions' such as demanding repentance and reformed behaviour, then one is not really forgiving the guilty party, but a changed or different person altogether.

> In order for there to be forgiveness, must one not on the contrary forgive both the fault and the guilty *as such*, where the one and the other remain irreversible as the evil, as evil itself, and being capable of repeating itself, unforgivably, without transformation, amelioration or promise?
>
> (Derrida, 2001, p. 39)

The 'unconditionality' and 'radical purity' of such forgiveness may be 'mad' in its very impossibility, but, when it does 'arrive,' it 'surprises, like a revolution, the ordinary course of history, politics, and law' (Derrida, 2001, p. 39). Hence, Derrida concludes (with only *apparent* self-contradiction) that 'forgiveness forgives only the unforgiveable' (Derrida, 2001, p. 32). We are really forgiving only when we forgive the wrong and the person responsible for it, without the expectation of reform or restitution.

One might similarly propose that *trust trusts only the untrustworthy*. To trust others must be unconditional and without negotiations or calculations about their future actions or how they may affect one's own interests. We cannot predict or calculate the other's actions; the other is radically untrustworthy; hence we trust. To say 'I trust' is an impossibility, and, in saying it, 'I betray what I mean to say.' *Trust enunciated is trust betrayed.* If trust is defined as a consciously calculated belief, judgement or decision (as it normally is in the social-science literature), then trust is already betrayed before we have begun. To say that I only trust in so far as I am confident that the other will act in my interests is not really to trust at all.

The proposition 'trust trusts only the untrustworthy' is contrary to the more widely used transactional models. It contradicts head-on, for example, Hardin's thesis that 'it is generally beneficial to trust only those who are trustworthy – not everyone, including the patently untrustworthy' (1999, p. 39). He assumes that we can distinguish between the 'trustworthy' and 'the patently untrustworthy,' as if people come in two kinds. We may indeed know of some individuals whom we regard as utterly untrustworthy, based on past behaviour, but human beings are more complex than such binary distinctions. Hardin's advice to trust only the trustworthy is outright question-begging, therefore, as the normative conclusion 'to trust only some people, not everyone' is hidden in the premise that one should first distinguish trustworthy from untrustworthy individuals. If I perceive you as trustworthy, I am already trusting you; if I perceive you as *un*trustworthy, I am already *dis*trusting you. In effect, Hardin advises us to 'trust' only when trust is *not* necessary: that is, when we already *know* who is 'trustworthy,' and who has our interests at heart – as if we can ever really 'know' that with certainty. The most 'trustworthy' person, by that account, would have been brainwashed to act always in our interests.

Instead, persons are trusted precisely because we cannot (and would not wish to) plan or predict their future actions. The other remains 'an unknown quantity' and is trusted due to the ineffability of other minds and the *un*trustworthiness of their mixed motives and fallibility. To trust one another we must regard one another as free agents – or, in the case of children, as learning to exercise free action. And so, we are forced to act *as if* we know that which eludes our knowledge, ignoring our own ignorance.

On the Derridean view, trusting 'does the impossible.' The more we trust one another, the more vulnerable we become, and the more harm we can potentially do to one another. The trusted other remains perpetually and irredeemably 'untrustworthy' in that one can never know an other's motives or predict all of his or her actions. If one *did* know all of that, one would not be acting on trust. Trust is a way of overlooking or acting in spite of uncertainty about others. It does not foreclose, eliminate, reduce or even mitigate the uncertainty; it does not ask the other to change or 'do as I say'; hence it does not overcome or negate its lexical opposite, distrust. As uncertainty and undecidability are the very conditions of possibility of trust, 'trust is haunted by non-trust' (Arfi, 2010, p. 203). And hence, in trusting, 'the ordinary course of history, politics, and law' is disrupted (to expand on Derrida's discussion of giving) because, like a gift, trust applies beyond the norms of calculable, predictable human transactions, and one proceeds 'as if' one's vulnerability had been resolved, with no questions asked.

One problem with the Derridean approach is that trust anticipates future actions, and an unconditional trust would never be broken. As there were no conditions attached, trust would endure no matter how the parties conduct themselves. Yet, relationships and political allegiances can and do end on the grounds of breach of trust, such as promises or vows not kept – and, as argued above, it is exactly such experiences that painfully bring trust to consciousness and into discourse. The Derridean approach would imply that only an unconscious trust, such as that of the child for the parent, can be considered to be trust as properly understood. Those capable of critically examining trust, or judging whom not to trust, are no longer capable of genuine trust, if we follow this pathway. So, it is not clear how Derridean 'impossibilism' can account for those painful incidents that bring trust to our awareness: the breach of trust that ends or limits a relationship and thus reveals a conditionality to our trust in others. Moreover, while Derrida says that giving and forgiving (and hence trusting) are 'mad' in their impossibility, he does not ask how 'mad' we would be to lose our confidence in their possibility. Despite the contradiction between the two, we may not have to choose exclusively between Mauss's and Derrida's theses, however.

Reconciliation

The ethical questions 'Who is trustworthy?' and 'When is it warranted to trust?' assume incorrectly that trust originates in *beliefs* that we form about people or in *choices* that we make in dealing with them. Instead, we should regard trust in terms of inter-subjective ethics of relationships, practised through mutual recognition and the observance of customs of promising, giving, forgiving, abstaining, etc. A capacity to choose consciously to trust only arises retrospectively – after we become aware of trust *through* its betrayal. And 'to trust' as if it were a calculated choice is already a betrayal of trust. There can be no definitive positive answers to the ethical questions of whom or when or how much we should trust, as the actions entailed in trust presuppose not knowing the answers. To persuade us of the rationality of trust, there is only the negative counterfactual of a complete lack of trust. If we *believe* that no one can be trusted, then we are suffering from the pathology of paranoia. If we all *choose* to trust no one at all, then we should fear a condition approximating a Hobbesian state of nature, which is much worse than the social norm. But this 'trustless world' is a state of affairs that never occurs, and so this negative counterfactual is equally an impossibility. It is a mere spectre that 'haunts' many texts on trust, scaring us into belief. It could, however, be equally nightmarish (and equally unrealistic) to imagine a life in which one trusts everyone all of the time. But, in sum, there is no need to fear a world without trust, nor to fear a world without distrust. It is, on the other hand, authentic *to fear the loss of those whom one trusts the most*. Conversely, it is unthinkable that a sane person would not trust at least some people some of the time.

In effect, we are *forced* to trust (at least) some others some of the time, and to trust in complex political and commercial systems. Not to do so is unwise, if not mad – but doing so embroils us in a 'mad' vulnerability to unpredictable events. A lack of necessary and sufficient justification *opens* (or simply *is*) the space for trust. In trusting, we embrace the unknown and inexplicable other; we are trying to perform the impossible, to engage in and sustain ethical obligation to one another, but without fully knowing or agreeing the terms and conditions.

According to Luhmann (1979), in trusting others we reduce the complexity that would come with accounting for all possible future outcomes of our engagements with others. But surely there is more to it than 'the reduction of complexity.' The 'services' performed by words and deeds of trust are also in the reduction of hostility and the increase of possibilities for an enriched life. Trustful action assists in peacefully governing and maintaining relations of power, prestige and recognition, whether between equals or between 'unequals.' Indeed, trust does not really reduce complexity; it is a name for action *in spite of* the uncertainty inherent in the complexity of events and the ineffability of others. The art of being trustworthy means making oneself harmless. But we never fully know how others may act, what their motives might be, or how they could change. We cannot predict all possible ethical dilemmas that may one day force us to betray someone's trust. We never know what harm a complex organization or system may cause due to policy, incompetence or sheer lack of control. Trusting others aids in *enhancing* complexity, such as the specialization of tasks in large communities, while making complexity, vulnerability and uncertainty mentally bearable.

Derrida's unconditional views of the gift and of forgiveness contradict the more commonly held 'transactional' views that extend from Mauss through to Fukuyama and Hardin. In the Derridean approach, the acts of giving, forgiving, promising and trusting appear impossible and disruptive. And yet such actions and relationships happen anyway; they appear to us pragmatically as 'naturally' possible and within our capabilities; indeed, many regard them as essential for social bonding, moral order and economic prosperity. The observable social facts of cooperation would thus contradict Derridean 'impossibilism.' The contradiction between unconditional and transactional approaches need not be resolved, however, by negating and cancelling out one in favour of the other. The truth of trust may be sought in the contradiction itself, or within the perpetual doubt that this contradiction reveals. The *aporia* posed by trust reveals that trust is (un) founded in the straddling of doubt. It poses doubt, hoping to depose it. The truth of trust is always '*in* doubt' – concealed within doubt itself – and not in the reduction thereof. By trusting, we can act in spite of causes for doubt.

The truth of trust

A cognitive ability to decide to trust or not to trust others is acquired only *after the performative development* of relations of trust in lived social contexts. The acquired consciousness of trust only occurs to us due to the painful *breaking* of the implicit or unspoken trust that characterized relationships we have grown within. A trust that is calculated to serve my interests is an already-broken trust. And a *politics* of trust must approach this paradox: that trust encompasses doubt. Distrust lives *with* – not against – trust, interwoven in the social fabric. The avowed aim of democratic constitutions is to entrust powers, but with limitations and with the sanction of the next election – because, without self-contradiction, we trust the untrustworthy. Trust, mistrust and distrust cut across one-dimensional models of social contract and representation whereby the people supposedly trust (or trusted) that powers be used for the security of all.

Trust and distrust are implicated in the ethics by which a society can realize itself as 'free' – consisting of freely willing and legally accountable subjects – and hence by which it can practise liberal-democratic principles. One of those principles is that political leaders speak sincerely and truthfully. But recently we hear of a 'post-truth politics,' due to instances of politicians' disregard for facts, disdain for experts, circulation of fake news, confusion sown by 'alternative facts,' and a widespread willingness to believe untruths or conspiracy theories. The notion of 'post-truth,' however, implicitly hypothesizes a past when politically significant untruths (lies, propaganda, secrets, spin-doctoring, etc.) were largely eschewed and the deliberative norms of 'accurate and sincere utterances' (Allard-Tremblay, 2015, p. 379) were more widely respected. An alternative hypothesis that in, say, 1916 or 1966, political rhetoric showed neither more nor less respect for the truth than in 2016 is also plausible. But it is beyond the scope of this book to test that hypothesis. The production of that which is treated as factual and truthful in a political community has never been a disinterested process, however, and neither are the political means by which selected figures or groups come to be trusted as sources of reliable facts and informed opinions, by some if not by others. Despite the intervening centuries and the radical changes in technologies, we witness today the same basic problem of political trust that troubled Thomas Hobbes: we doubt people's abilities to judge what to believe and in whom to trust.

It may be more pertinent to say we are witnessing a 'post-*trust* politics': a moment when political trust is not just weak, it is not even expedient, as those who 'win' can do so by assuming and spreading distrust. We could, alternatively, pay heed to a Hegelian view of the state and distinguish people's *opinions* about governmental institutions from 'what they genuinely will,' or the basic sense of order that they actively rely upon.

> They trust that the state will continue to exist and that particular interests can be fulfilled within it alone; but habit blinds us to the basis of our entire existence.
>
> (Hegel, 1991, p. 289, §268)

From that point of view, public opinions about trust are no more than opinions, whereas everyone who makes lawful use of the public roads, the legal tender, the meteorological service, etc., is enacting a shared trust in the state. The state produces, preserves and regulates itself through its differentiated powers and functions. All of the particular institutions and individuals that are its members rely upon the state for their security and their duties, and for the free pursuit of their aims, but none of them can voluntarily opt out. Grounded in such a 'political disposition,' trust is a necessity underlying our continued social existence, and yet it does not banish distrust.

Dis/trust is 'constitutional' within a democracy, as the separation of powers ensures that we entrust limited powers to some because we trust no one if left unchecked. There undoubtedly is a politics of trust, then. To address it, however, we need to understand the doubts that are encapsulated in our consciousness of trust as a political factor. We may begin by re-examining the constitutional and social obligations and the moral economy that sustain popular belief in nations and states, making them recognizable to themselves and to others. Even the most carefully crafted democratic constitution may fail if too many voters indulge in cynicism and distrust, possibly egged on by a demagogic and vulgar leader, such as a Berlusconi or Trump, or angered by the consequences of economic inequalities and stalled or downward social mobility. One cannot overlook or deny the manifest scepticism, conflicts and protests (in the streets and at the ballot-boxes) that have swept through democratic countries.

Antinomies of political trust

The radically different approaches to trust presented above (a conditional, transactional trust, contrasted with an unconditional, impossible trust) can be rephrased in terms of the political compromises achieved by a nation-state.

The traditional justifications for taxation, redistribution and social security in modern states have often been based on ideas of a social contract, or a class-compromise, or simply a deal such as America's New Deal. A trade-off is said to occur wherein the citizen accepts the burdens of taxation and obedience to the law in return for a suite of public services and the promises of security, protection of life and property, gainful employment, and provisions for individuals and families in times of misfortune or disability. While opposing interest-groups and political parties may argue and bargain over the details of the 'deal,' there is an underlying consensus (at least among a sufficiently large majority) that the nation's people and its system of government are secured and bound together by the fundamental social contract or compromise, in the knowledge that they may make bids to change law and policy according to changing values. The rights and freedoms of citizens are recognized by the state, in law and administration; citizens reciprocate by undertaking duties and abiding by laws. A political trust is embodied in such a deal, in that it creates mutual obligations between political actors and state institutions on one hand and citizens on the other. The parties are mutually bound and limited in their freedoms, but everyone is (ideally) better off as a result. Following Rawls (1999), such a society is just if inequality of power or wealth is not the result of discrimination, and if it works to maximize the status of the worst-off members. When, on the other hand, an economic crisis, such as in Greece, is so severe that it challenges the capacity of the state to compensate for hardships, then the 'breach of the social contract is accompanied by declining levels of trust in state institutions, resulting in party system collapse' (Halikiopoulou and Vasilopoulou, 2018, p. 45). Hence, we may regard political trust in transactional, conditional terms, as a reciprocal deal between the state and the individual.

An unconditional or 'impossible' view of political trust can also be described, however. In this case, the state's benevolence and the citizen's debts or obligations to society, while finite, are incalculable. All human beings are fundamentally equal in worth and dignity – 'in the eyes of God,' as it is often said, underscoring the human impossibility of putting that principle consistently into practice. Nonetheless, a principle of radical equality would be our starting-point, according to which every individual holds an inalienable right to an unconditional guarantee of a standard of living that (at least) averts indignity and exclusion from the community. Any citizen who is unable, for any reason, to meet the normative standards of economic self-sufficiency and autonomy is automatically 'forgiven' and hence supported. No child is left in poverty. Everyone is assured that a lifetime of work and contribution to society will not end in poverty and indignity. The state always holds 'behind its back' the legitimate uses of coercion, but it chooses benevolence before punishment. There is no prison for debtors. But the individual's debts to the state are incalculable and unrepayable in a lifetime.

One may see such a view as 'Utopian,' which is another way of calling it 'impossible.' When such unconditional forgiveness of incapacity does 'arrive,' however, it is politically transformative, as it is not motivated by desire for political gain or personal aggrandizement. In terms of political economy and social policy, it would mean that labour is radically 'de-commodified,' and no one becomes an economic hostage in a labour-market (Esping-Andersen, 1990). Concern about a social 'trust gap' (Smith, 2010) related to discrimination and inequality may be taken as a precursor to this thorough-going, if 'impossible,' political claim. The postulation of equality is both necessary, as a political act, and yet impossible – just as the infinite is necessary for our understanding of finite numbers, and yet impossible to apprehend (Badiou, 2005).

These are ideal representations, however. Inequality, conflict and distrust are also commonly observable features of real-world political events. Western societies that had achieved post-Reformation toleration and an internal sense of solidarity, often reliant upon a degree of ethnic or religious homogeneity, have encountered problems in extending unconditional rights (to reside, settle, work, worship and claim social security) to newcomers who are perceived as different and alien, who have no record of contributions, whose presence appears to breach the mutual promises and duties of the state's 'deal' with its citizens. Resentments surrounding pre-existing regional and cultural differences may also surface. At worst, we see some nations internally divided, to the extent of breaking apart.

Consider, then, the following two examples of Catalonia and the Donbass, in which political trust failed. In 2017, Catalonia was divided by a political movement to secede from Spain. Many Catalans argued that, as well as their cultural and linguistic differences, the region contributed more to the national exchequer than was provided in return through public services. This pitted pro-independence Catalans against those who supported union with Spain, and it pitted the Catalan regional parliament – led by pro-independence politicians – against the government in Madrid. When the regional government staged a referendum on independence, the Spanish government refused to recognize it, and police-officers forcefully entered polling-booths, prevented people from voting, seized ballot-boxes, and later imprisoned some elected regional representatives. Madrid then took control of the Catalan government and ordered a fresh regional election, at which the majority of seats were won by pro-independence representatives, thus continuing the political deadlock.

A much more violent secessionist conflict flared up in the eastern provinces of Ukraine (the Donbass) in 2014. The year before that, former president Yanukovich had dropped negotiation of a trade agreement with the European Union in favour of a financial bailout and gas deal with Russia. This sparked the so-called Maidan Revolution in the winter of 2013–14 that ousted Yanukovich. In the following few months, Russia annexed Crimea and counter-Maidan pro-independence protests erupted in the eastern provinces of Donetsk and Lugansk. A civil war resulted, with covert support from Russia. Rebels within the two provinces fought to establish independent republics, while the Ukrainian government described its military reaction as an 'anti-terrorist operation.' Ukrainian militias shelled the cities and villages held by the rebels, resulting in thousands of civilian casualties, and as many as two million people fled their homes (Katchanovski, 2016). On 17 July 2014, a Russian anti-aircraft system shot down a Malaysian Airlines flight, killing all on board, having most likely misidentified a target. A ceasefire was put into effect in 2015, but the shooting from both sides continued and the region became sealed off by (in effect) an armed border between hostile nations (OSCE Special Monitoring Mission to Ukraine, 2017). The self-proclaimed Donetsk People's Republic started issuing its own passports and vehicle registrations. It began to teach children in schools its own principles of citizenship and changed the language of education from Ukrainian to Russian. But the republic was not internationally recognized – not even by Moscow.

In each case, the implicit will to belong to and identify with a nation-state has been lost for many people – sufficiently many, with sufficiently strongly held belief, that they take actions to try to separate themselves as a new political entity. The state may react with force, however, to prevent such a loss. It is fair to *describe* these situations metaphorically as a 'breakdown' of trust, although this will not suffice as an explanation for such complex events. Distrust is a descriptive factor, not a causative factor. The rise of conflict and the decline of political trust are simply two different ways of describing the same situation. The political trust that had sustained a commitment to shared nationhood has (metaphorically) 'broken down' nonetheless. The loyalties of the people become divided and many take active steps to secede – seizing and taking up arms against the state in the Donbass. In its turn, the state resorts to violent means – police brutality, political intervention, and, if necessary, military force – to preserve territorial integrity and economic assets.

So, for some hard-headed advice, let me return to the rewording (in Chapter 1) of the Machiavellian question, 'Is it better to be *trusted* or to be feared?' It would be better to be both trusted and feared, as the people's loyalties to the state are strictly conditional (unless inspired by true nobility of leadership) and the state must always reserve its rights to punish and coerce. When the 'deal' works, the people will support you, but, when it fails, they will turn their backs on you. A ruler is trusted only 'for the time being' – as long as the benefits of subjection last. When things go wrong, it is much easier for the people to risk offending a ruler whom they trust (or trusted) more than they fear than one whom they fear more than trust. Hence, for hegemony over and subjugation of peoples, fear of punishment and (as necessary) armed violence are indispensable. It is preferable to instil trust, and not to use guns, to *maintain* order; it is nonetheless essential to have enough guns under one's command in case the need should arise to *restore* order.

The problem is then how to use fear without making the people hate you. But the long-term problem of restoring political trust (a consensus that 'we are all in this nation together for our own good') is much harder, once force has been used. It is not clear, for instance, whether political trust between Catalans and Madrid will return. In the case of the Donbass, reintegration with the government in Kiev on a basis of trust, given the violence that was unleashed and the corruption rife within that capital, presently looks impossible. But is such political trust paradoxically possible precisely *because* of its apparent political impossibility? Or, is it only realistically possible through a series of careful calculations and negotiations that might be understood, for instance, in the terms of game-theory?

'Thoughts on the present discontents'

Divisions of political opinions, and active divisiveness, between 'the people' and the political class (or 'the establishment') may appear to constitute, in rough terms, the structure of much of the discontent and distrust of recent times. But 'the people' are never united in opinion, and so this discontent encompasses deep divisions of opinions between large factions of 'the people' themselves, accompanied often by party fragmentation that confounds government-formation, for example in 2017 in the Netherlands and Germany. Factionalism among the people and their representatives, and consequent dysfunction in the executive and legislative branches of government, have been profound in the United States, even before the advent of the remarkably dysfunctional Trump administration (Hetherington and Rudolph, 2015). The Brexit referendum also revealed deep political divisions, and its consequences have embroiled the UK government and the EU in a multitude of apparently intractable and irreconcilable policy problems, such as the Irish border. It even raised an ancient constitutional debate about the relative powers of royal prerogative and parliamentary sovereignty.[2] A bitter political debate, not just between but within political parties, continued in full public view.

Although the constitutional and political problems of eighteenth-century England were entirely different from today's, Edmund Burke lived through, and eloquently commented upon, equally dysfunctional times. He attacked courtiers for choosing ministers who would be servile to the King, that ensured parliament would not control the Crown's expenditure, that treated the interests and opinions of the people with contempt, and that lacked an effective opposition to hold the executive to account (Bromwich, 2014). He exposed a House of Commons that put forward 'men without popular confidence, public opinion, natural connexion, or mutual trust, invested with all the powers of Government' (Burke, 1981, p. 321). Burke's constitutional remedy featured a ministry formed independently of the King and accountable to the House, and a House that is accountable to the people. A unified ministry 'composed of those who recommend themselves to the Sovereign through the opinion of their country, and not by their obsequiousness,' will serve the King more effectively, and 'with affection and fidelity; because his choice of them, upon such principles, is a compliment to their virtue' (Burke, 1981, p. 322). Faithful service, trusted by the people, would thus be reciprocated by regal recognition.

Burke was arguing for separation of powers and for comity between 'the people' and 'the establishment.' The constitutional model of political parties forming, on one hand, a loyal opposition, and, on the other, a majority whose leader, by convention, is invited by the Sovereign to form a government, is more or less what has evolved, with historical impetus from Burke and many others, in Westminster systems (Galligan and Brenton, 2015). And Burke's nascent theory of representation – that the elected member is not bound to seek mandates from constituents on every matter, but acts as their trustee – influenced the founders of the American constitution, as 'a decade later, [James] Madison followed the footsteps of Burke' in the *Federalist Papers* (Bromwich, 2014, p. 225).[3] Along the way, though, the British had lost the loyalty of the American colonies, in no small part due to breaches of the constitutional convention of 'no taxation without representation.' The Americans won their independence and then set the modern standard for a written constitution with clear separation of powers. It is thus with some historical sense of irony that we may now observe both constitutions – the unwritten British and the carefully crafted American – challenged and undermined by comparable forms of political distrust and by 'the present discontents.'

The full and original title of Burke's famous polemical essay is 'Thoughts on *the Cause* of the Present Discontents.' At a time of increasing national wealth, and in the absence of any national calamity or defeat in war, why were there such 'convulsions' and 'distemper'? Were the people just 'malignant' and 'ungrateful'? It is much harder, however, to judge the causes of present events than those of the past which we can observe more coolly from historical accounts. 'It is very rare indeed for men to be wrong in their feelings concerning public misconduct; as rare to be right in their speculation upon *the cause* of it' (italics added). But Burke was convinced that there is nothing to be gained from blaming the people. We should look to 'the trustees of power,' 'because it is more easy to change an administration than to reform a people' (Burke, 1981, p. 256).

Distrust, and conversely a decline or crisis of political trust, can mean many different things in practice, but they are meaningful terms with which to describe 'the present discontents' of the early twenty-first century. They do not provide us with a diagnosis of the cause, however. Burke is right, though, that we need to look critically at the conduct of 'the trustees of power' when seeking suitable change or reform. There is nothing to be gained from blaming the people for not trusting their leaders, regardless of how irrational, ungrateful or malevolent some of their opinions and conduct may appear to be from a privileged perspective.

Conclusion

The guiding concept of 'moral economy' assists us in thinking more holistically about the social, cultural and economic aspects of the actions and relations in which trust matters the most, or through which trust is experienced. At the height of the era of neoliberalism, in the 1990s, it was common to hear enthusiastic talk of a globalized competitive economy with open borders, global citizenship, deregulated government, multi-national networked business models, and freedom of consumer choice, and hence to hear that nationalism and the nation-state were in decline (Fukuyama, 1992; Ohmae, 1996). A vision of a global free-market neglects, however, that, for any organized group or business or community to cohere and flourish, individual members need to believe that what they have to *give* will somehow count or be valued by that to which they belong, beyond the utilitarian terms of immediate market transactions, and that they will receive in return enough for their security, or at least hope for the future, such that their efforts are neither in vain nor regarded disdainfully. Such localized or nationalized solidarity – among a community of 'mutually recognized' members – is quintessentially political. Disagreements do not threaten the system itself if there remains a basic comity or connection between people, organizations, institutions and state and a degree of cooperation between opposing parties.

A politics of *dis*trust arises and predominates within a community, an organization or a nation when such a sense of reciprocity and solidarity has declined, and when 'the forgotten people' believe that normative cycles of giving and receiving – or the creation of bonds, security and trust in the networks to which they should belong – have somehow failed. The over-powering effects of disruptive technological change and the sense that the individual's trust in institutions no longer even matters within a regime of 'surveillance capitalism' may be contributing to these discontents (Zuboff, 2015). If enough people feel as if the 'deal' implicit in their loyalty as citizens of a nation-state has been betrayed, then they are likely to react angrily, to respond to calls to 'take back control' and put the nation's native inhabitants first, no matter how futile that reaction may prove to be. Their search for an explanation for their frustration and disillusionment can lead them to mis-identify its antecedents and to target an 'alien' or 'exceptional' social group for blame, as well as to look critically at the conduct of 'the trustees of power.' Even though their economy may be relatively affluent materially, the rule of law and basic rights observed, and public services functioning, the people's distrust means that they may heed calls for change, supported all the while by an implicit trust that the apparatuses and services of the state on which they rely will continue undisturbed – for themselves, but not for 'others.' If distrust becomes even more profound, then people may take active steps to separate themselves from a nation-state to which they no longer wish to belong, or they may turn to revolutionary actions to seek to change the regime itself.

Political trust may be understood 'with or without conditions.' It is normal in the social sciences to speak of trust in conditional or transactional terms. But radical ideals of equality and justice, and the *aporia* of trust itself, must leave open the possibility of an *im*possible political trust that overcomes barriers, divisions and conflicts. We do not have to make an exclusive choice between these contradictory approaches to political trust if we think dialectically.

Notes

1 'Not all economic activities are treated as economic activities and included in the production boundary of the System of National Accounts. Except for the services of owner-occupied housing and paid domestic staff, all personal and domestic services that are produced and consumed within the same households, such as cleaning, decoration, cooking, caring for and educating children, caring for sick and old people, maintenance and repair of dwellings and durables, transportation of household members etc. are excluded' (United Nations, 2003, p. 20).
2 Following the non-binding referendum ('the will of the people'), could the Prime Minister on behalf of the Crown give notice of the government's decision to exit

the EU, or did this first require parliamentary approval? The courts decided that parliamentary approval was required by law.

3 Alexander Hamilton in *Federalist* 71 (1788) also took a distinctly Burkean outlook: 'The republican principle demands that the deliberate sense of the community should govern the conduct of those to whom they intrust the management of their affairs; but it does not require an unqualified complaisance to every sudden breeze of passion, or to every transient impulse which the people may receive from the arts of men, who flatter their prejudices to betray their interests' (Jay, Goldman, Hamilton, and Madison, 2008, p. 351).

References

Allard-Tremblay, Y. (2015). Trust and distrust in the achievement of popular control. *The Monist, 98*(4), 375–390.

Arfi, B. (2010). Auto-immunity of trust without trust. *Journal of International Political Theory, 6*(2), 188–216.

Badiou, A. (2005). *Metapolitics.* London: Verso.

Booth, W. J. (1994). On the idea of the moral economy. *American Political Science Review, 88*(3), 653–667.

Bromwich, D. (2014). *The intellectual life of Edmund Burke: From the sublime and beautiful to American independence.* Cambridge, MA: Belknap.

Burke, E. (1981). *The writings and speeches of Edmund Burke* (Vol. II). Oxford: Clarendon Press.

Caillé, A. (2010). Gift. In K. Hart, J.-L. Laville, and A. D. Cattani (Eds.), *The human economy: A citizen's guide* (pp. 180–186). Cambridge: Polity Press.

Derrida, J. (2001). *On cosmopolitanism and forgiveness.* New York, NY: Routledge.

Derrida, J. (2007). A certain impossible possibility of saying the event. *Critical Inquiry, 33*(2), 441–461.

Esping-Andersen, G. (1990). *The three worlds of welfare capitalism.* Cambridge: Polity Press.

Foucault, M. (2007). *Security, territory, population: Lectures at the Collège de France 1977–1978.* New York, NY: Picador.

Foucault, M. (2008). *The birth of biopolitics: Lectures at the Collège de France, 1978–1979.* New York, NY: Palgrave Macmillan.

Fukuyama, F. (1992). *The end of history and the last man.* New York, NY: Maxwell Macmillan International.

Fukuyama, F. (1995). *Trust: The social virtues and the creation of prosperity.* New York, NY: Free Press.

Galligan, B., and Brenton, S. (2015). *Constitutional conventions in Westminster systems: Controversies, changes and challenges.* Cambridge: Cambridge University Press.

Gambetta, D. (Ed.). (1988). *Trust: Making and breaking cooperative relations.* Oxford: Basil Blackwell.

Giddens, A. (1990). *The consequences of modernity.* Stanford, CA: Stanford University Press.

Halikiopoulou, D., and Vasilopoulou, S. (2018). Breaching the social contract: Crises of democratic representation and patterns of extreme right party support. *Government and Opposition, 53*(1), 26–50.

Hann, C. (2010). Moral economy. In K. Hart, J.-L. Laville, and A. D. Cattani (Eds.), *The human economy: A citizen's guide* (pp. 187–198). Cambridge: Polity Press.

Hardin, R. (1999). Do we want trust in government? In M. E. Warren (Ed.), *Democracy and trust* (pp. 22–41). Cambridge: Cambridge University Press.

Hardin, R. (2006). *Trust*. Cambridge: Polity Press.

Hegel, G. (1991). *Elements of the philosophy of right*. Cambridge: Cambridge University Press.

Heilbroner, R. L. (1973). Economics as a 'value-free' science. *Social Research, 40*(1), 129–143.

Hetherington, M., and Rudolph, T. J. (2015). *Why Washington won't work: Polarization, political trust, and the governing crisis*. Chicago, IL: University of Chicago Press.

Jay, J., Goldman, L., Hamilton, A., and Madison, J. (2008). *The Federalist papers*. Oxford: Oxford University Press.

Katchanovski, I. (2016). The separatist war in Donbas: A violent break-up of Ukraine? *European Politics and Society, 17*(4), 473–489.

King, M. (2016). *The end of alchemy: Money, banking, and the future of the global economy*. New York, NY: W.W. Norton.

Luhmann, N. (1979). *Trust and power*. Chichester: Wiley.

Mauss, M. (1990). *The gift: The form and reason for exchange in archaic societies*. London: Routledge.

Misztal, B. (1996). *Trust in modern societies: The search for the bases of social order*. Cambridge: Polity Press.

Offe, C. (1999). How can we trust our fellow citizens? In M. E. Warren (Ed.), *Democracy and trust* (pp. 42–87). Cambridge: Cambridge University Press.

Ohmae, K. (1996). *The end of the nation state: The rise of regional economies*. New York, NY: Free Press.

OSCE Special Monitoring Mission to Ukraine. (2017). *Hardship for conflict-affected civilians in Eastern Ukraine*. Organization for Security and Co-operation in Europe.

Polanyi, K. (2001). *The great transformation: The political and economic origins of our time*. Boston, MA: Beacon Press.

Rawls, J. (1999). *A theory of justice*. Cambridge: Belknap.

Smith, S. S. (2010). Race and trust. *American Review of Sociology, 36*, 453–475.

Thompson, E. (1971). The moral economy of the English crowd in the eighteenth century. *Past and Present, 50*(1), 76–136.

United Nations. (2003). *National accounts: A practical introduction*. New York, NY. Retrieved from https://unstats.un.org/unsd/publication/SeriesF/seriesF_85.pdf

Uslaner, E. M. (2002). *The moral foundations of trust*. Cambridge: Cambridge University Press.

van der Meer, T., and Zmerli, S. (2017). The deeply rooted concern with political trust. In S. Zmerli, and T. van der Meer (Eds.), *Handbook on political trust* (pp. 1–15). Cheltenham: Edward Elgar.

Zuboff, S. (2015). Big other: Surveillance capitalism and the prospects of an information civilization. *Journal of Information Technology, 30*(1), 75–89.

8 Conclusions

A problem – or a crisis – of political trust is said to be at the heart of the electoral disruptions and public dissatisfaction experienced recently in democracies. This problem has been misconstrued, however, due to reductive definitions and misrecognition of trust itself. This critical concept stood in need of reformulation.

The disruptive events of 2016, particularly the Brexit referendum and the election of President Trump, provided a live historical backdrop against which to re-examine trust as a concept in political theory. Those and other unanticipated electoral results were typified as reactions against 'the establishment' – especially against a liberal political élite. They were seen as victories for 'the people' – the forgotten people, the little people, the real people – who had purportedly been hoodwinked for years by political and business élites that pushed for open borders, more immigrants and tolerant multiculturalism. A lack of political trust in liberal-democratic (and flawed-democratic) countries is manifested in suspicion of foreigners and resistance to globalization, as well as left-wing critiques of unjust and unmerited privileges, inequalities and social disadvantage. Traditional political parties, ideologies and models of representation have lost their legitimacy in the eyes of many citizens, and consequently many have either supported populist alternatives or abstained from voting.

It is not only recently, though, that people have been forced to think about political trust. In the late eighteenth century, for instance, the struggles that Edmund Burke went through to uphold what he regarded as the 'high trust' incumbent upon him (and on all those in positions of power) are as compelling as anything we see today. Indeed, Brexit is arguably less catastrophic than the ruptures that Burke sought (and failed) to avert, notably the loss of the American colonies and the gross injustices committed by the East India Company. The present global-historical turn against liberal democracy is disturbing – but, taking the long view, it may be a turn in history's spiral.

Our trust involves a sense of belonging with others or to a group, be it family, community, nation or state, the latter entailing the legal status of citizenship with rights and duties. The duty incumbent upon the state is to maintain that common consensus of belonging among a sufficient majority such that people can prosper and opposition to the state is minimal. Political contestation occurs around questions of who belongs to the state and how governments should maintain the social well-being of citizens. Who should be able to benefit from 'our thing'? Should 'we' continue to belong to the nation (or union of nations) that we happen to belong to, or separate ourselves into an autonomous entity?

Divisiveness and conflict within and between nations, if we follow the headline-news, are ever-present. But a further political struggle of our times is occurring around people's lack of control over the automated and perpetual data-gathering about themselves, and over 'digital alter egos' compiled by business corporations and agencies of state. Purchases, consumption of news, sharing of events and ideas through social media and the aimless or curious browsing of websites are all being recorded somewhere by someone's automated digital systems, and profiled by means of complex algorithms for advertisers, online reputation managers and intelligence officers. We have little control over 'who we are' and 'what we believe,' as represented in cyberspace, nor over how this is commodified. The contested models of regulation of the internet – including openness, competition, privacy and surveillance – are a global political question, posing new and unfamiliar problematics of trust.

Furthermore, political trust needs to be considered alongside material inequalities. If we regard economies in political and moral terms, taking into account the distribution of incomes, wealth and opportunities, then the structures that determine people's livelihoods will affect whether they perceive 'the system' as fair, or as rigged against them. Political trust is related to the (actual or perceived) justice of the 'deal' or the institutional exchanges between government, private enterprise and those they serve or employ. Poverty, reduced social mobility and resentment of the wealthy erode political trust and lead to calls for alternative economic policies. These alternatives may be of the social-democratic variety (redistribution) or the conservative-nationalist variety (less immigration), but both resist globalization and reassert the mutual obligations of belonging to particular versions of 'the nation.'

Besides a traditional politics of socio-economic class, however, polarization occurs across a range of dimensions and cultural values. Inequities of political significance have emerged between the generations, between racial and religious groups, between native-born and immigrant, between those with and without higher education, and between the globally mobile and those who cannot afford (or do not want) to leave their home-towns. These politically salient social cleavages resulted in party-political fragmentation, the obliteration of some traditional parties of the centre-left and centre-right, and the disruption of formerly predictable electoral pendulum-swings. The rise of right-wing populist parties and protest-voting in countries such as Germany and Italy made government-formation difficult. In others, such as Hungary, Turkey and India, it delivered successes to nationalist 'strongman' leaders.

While the real material and social impacts of ethnic cleansing, civil war, colonization, exploitation, restructuring, digitalization and automation occur around the globe, from time to time an intangible quality of social relations called 'trust' is invoked as something vital that is broken or missing. Trust and the lack of it look like an explanation for deeper local and global divisions. But if 'more trust' were an effective solution, then someone should have shown us how to get there by now. There has been no shortage of surveys, research and policy documents on the matter – but still no applications or solutions that can be predicted to work. Many communities are affected by distrust or they are trusting in hard-liners, given the threats and the inequities that they see. Political trust is a text-book example of a 'wicked problem,' and furthermore, without political trust, no other wicked problem (such as climate change or unemployment) can effectively be addressed.

There are of course many recommendations for 'rebuilding' political trust. There should be strict limits on political campaign donations and spending, stand-down periods between leaving public office and working for private lobbyists or think-tanks, and better resourcing for legislators (especially those in opposition) to reduce reliance on lobby-groups. In the US, the elimination of gerrymandering and voter-suppression would help. In the EU, less regulation and greater responsiveness to the people are called for. Better civics education in schools is on many people's lists. But, to get such policies implemented effectively, majorities of law-makers need to agree to such self-limitations and transparency. It requires major political figures to negotiate, 'agree to disarm,' and 'play by the rules of the game' (Mounk, 2018, p. 242). But this presupposes that they trust enough to agree on what 'the rules' are, that they can safely admit to past unfairness, and that there is political capital to be gained from fair play. It takes political trust in order to make the tools with which to build political trust, it seems. When we assume that trust is something distinct that we can literally 'rebuild,' we forget that the actions that are said to 'rebuild trust' are in themselves actions that entail and exemplify what we mean by trust.

Social sciences have misinterpreted trust, asked too much of it, or asked the wrong questions. A basic conceptual confusion (which has been easy to identify but difficult to clear up) defines trust in an essentialist manner as a mental state or attribute, as 'something that goes on in us' such as 'our beliefs about others.' Social scientists have reified the results of surveys that ask for individuals' opinions or beliefs about trust in others, in governments or in politicians. Such surveys are informative, but, properly speaking, trust is not fully comprehensible as a belief or opinion. One's *belief* that a person is speaking the truth or acting with good intentions is a common, but neither necessary nor sufficient, feature of a relation of trust. Similarly, a belief that someone is *trustworthy*, based on past conduct, *may* be a feature of a relationship of trust. But many social scientists have generalized such beliefs or opinions, treating them as sufficient evidence of trust itself. Instead, I have described trust performatively in terms of the ethical qualities that normalize interactions between and among people.

One significant benefit of reprising the original and evolving political uses of the term *trust* is to appreciate the diverse actions that may be characterized as forms of trust, and hence to caution us not to overuse the abstract noun nor to reduce it to either a mental state or a 'social reality.' The more that trust and distrust have been called upon to account for the troubles of our times, the more important such a critical reappraisal has become. This re-examination of political trust has been sceptical at first, as it should not be taken for granted that trust applies readily at the level of societies and politics, or, even if it does, that it helps us to do more than describe such complex situations. Trust and distrust are characteristic or descriptive of the politics and ethics of situations, but they are not explanations that point to remedies.

Nevertheless, it does make sense to talk of political trust and of a politics of trust. And it is worth our while attending to the public ethical requirements incumbent upon us as 'trust' when we aspire to social progress.

Political trust re-thought

Some may say that Thomas Hobbes offers no useful insight into political trust, but, on close reading, he does. He would have comprehended the political vulnerability of our times: that folk are gullible. Unwisely trusting favoured persons as authorities, they are inclined to believe blindly both the facts and the falsehoods that they are told. Even if what they hear is largely false, sufficient numbers of people will accept it anyway, if it is repeated with conviction and addresses their cultural malaise. The basic political question Hobbes posed may be, 'In whom should you trust?' or, 'In what should you believe?'

The sovereign should 'settle' or standardize the definitions of words, especially politically and religiously contentious words, and control the publication and dissemination of doctrines, according to Hobbes. He wanted to get rid of 'fake news.' Nowadays, such state control of ideas and their publication is undesirable and impossible in democracies – although state and corporate observation or surveillance of what and whom we believe, or like or follow, and of our innermost doubts, or our Google searches, is now routine. Due to an explosion of information sources, we live now in an age of *dis*information, dissent and doubt. We witness the deliberate *creation* of confusion, alternative facts, fake news and conspiracy theories, when one person's 'failed' news source is another's defender of 'truth and democracy.' Post-truth politics – or post-*trust* politics – poses anew the Hobbesian problem, not in the form of an outright condition of war, but a condition of confusion, distrust and discord over whom and what to believe and to follow.

This book owes a lot to Ludwig Wittgenstein (who did so much to cut through philosophical confusions) and to Wittgensteinian readings of Hobbes. But it has identified John Locke as the conceptual progenitor of a properly political form of trust. Close attention to the syntax in which trust occurs revealed a significant shift from Hobbes to Locke – a reification of trust as a thing we give, and its attribution to institutions and practices of government. In the subsequent two centuries, we have observed, the uses of trust expanded, as illustrated in the works of Burke and Mill. Burkean political trust has lately become narrowly interpreted in the context of theories of representation, while the present exploration has rediscovered Burke's providential meaning. In contrast, J.S. Mill demonstrates a political grasp of trust that is more compatible with secular contemporary literature. But both Burke and Mill also speak of 'a trust' as a significant public office or duty – a meaning that is less used today. The further important shift that occurs in the late twentieth century, however, is the realization of an impersonal, generalized or abstract trust that pertains to, and is distributed by and through, entire networked systems. Money is the most well-charted exemplar. But retracing the roots of the idea of 'trust in money' raised some important doubts. The attribution of a systemic distributed trust begins to look like a quasi-religious idea, or a faith in an immanent and intangible force that pervades all. It lures writers into trying to explain a poorly defined 'trust' in equally poorly defined terms such as faith, values, belief – or even capital. Moreover, we may choose between objects in markets, but we have no choice but to trust 'in the system,' or else we are lost to 'normal social life.' How many times, for instance, have we 'agreed' to hand over our personal details to big data firms? If it is a choice, political trust is fundamentally a forced choice.

The best approach is to keep trust grounded in the observable and ethically significant things that we do and say in relations with one another and in our participation in social-political-economic life. This may be as basic as the civility of introducing oneself to a new acquaintance and sharing some ideas to make conversation. Trust actively encompasses the reasons for our relatively patterned mundane conduct, in doing things like settling bills, overlooking one another's minor mistakes, talking about political events, or assisting others without expectations of repayment. The idea of a properly political trust, moreover, makes descriptive sense of the complex arena of mutual obligations, public legal duties, social protections and so on, that we all observe or enjoy, or complain about, from time to time. As Hegel might have put it, in adopting duties, we discover our freedom in the context of an ethical social life that makes the realization of personal aims conceivable. The governed, regulated and patterned conduct of people in the streets, shops, offices, etc. – their political disposition – as they go about their lives, observing these constraints and opportunities, enacts what we may rightly call a political trust. Because we cannot do without others, we cannot get much done without trust.

To draw conclusions

'Unspoken tacit trust' is only spoken of retrospectively. It precedes, logically and developmentally, our speaking about it, which undoes it. Unspoken trust is the strongest and most basic form of trust, arising without or before conscious thought. So, when setting out to think, talk or write about trust, a subject that speaks has already asserted and interposed itself, as both subject and object of the verb, 'pre-occupying' the place of trusting and being trusted. The *subject* that trusts is already mediated by language.

We should not let grammar and figures of speech confuse us about what goes on when we trust. The model of 'A trusts B' should not predetermine our understanding of trust, as if it were something that goes on in one person, with regard to another. Neither should we take literally our metaphors, such as 'building' and then 'breaking' trust or speaking of it as a 'glue' or a 'lubricant.' Trust is no such object or thing. Moreover, to say 'we trust machines' is metonymy, substituting an inanimate object for the myriad of people whose principles and work are being trusted.

Trust ultimately eludes representation in either symbols or images. It is inherent in human sociability, representable as neither nature nor culture alone. As trust is neither an emotion nor an idea – nor does it depend upon our having any particular emotions or ideas – and because it entails what happens between and among people, it cannot be definitively located within or attributed to the individual. The troubling ineffability of trust reflects the absence of a fully comprehensible truster–trusted relation. We can describe what people do in relations with one another, but this is infinitely variable, being situationally, culturally and historically contingent. The description of particular kinds of relationships or actions as forms of trust becomes hair-splitting and confusing at times simply because trust may relate to virtually *anything* that is non-coercive and that governs our conduct.

The parties to a relation of trust do not conform to any particular prescribed set of understandings. Trust is ethical, but a rule-book would not help. And the vulnerability of those who trust one another is always a cause for doubts, especially if one thinks too much about it. Thus, to speak *of* trust is to doubt, to speak with doubt, to put trust reflexively into doubt, or to betray one's own trust. Trust enunciated is trust betrayed. And similarly, trust and distrust are not opposites in practice; they are dialectical counterparts and mutually constitutive. It is this *aporia*, announced in any proposition of trust, that leads us towards (not away from) the unsettling truth of trust.

The political resolution lies in neither trust nor distrust, then, but in both at once – to adapt words from Hegel. Distrust in political life is institutionalized and rational, but this neither rules out nor negates trust, and vice versa.

In trusting, we mutually recognize ourselves as free, and hence extend our freedom; but freedom and trust emerge from forced choices. The fundamental choices have been made in advance, and we act *as if* free to choose, and as if choosing to trust the state and its currency. But in as much as this 'free' subject of trust/risk/choice appears natural or self-evident, it is only retrospectively, after suspending any deeper political doubts. The free subject of modern political trust is not looking for an *exit* door, unless political trust has truly been 'broken,' and, even then, there may be no exit in sight, so long as one wishes 'to have a life.'

Definitions of trust tend to see it in terms of my wager or belief in the other's predictably acting in my interests, or (which amounts to much the same) my judging them trustworthy. We would then be trusting only the 'known' trustworthy, a circular and redundant conceit, by any logical account. Such definitions overlook the indefinable moment of trust, as we act beyond the calculable, or without the information needed to minimize vulnerability. If one stays within the range of the cognitively calculable or estimable, based on experience or past deeds or reputation for reliability, then it is not yet trust. But neither is it satisfactory to attribute trust to a non-rational 'leap of faith,' as this too is circular. We trust *in* the incalculable and the dubious. Trust trusts only the untrustworthy – the aspect of otherness that eludes 'safe' estimation or prediction.

There *is* a politics of trust, as trusting one another means governing and moderating our reciprocated actions. We limit our conduct, without coercion, making it possible to cooperate. We monitor one another's debts and promises, we self-regulate our emotional reactions, and we set aside many questions, doubts or suspicions about what others could do. But these doubts are not eliminated; they are only unthinkable or forgotten for the time being.

At a systemic political level, trust is a quality of power-relations, observable in numerous institutional exchanges, rights and duties. Implicit or explicit, any claim to legitimately occupy governmental offices entails promises, obligations and credits. The power to tax is accompanied by the promise to use those resources for defined beneficial policy aims, as well as for an indefinable popular sense that the country is 'heading in the right direction,' or at least not heading for disaster, and that 'we' have a lot at stake and in common. The authority to speak for or to represent a nation is premised upon perceived credibility, derived from a recognized basis or procedure for achieving that role. And distrust is not abnormal or dysfunctional, as we learn from history that it's unwise to trust anyone with unchecked powers.

If we think in active human terms of 'the moral economy,' then trust is a vital, albeit intangible, ethical quality of our interactions with, and our obligations to, one another. In any political-economic arrangement, there is a 'moral orderliness' at stake; there is a contestable set of norms about the justice of reciprocal rights and obligations, the circulation of goods and rewards or penalties. One may talk of such responsibilities, as Burke did, in abstract terms as 'a trust' – as moral obligations incumbent upon decision-makers and institutions – or in the active terms of 'trusting' – that is, the normalized ways and means or practices by which we recognize obligations to one other as free subjects with needs and rights.

Every stable country strikes a kind of 'deal' in political economy that suffices for 'a multitude' not to question its appearance as 'a nation,' at least to a degree that people prefer to ignore thoughts of secession or rebellion. But if this 'deal' is perceived to have been broken or abandoned, distrust is likely to prevail. Then a leader who speaks up for 'the forgotten people' and against 'the establishment,' and who wants to 'reclaim' the nation or to make it 'great' again, may find an enthusiastic audience. In practice, this strategy has proven in some countries to be sufficient to command a majority (in a referendum or an electoral college), or in others sufficient to straddle the balance of political power and hence to determine or to frustrate the formation of a government.

When thinking of political trust, most writers have been concerned with promises made to 'the people,' and either kept or not kept. And the promise has been treated as 'merely' a transaction, overlooking the 'impossibility' of the promise as it puts our relationships at stake, creating obligations based upon an uncertain future and a willingness not to forget.

Not enough attention has been paid to the exceptional sovereign power to forgive, and this power is all too often held in reserve. The abandonment of millions of people to violence, displacement, statelessness and calculated suffering is 'normalized' by force and by propaganda, observable for example in the reappearance of 'the camp' (from Nauru to the Calais 'Jungle'), or in fences and walls built to keep 'unwanted' people out (from the Hungarian–Serbian border to the Mexican–US border). And a loss of individual autonomy or self-reliance is nowadays often treated as a personal moral failure, or as fraudulent, thus legitimizing the abandonment of many members of affluent societies to disenfranchisement, poverty, illness and early death. The loss of security and trust among those who suffer from such misfortunes goes unremedied by the state's power to forgive and to redeem. In practice, not all human beings are of equal worth or dignity in the eyes of the state. Not all lives are equally 'grievable' (Butler, 2009). Millions exist outside of the frameworks of recognition, beyond politico-legal redemption. But the power to forgive is as vital to political trust as its flip-side, the power to promise.

A theory of political trust needs to be grounded in mutual recognition. This is more than a one-way matter of the state, through the law, recognizing the rights, needs and liberty of the people – most crucially, recognizing minority groups. Recognition is *mutual,* and hence the theory needs also to take account of the ways in which people recognize the state and its institutions and participants, and how people recognize those they see around them – as fellow citizens, or as alien. How, if at all, do I belong to the state? How do you belong? To what does one belong? Or, to which version of the nation-state (as there are always at least two main versions) does one regard oneself as belonging? And is it safe or beneficial to belong to it? How does the state pull off the 'trick' of suspending our disbelief in the plural 'we' forming a single 'nation'? *E pluribus unum* is not a one-off historic achievement but requires continual political work.

Political distrust comes to consciousness due to disruptive events and popular discontent. It is a symptom of the uncertainties that multiply with conflicts and migrations, the emergence of new technologies and the effects of a highly competitive 'attention economy.' When images are infinitely fungible, identities are easily expropriated or feigned, and beliefs are readily manipulated, our trust calls for reformulation. A dialectical apprehension of trust is needed to address these transformations, to comprehend the contradictions and paradoxes of political trust.

To conclude the rest

> When any number of Men have so consented to make one community or government, they are thereby presently incorporated, and make one body politic, wherein the majority have a right *to act and conclude the rest.*
>
> (John Locke, 1980, p. 52, §95, italics added)

The conventions of a chapter such as this call upon me to summarize the main points of what has gone before, without introducing any new or unexpected evidence or arguments, and also to bring the text to a close with (to conclude is 'to close with') a summation of what the foregoing argument purports to have illustrated or demonstrated. But I shall close with Locke's usage of the verb *to conclude* which closes in upon a meaning that is now mostly abandoned, except in some legal usages, and that is, 'to constrain to a course of action, to bind, or to oblige,' in other words 'to trust.'

Who are 'the rest' who are so *concluded* by and with a supposed 'majority'? Clearly 'the rest' are a political minority, left outside of the decision, even if they are not statistically a minority of the population. (Think of children, as minors and hence in the minority, *concluded* by their elders, and women *concluded* by the majority of Locke's 'Men' who 'consented' to a government.) 'The minority' are bound by a decision that they were unable to refuse.

Locke would have us conclude that, to be *in*cluded in the body politic, the subject consents that matters be *con*cluded by a majority – over-ruling 'the rest' who did not even consent to be ruled. And the will of a majority then bestows the right to act, and so 'to conclude' the exceptional non-consenting subjects, *as if* they had consented. Any effective political act is such a conclusion. We are all, including the dissenters, concluded by the sovereign decision, whether by means of the executive orders of the president and commander-in-chief, the acts of the legislature, the choice of a majority of those who voted, the impersonal administration of law or the royal prerogative.

If to act politically is to conclude, may I also reason commutatively that to conclude is to act politically? Is the chapter called 'Conclusion' a political act of the author, as trusted authority, to conclude or bind the reader as if the latter were in the minority, or a subject who has tacitly consented to be ruled? In reading the text, do readers consent to being incorporated, as one body politic, and concluded by its rule?

If I may act politically and 'conclude the rest' (including those who dissented), then to what was the reader supposed to consent? It was to look upon and to observe some aspects of trust in the field of the political. And this was meant not in the tendentious sense of 'bearing witness,' but rather in the original sense of *theoría* as contemplating by viewing or observing. I have drawn the reader's attention closer to the continual exchanges between political belonging and subjectivity through the lens of trust and distrust.

References

Butler, J. (2009). *Frames of war: When is life grievable?* London: Verso.

Locke, J. (1980). *Second treatise of government.* Indianapolis, IN: Hackett.

Mounk, Y. (2018). *The people vs. democracy: Why our freedom is in danger and how to save it.* New Haven, CT: Yale University Press.

Index